"Johnny's Such a Bright Boy, What a Shame He's Retarded"

KATE LONG

"Johnny's Such a Bright Boy, What a Shame He's Retarded"

HOUGHTON MIFFLIN COMPANY BOSTON

1977

Library of Congress Cataloging in Publication Data

Long, Kate.
  "Johnny's such a bright boy, what a shame he's retarded."
  Bibliography: p.
  Includes index.
  1. Handicapped children — Education — United States. 2. Federal aid to education — United States. I. Title.
LC4031.L66   371.9'0973   77-5815
ISBN 0-395-25346-2

Printed in the United States of America

P 10 9 8 7 6 5 4 3 2 1

To the child inside each one of us

2912326

"I would like to see special education used to expand the definition of normal, rather than to expand the definition of abnormal."

— Edwin Martin, director, U.S. Bureau
of Education for the Handicapped

Preface

THE FIRST TIME I heard the word "labeling" in a teacher-training class, it brought up a mental picture for me of rows of jars with stickers on them telling what's inside. I told a classmate that the idea of labeling people rather than objects seemed odd. She called me one of her favorite names, after making the point that people label each other every day. If somebody calls you a turkey, a genius, or a creep, you've been labeled for that minute, sure enough. But even though a name can hurt as well as feel good, it's just an opinion and usually doesn't permanently affect your idea of who you are and what you can do. When a child in public school is officially labeled retarded, emotionally disturbed, brain damaged, or learning disabled, however, the label is regarded as a factual statement about the child. Because the weight of the school system's judgment is behind the label, it is hard for the child and those who know the child to disregard the label, particularly if it is used to segregate him or her from unlabeled classmates. Such labels often adhere to a person throughout life.

Labeling usually occurs within the context of what is known as special education. Special education was created to provide programs for those children the general school systems weren't willing or able to deal with, for whatever reasons. Originally, the children were very clearly mentally or physically handicapped and the programs were quite specialized. Over the years, however (especially since the late 1960s), more and more children have been labeled handicapped. A child who is misbehaving or having trouble learning to read can now be put into special education, as much as a blind child or a child with cerebral palsy. This diversity creates a very odd and difficult situation. On one hand, special programs make it possible for genuinely handicapped children to receive much-needed programs they would never otherwise have. On the other hand, loose definitions of categories like "behavior disorders" and "learning disabilities" have made it possible to label and segregate almost any child with any difficulty whatsoever. The extent to which this happens depends on an individual school system.

I started working on *"Johnny's Such a Bright Boy, What a Shame He's Retarded"* almost four years ago, when labeled segregation of all special education children was still a fairly automatic practice in most school systems. I originally began writing to help myself sort out some deep feelings created by work experiences with children who had been labeled and segregated. At that time, my work had brought me into daily contact with dozens of children who had been labeled retarded and segregated on a very small amount of evidence. There was much room for error in the labeling process, and the consequences for the children were serious. Published materials and contact with people working in the schools in other parts of the country told me that this near-arbitrary labeling (and all the negative consequences that go with it) had become commonplace in all regions of the United States. In programs for the "retarded" and "emotionally disturbed," for instance, the question "Why is this child here?" had by all reports almost become a cliché.

Labeling and segregation of children is a subject that arouses much strong feeling. When I first began writing, my sympathies were almost totally with the children, and my frustrations were for the most part pointed toward the usual target — other adults in school systems. In the course of researching the book, however, I participated in a variety of programs and talked with a number of people, adults and children, who were involved in special education from many different perspectives. The more I learned about the regulations, politics, and economics that govern special education programs, the more clearly I understood that the complexity of the system itself often traps adults into procedures and situations they themselves would not have chosen.

As one Maryland grade school principal put it, "Don't forget that the intentions for these labels and separate classes were very good in the beginning. But many assorted pressures enter in, and what can actually happen to a child, in my school system anyhow, often doesn't much resemble the original intentions." For years, he explained, the segregated classification system in the schools has been supported by a complicated web of economic, political, legal, and social considerations that are often irrelevant to the educational needs of the child or the natural inclinations of teachers. "There isn't any point in taking out frustrations on each other if we don't like what's happening," he emphasized. "Better to get together and try to do something about it. But then again, you know how hard *that* is." It isn't easy to work together for change, but in many states during the past four years, people have been trying to alter the way children are labeled and segregated.

A few of the major objections to the labeling and segregation approach are worth noting here. Those who look at the nature and future of entire school systems, for instance, have argued that schools that can send children with problems "somewhere else" can also say, in effect, that those children aren't learning because *they* are defective, not because the system itself has faults. There is no doubt that large numbers of children in schools are having day-to-day problems, but the question becomes: Should the system reexamine its programs or should the child be blamed for his lack of progress? Under the labeling/segregation system, it has been too easy to shift responsibility onto the children themselves, without actually doing anything substantial to help them.

The labeling process has also been heavily criticized because it is weighted against low-income and minority children.* Pressure for change from parents and legal advocates has been strongest where labels were used as a justification for segregating the children of groups that were already subjected to discrimination in their communities. The children who had been labeled retarded in this book, for instance, came primarily from white, low-income families. In

*Since the early seventies, lawsuits have been filed in all parts of the United States on behalf of minority and low-income children who have been labeled and segregated through shaky procedures based on white middle-class standards. The Office for Civil Rights has documented widespread excessive labeling of children from minority families. See p. 335.

other parts of the country, they might have been Chicano, black, Oriental, Indian, or other minority-group children.

Many people have agreed that the nature and self-esteem of any group could be negatively affected if the practice of labeling and segregating significant numbers of children in the group was to continue indefinitely. People have also wondered what it will mean to our entire society to have a generation of children — those who are not labeled, as well as those who are — learning that anyone who is different or who has problems will be "evaluated," categorized, and possibly segregated. For me, this often-overlooked argument is particularly powerful. Increased pressure to conform and acceptance of negative attitudes toward those who are different is, I think, one of the most significant impacts of the classification system as it has been put into effect in the past.

If logical solutions were possible, schools would be hiring more elementary-school teachers to reduce the student-teacher ratio, raising teachers' salaries, and improving teacher-training. But the most reasonable solutions aren't going to be possible until some of our basic social priorities are reversed, and school systems are as well funded as, say, the military.

For now the only large available funds for school "reforms" are in special education and other "compensatory education" programs. As long as the funding remains this way, any attempts to deal with children's problems are likely to come through those channels. The extent to which this is true can be seen in the fact that, as early as 1975, at least four states reported to the Bureau of Education for the Handicapped that 25 to 30 percent of their school population was handicapped. Though the government did not accept that figure for funding, the size of those percentages amazed many people. Others who were not so surprised pointed to the fact that, in a time when it is extremely difficult for school systems to get adequate funds, schools can get extra money for labeled children.

It follows then that, partly because of the economic situation, most of the present attempts to find alternatives to labeled separate classes come under the heading of special education "mainstreaming" (also known as "normalization," "least restrictive alternative," and "least restrictive environment"). Mainstreaming means, first of all, that every child has a right to be educated in as normal a situation as possible and appropriate for that child, and, second, that all children will benefit from learning to appreciate differences among people on a daily basis.

Mainstreaming is practiced differently in different school systems. In many schools, a child who is having trouble learning to read might have been labeled and segregated. Under mainstreaming, she could spend most of her day in the general education classroom and visit a special education resource teacher in her school for an hour every day or every other day for intensive help with her reading problem. The resource teacher would work with the general teacher to help adjust the child's total program. In another school, a special education teacher might teach on a team with several general education teachers. However mainstreaming is practiced, it does not mean that every child can or should be put in a general education classroom, but that each child should be placed in as near-to-normal a situation as constructively possible.

Though special education was originally created to provide educational programs for children with easily identifiable physical and mental handicaps, special education in actual practice today is very hard (and maybe impossible) to define. Like blind men feeling an elephant, five different people might experience special education in five totally different ways. The diversity is as great as diversity among schools, from highly specialized clinic to third-rate "dumping ground."

Because of the wide range of children included in special education, professionals now use the words "minimal," "moderate," "severe," and "profound" to indicate the level of seriousness of a child's problem, e.g., "minimally retarded," "moderately retarded," "severely retarded," "profoundly retarded." As it stood in 1976, approximately 80 to 85 percent of all children in special education nationwide were considered severely or profoundly handicapped.*

*This percentage will most likely increase significantly due to new federal and state laws requiring schools to provide programs for all children, regardless of severity of handicap.

Another smaller percentage were in programs for "gifted" children.

In the early seventies, conversion of school systems to mainstreaming was promoted by people within special education who felt that prevailing policies were having the ironic effect of isolating and stigmatizing each of these groups of children far more than was necessary. The greatest irony of all may have been the fact that, at the same time as questions were being raised about the segregation of millions of "minimally" and "moderately" handicapped children, children who badly needed special programs had often been segregated out of school entirely. At that time, the Council for Exceptional Children had arbitrarily been denied any entrance whatsoever to the public schools on the basis of the severity of their handicaps.*

In the highly complex atmosphere since 1970, more major developments have occurred in special education than in any comparable period since it began. The first significant action came from courts of law. Parents and advocates for mislabeled children sued for damages and demanded that their children be educated within the general school system. Parents of excluded children sued to force schools to provide their children with appropriate special education programs. In combination with the legal decision, organized parent groups caused most state legislatures to pass laws that greatly increased state funding possibilities for special education and made other legal provisions for the operations of the programs. Within a few years, however, increasingly complicated civil rights questions were raised. It became obvious that, at the same time as it became possible for genuinely handicapped children to get badly needed special programs, new funding provisions were simultaneously encouraging schools to pack special classes in the minimal/moderate range.

In late 1975, partly because the state laws varied so widely, the federal government passed Public Law 94–142, which is bound to

*An important aim of a good mainstreaming program is to have a variety of options for a variety of children. Because of the complexity of the needs of most severely and profoundly handicapped children, appropriate mainstreaming for most of them would mean entrance into the intensive specialized situations.

have far-reaching ramifications on entire school systems in years to come. Under the law, which goes into full effect in 1978, it is no longer legal anywhere in the country to exclude any school-age child from publicly funded education, no matter how severe the child's handicap may be. At the same time, the availability of federal funds for special education will be increased yearly into the 1980s, which may make placement decisions more financially motivated than ever. School employees will have to deal with vastly increased federal regulations and paperwork. Within the context of this book, the most significant aspects of the law may be the due process requirements and the fact that the law strongly encourages (but does not require) mainstreaming.

The passage of a law alone can't make good mainstreaming happen. Children can be transferred into different situations, but the spirit in which a program is carried out determines what happens to the children as much as the technical know-how, resources, and planning. Though separate special classes are still the predominant program structure for "minimally handicapped" children in many school systems, some systems have already achieved excellent results with mainstreaming. Others have had problems.

This book was written "in support of mainstreaming in the public schools," not because I don't see the problems involved but because I hope very much that mainstreaming works well. It seems inevitable, given current legal trends, that mainstreaming will be tried on a wide scale, whether it's practiced well or not. Since 1974, there has been a sudden tremendous increase in school systems involved in mainstreaming. Where the motivations have been in good part legal or economic, general education and special education teachers have been too often ordered to "mainstream" without being given an adequate chance to understand the goals behind the practice or to learn effective ways in which it can be carried out. The resistance and resentment that often results quite naturally can seriously handicap any mainstreaming effort. As one third-grade teacher told me at a mainstreaming conference, "Five years ago, you special education people were telling us we couldn't handle children with problems and saying we should send them to the special classes instead. We got used to referring kids out. Now you've turned around to say that the children do much better in as normal a situation as possible. Maybe that's true, but I find this turn-around very confusing. There's a resource teacher in my school who's supposed to help me, and we'd better get the kind of support I think we ought to have to make it go."

Experience over the past five years has shown that, without mutual sympathy, cooperation, and support among teachers and administrators, the best mainstreaming plan will be seriously handicapped. The mainstreaming process is especially complicated at first, and people need to be able to work well together to make it succeed. People need to understand and believe in mainstreaming. They also need to have some idea of the pressures other adults are facing.

The friction among adults that threatens the success of mainstreaming efforts in many schools follows a pattern that occurs in other situations. A friend of mine who works in a poorly funded mental institution has a sign in his office that says DON'T FORGET THE REAL PROBLEMS. He and his co-workers put that sign up to remind each other to channel their frustrations into attacking basic shortages rather than into blaming and demoralizing each other.

Talking to a reporter at the height of the Boston busing controversy, a South Boston woman echoed the same message. "This is crazy," she said. "What we've got here is poor people fighting poor people. Our interests are more the same than they're different. Instead of tearing into each other, we really ought to be sticking together to ask why all our kids have to settle for third-rate schools. We're fighting over our little piece of pie and have forgotten that it ought to be big enough for everyone."

If it were possible, maybe there should be a message printed on all materials dealing with labeling and mainstreaming saying DON'T FORGET THE REAL PROBLEMS. Some "make-up" measures are definitely better than others for children, but none can really substitute for a direct approach to the fact that so many children are having problems in school. The mainstreaming movement may well cause school systems in general to move closer to dealing with deeper problems. In some schools already, adults have combined forces, worked together, and insisted they be given the support they need to make the new approach work. This is very exciting to see when it happens.

Johnny was written to provide an easy way to bring some of the basic motivations for mainstreaming alive, to help readers see the complexities of the labeling/segregation situation, and to increase the possibility that readers will want to support constructive efforts for change. The book has been written in fictional story form, with research and factual information woven in. The story describes a school system that is just beginning to move toward mainstreaming. It may be seen as a historical explanation of current efforts to create alternatives or as a description of existing reality, depending on which school system (or school) you're looking at.

I hope that the arguments in *Johnny* against practices that harm some children will not be used to criticize the advances that have been made on behalf of children who do need specialized programs, full-time or otherwise. I do not intend these arguments as a means of saying that nothing should be done for children whose problems are considered to be minimal or moderate or that existing programs in that range are automatically less than worthwhile. Likewise, nothing that follows is meant to detract from the respect due people who have made wonderful differences in the lives of children while teaching educable mentally retarded (EMR) classes. If I am adversely critical here of the EMR category and the classification system in general, I do not intend criticism of individuals like these. Many have little or no control over the structure of the program in which they make a living, though many would be the first to object to the kind of situations described here. If it's been at all possible to translate feelings into words, there can be no real good guys and bad guys in the story. There are just people, trying to deal not only with educational problems, but also with each other.

The process of writing this book has been something like a five-pound hen trying to lay a ten-pound egg without breaking it. It goes without saying that I haven't been able to do this complicated subject justice and that many of the most worthwhile aspects of the book have been produced thanks to the insight and contributions of people like Sue Williams, Anne Robinson, Anne Hocutt, Skip Jason, Barbara Miller, Tom Irvin, Laura Long, Elizabeth Grafton, Ginny Murphy, Burton Blatt, Whyla Beman, Patricia Forsythe, Carol Robeck, Hugh Ripman, Sara James, and Andy Andersen.

Thanks to the personnel of the Council for Exceptional Children, the Senate Subcommittee for the Handicapped, the President's Committee on Mental Retardation, and the Bureau of Education for the Handicapped (a remarkable government unit) for their help in research, as well as to all the people who donated their time for interviews and visits. Special thanks to Annette Cothran, Doyle Gaines, and all associated with them. Dr. Joe Cunningham of George Peabody College for Teachers in Nashville helped me integrate the nonfictional information into the first half of the book, and deserves much credit.

Most of all, this book could never have been finished without the support and encouragement of my friends. I feel special appreciation for my editor, Anita McClellan, who stayed right there through all the thicks and thins and invested a great deal of herself in seeing this book hatched. There just aren't enough thanks to cover that kind of support.

Contents

"Johnny's Such a Bright Boy,
What a Shame He's Retarded"

1. Special and Regular

"What is true mental retardation? Who is really mentally retarded? What is the real prevalence rate for mental retardation? All of these are nonsense questions, which cannot be answered . . . The answers to these questions depend on the definer's perspective, his assumptions, and the tactics which he uses in the pursuit of meaning. There is no single answer. There are no 'true' responses. The human intellect can organize the empirical world into myriad categories and sort people according to an indefinite number of characteristics. The definer selects the system that best serves his purpose."

— Dr. Jane R. Mercer, *Labeling the Mentally Retarded,*
Clinical and Social System Perspectives on Mental Retardation, 1973

LONG AFTER the last school bus had crossed the bridge and started up the mountain, Maggie Callahan and Peggy Adkins sat talking together on the steps of Dummy Tech. A couple of girls were playing in a big pile of fallen leaves on the playground. While watching them tunnel and roll through the leaves, Peggy and Maggie were also comparing notes. Maggie had become supervisor of the county special education program the week before, and Peggy had already been teaching a few months at Gateway School.

"Half the time, people don't call it Gateway, they call it Dummy Tech,"·Peggy told Maggie. "The story goes that, a couple of years ago, some hot-dog kid got into hollering 'Dummy Tech!' whenever the school bus would stop here, and kids've been doing it ever since."

"I've got a lot of mixed feelings about this situation," Peggy continued slowly, flipping a pebble across the road, where a little puppy was nosing around in the dirt. "I mean, these kids are supposedly separated from the others, so they can get something special, right? Something that makes their lives better? That sounds good when I think about it, but then I look at what's really happening with most of them, and I'm not so sure . . ."

Peggy leaned back against the stucco wall. There was a big

spray-painted heart over her head with "Sweet Stevie + Big Bren-ner" in the middle of it. "It's like a bad joke," she sighed. "You know, I'm not trained as a special education teacher myself. I'm a high school home ec teacher, and this is my first year of teaching. The superintendent has promised to put me in home ec next year, so, in the meantime, I'm doing what I can with these kids."

She looked up and pulled on one of her ponytails. With her red hair and freckles, Peggy looked like a high school student herself. "Even putting *me* down here shows what people think about these kids. I mean, they sure wouldn't have put me with the third grade . . . I'd be good at high school home ec, but I feel a little lost here . . . ." She looked at Maggie questioningly. "These kids ought to get good elementary-level teachers, at the very least."

Another pebble sailed across the road and hit the puppy on the rear. Peggy smiled, raising an eyebrow. "Yeah, these are the re-tarded kids, we've ended up being the retarded teachers, and you're going to be the retarded supervisor. All off here in our own little box."

A hawk circled overhead. They both watched it sail and dive, ad-justing its wing slant to the air currents. "Anyhow," Peggy Adkins continued, "some of us don't know that much about teaching read-ing and things like that, and the office won't give us the materials we need. We get way less than the regular classrooms do. If people really thought these kids were special, all this wouldn't be happen-ing.

"It's worse than crazy, because basically most of these kids aren't so much different from anybody else, as far as I can see. Sure, they have all kinds of problems, but I can't for the life of me figure out why they're all called retarded."

She began to flip pebbles with greater energy. The puppy went scrambling and yapping. Peggy turned to face Maggie. "Did you know that a lot of the other kids won't even sit by our kids on the bus? One of my girls told me today that the other kids were calling them 'cooties.' If we were the best teachers in the system, I don't see how we could make up for that sort of thing."

She picked up a stick and scratched in the dirt. "Shoot, you know what happens, Maggie. If a kid's not retarded when he gets here, he *gets* retarded after a while. Some of them develop emotional problems too. They know what all of this means. And the worst part of it is that most of these kids already had a couple of strikes against them when they got to school, not having had the advantages a lot of kids have had. School's supposed to be their chance to get a leg up."

She dropped the stick and sighed. "Are all these kids retarded? I used to get a lot more upset about it than most of the other teachers. Maybe because I'm new, maybe because I'm a lot closer to being a kid myself.

"But I got tired of people saying stuff like 'Welcome to the real world,' so I don't talk about it much anymore. I guess they're right. After a while, you get used to it, and it just seems normal." She watched the hawk sail out of view, then added, "But still, most of these kids could have been me, if I hadn't had the advantages I did, and I can't help but think that there's got to be a better way of doing things."

Maggie was having even stronger reactions than Miss Adkins had had, because she was seeing how special education was working in relation to that particular school system. A few days later, she got a message to call the principal of Little Creek Elementary School. "He said something about getting a special ed kid when he doesn't have any special education at his school," the secretary told her.

"Yeah, that's what I wanted to talk to you about," said the principal, an easygoing fellow who also doubled as the fifth grade teacher. "Callie Peale's her name, nice quiet little kid, always singing funny little songs about frogs and things. She used to be in one of those retarded classrooms out behind Stockdale School before she came over here.

"So we had her for a while, only now she's gone. Five days ago, her mother sent over a note saying she was transferring the girl over to Page School. Said she'd come in and talk about it, but she didn't. Anyhow, the kid's not here anymore. I guess she's over at Page School."

Maggie called Page School and got the principal, a Mrs. Williams, on the line. The words "special education director" had barely escaped her lips when Mrs. Williams knew the call was about Callie Peale.

"Look here, we don't have any special ed here," she cut in. "The principal from over at Little Creek called up and warned me that the girl was coming . . ."

"Warned?"

". . . and so, when this kid showed up, I met her on the sidewalk and told her she didn't belong here. I told her she belonged at Gateway School with all those other kids like her. I even showed her where to catch the bus. So I have nothing to do with her. We don't have special ed here."

Maggie stuck a verbal foot in the phone before Mrs. Williams could hang up. "Mrs. Williams, do you happen to know where she is? I'm trying to find the girl."

"No," she said impatiently. "We don't have anything to do with the girl. She's special ed. I sent her down to Gateway. That's where those retarded kids belong."

"Did she get on the bus?"

"I don't know. I showed her where the bus stop was."

Maggie sat staring at the phone, trying to imagine the jangle an encounter like that would have on a child, and trying to understand the meaning of what Mrs. Williams had had to say.

Callie's file records didn't make things any easier. There was a nondescript two-paragraph psychological report saying that Callie was neatly dressed and that her IQ score qualified her for special education. There was also a report from child welfare describing a chaotic home situation, the child's deteriorating self-esteem, her progressive withdrawal, and her tremendous need for stability.

According to the report, Callie had already lived in two foster homes, and whoever wrote that report had recommended that another be found for her. There was no address or telephone number in the file. Maggie began to feel slightly panicky.

An insane kind of telephone and car chase followed, beginning with the news from Little Creek that Callie had taken her records with her when she left. Nobody knew where Callie was. She hadn't showed up at Gateway School, and her former teacher didn't know where she was either. "She's eleven years old, and she only reads on second grade level," he commented. "I think she's been in special ed for about three years."

The superintendent said to call the truant officer. The truant officer, a kindly fellow named Mr. Morris, who doubled as director of transportation, was down at the school bus garage. He said any arrangements depended on how Callie's new location fit into the existing bus schedule. "If she's moved outside town, we can't bus her back to her old class. It gets too complicated." A note of irritation crept into his voice, and there was a long pause. "Well . . . I know the girl's father," he relented. "I'll find out where they're living now, and we'll go over there and see what's up."

The school nurse came by Maggie's desk while she was waiting for Mr. Morris to call back. "Why, that's the last little child this should happen to!" she exclaimed. "This family, I know them well, from work. The father's often drunk and violent. Mrs. Peale and the little girl are scared to death of him. One of Callie's brothers is living with relatives now, and the other ran away. The mother cares a lot about her kids, but she's constantly laid up with one thing or another . . . that poor little girl . . .

"As for Mrs. Williams over at Page School," she continued, "that woman told me last fall that she wasn't having any more special ed kids in her school. She said she's trying to build up Page's achievement test rating, and she's got enough problems already. She had an odd way of putting it. Said something to the effect that you can't stuff two hundred worms in a twenty-worm can."

Callie's father worked as a mechanic out of the Chevrolet garage. He told Mr. Morris that the girl was at home, had been for days, and was going to stay right there rather than go to Gateway. "School's for crazy kids," he said shortly.

Callie's rambling frame house, balanced on a steep hill, was located about a mile out of town. A little girl was standing in the window, half hidden by the curtain, when the truck pulled up. Maggie waved and she disappeared.

Mr. Morris and Maggie were both puffing by the time they reached the front porch. The dog on the end of the chain wagged his tail and rolled over in the dust. Mrs. Peale opened the door as soon as Mr. Morris touched it. She looked to be about forty-five, was wearing a shapeless green dress, pink fingernail polish, and tennis shoes. She apologized for having only one chair. "Just moved in and all." Mr. Morris and Maggie told her how sorry they were about what had been happening to her girl.

Callie was pressed silent and motionless against the kitchen wall, shoulders hunched, shrinking away as if she were afraid that somebody would touch her. She was standing under a 3–D picture of an equally pale Jesus.

Mrs. Peale started talking right away. "I thought maybe somebody might come sooner or later to see what happened to the girl. I didn't rightly know what to do when she came home crying a few days ago. She was saying that they didn't want her at that Page School, and she's been crying off and on ever since. She's not skipping school, she just don't know where she can go . . ."

Mrs. Peale kept twisting a chain around her neck as she shifted from foot to foot. "I don't know why they wouldn't want Callie over at Page School," she said softly. "Do you?" Callie had closed her eyes. Mrs. Peale was staring first at Maggie, then at Mr. Morris, who was busy lighting his pipe.

"I'm so nervous," she continued, forgetting about the question hanging in the air. "I get upset. And Callie takes after me. She's nervous too. You can see it just to look at her. I couldn't get her to stop crying when she come home the other day." Her eyes widened. "She said that Page woman told her she had to get on the bus and go over to Gateway School." Maggie edged closer to Callie, who opened her eyes.

"Gateway!" repeated her mother, still twisting her chain. "Why, that's the place where they send kids who don't have good sense. Why, Callie figured she had good sense, and she don't belong there. So she came home.

"I think she does have good sense," she continued, apparently to herself. "Don't you?" she asked Maggie.

"I know she has very good sense," Maggie said to Callie, who closed her eyes again, maybe wondering who the strange woman was.

Mrs. Peale brightened. "Of course, she's very nervous, delicate like. Like me. She's nervous. Look at her." Callie had actually begun to tremble slightly.

"Why, she's a fine-looking girl," said Mr. Morris. "Now, Mrs. Peale, we want to get her back in school, and this lady here is going to try to get her into the place where she'll be the happiest. Now that you've moved, she'd have to walk it if she wanted to go to her old class behind Stockdale School."

"Where would you *like* to go, Callie?" Maggie asked her. Callie edged away a little.

"Little Creek," she whispered. "I want to be at a regular school." Maggie told her that her teacher at Stockdale School missed her and would like to have her back.

"No!" Callie said, jumping at the sound of her own voice.

"And, she's too nervous to walk all the way over to Stockdale," her mother said. "We won't let her. She can't. It's over a mile, and she's pretty weak. And nervous. She doesn't want to go there."

As they drove back down the hill, Mr. Morris said the school system absolutely couldn't go against the parents' wishes, especially when there was no bus. After he dropped Maggie off, she talked to the superintendent. He said that if the parents didn't want Callie going to Stockdale, the system couldn't send her there. Maggie wasn't sure that the classroom behind Stockdale School would be any better for Callie. She wasn't sure what to do, so she went back down to Little Creek School.

"Sure, we'll take her," said the principal. "We're a pretty easygoing crew here. I can't guarantee she'll learn anything, but we'll give it a crack. She'll have to be with Miss Mullins, third grade. She's on second grade level, so that's the closest we can come."

Third grade. Best of three inappropriate alternatives, none of which suited Callie. She's eleven years old, but looks like she's eight.

Maggie cornered Miss Mullins and bent her ear about Callie's need for encouragement. Miss Mullins gave her a slightly sour look and promised to do her best for the little girl, though she already had twenty-nine kids to contend with. Maggie promised to check on Callie periodically, and Miss Mullins gave her a "big deal" look.

"Well, I guess she's not your responsibility anymore," she said, as Maggie went out the door. Maggie's stomach did a flip-flop.

Back up at the Peales', Maggie told Callie that she'd be going back to Miss Mullins' class at Little Creek, if she felt ready to tackle school again. Callie smiled softly for the first time and disappeared through the curtain into the back room. Mrs. Peale let go of her chain and revealed a silver-colored heart that had "key to my heart" written on it in red.

"Why didn't they want Callie over at Page School?" Mrs. Peale asked again.

Outside it was a beautiful clear day. The sun was shining with the lovely winter light that makes the tree trunks look like they have a glow of their own. A train went by, and the engineer waved and called, "Hi there, sweetheart!"

Life was going on as usual, but Maggie's head was going round and round, thinking about what Miss Mullins had said. Did I just dump a kid? she wondered. What exactly have I done for that child? She went up to the school board office, where she was thanked for taking care of the matter. There was a lot of excitement around the office. Somebody had just sideswiped the assistant superintendent's car.

Maggie shared an office with the reading supervisor, a woman in her forties named Abigail Robin. Abigail was sitting in a cloud of cigarette smoke, scribbling on papers. "Well, you look like you're ready to babble," she said. "So come on in, and babble away."

So the whole story got babbled, ending with "I guess she's not your responsibility anymore."

"O.K., kid, calm down," began Abigail, running her hand through her short graying hair. "Let's sort this thing out. You've just run into the hard reality of what happens when one part of a school system's used as a place to dump children. That's always pretty hard on new people. But the first thing you've got to do is stop getting so wound up."

"Well, look at what happened to that little girl!" Maggie said, scratching her head. "She was practically a Ping-Pong ball! One school wouldn't even let her in the door because she was special ed. Not because she was Callie Peale, but because she was special ed. As though she had some contagious disease that would contaminate the school's achievement test scores. And then, even though she was special ed, Callie would rather stay home than go to Dummy Tech. Neither her parents nor Callie wanted her to go back to her old class, and, besides that, the bus schedule got in the way. So, what happens is that the best we have to offer her is third grade, and that means she'll be fourteen before she gets out of grade school, if she's lucky."

Abigail leaned forward. "Well, at least you aren't claiming you mainstreamed her." She smiled. Maggie missed the humor. Below the office window, a used car salesman was helping an older couple check out a Chevy. The old guy gave the rear tire a good kick. Abigail sat there staring at her nails.

"So what can we do for Callie? Have you got something to help her out?" Maggie asked. "I mean, for sure, whose responsibility is she?"

"Well, frankly, no, I don't," Abigail said. "What's more, I see kids in the same situation all over the system. As reading supervisor, I cover seventy classrooms — stretched thinner than an old piece of bubble gum. I can lend the teacher a few materials, and maybe come by every three weeks, but that's about it. It's not really help, and you run your rear off, and then the teachers resent you for not doing anything.

"Anyhow, I'm as much at a loss as you are. This is a very traditionally structured system. We don't have team teaching, multigrade arrangements, reading specialists in the schools, or special ed mainstreaming at this point. There are a lot of people who would probably like to see that sort of thing happen, but it takes a lot more to change systems than just liking the idea. For one thing, we don't have the community involvement we should. You get a lot of complaints and pressures about achievement, but the taxpayers just voted down the school levy."

She shrugged. "What all this means is that the whole system is handicapped. Everybody's feeling inadequate, and people like me are running around trying to put on Band-Aids. That doesn't help Callie Peale, but that's what's happening."

Abigail pulled out a cigarette and tapped it on the table. "We're all stuck," she continued, "because we're supposed to make up for the lack of resources, alternatives, teacher training, low salaries, and the whole kit and kaboodle. We can't do that, so your part of the system is getting used as a dumping ground, and that's tough on a lot of people. Vicious things happen to kids, and us grownups don't have it so dandy either."

Maggie couldn't pay close attention. There was a tape recording playing in her head. It kept saying, "Something's got to be DONE, something's GOT to be done. SOMETHING'S got to be done . . ."

Abigail started talking about a school system in Texas where kids were on several levels in each classroom and the special ed and reading teachers worked together to help the regular classroom teachers so that most of the kids could stay in as near-to-normal a situation as possible. "That really cut down on the dumping. And they used team teaching to —"

"How the hell could that principal do that to Callie?" Maggie interrupted. "All that really matters is what's happening right here, not what's going on in Texas or even fifty miles away. What we call special ed might not have much to do with what someone else is calling special ed."

"Mrs. Williams didn't see what she was doing," answered Abigail, shifting gears easily. "As it happens, that woman is very well thought of in this town. I know her, and believe it or not, she's quite a nice person. The pillar of the Presbyterian church. That's what makes it so hard."

She paused and lit her cigarette. "She didn't see what she was doing," she said slowly, "because she didn't see a little girl. She saw a stereotype . . . and all the associations attached to that stereotype. She didn't see Callie. She saw 'retarded.' I'd lay you twenty to one on that.

"O.K., that's the end of my broadcast," she added, standing up abruptly and stubbing out her cigarette. "I'm off like a herd of turtles. Got some stuff to take home tonight." She reached over and patted Maggie's arm. "Look," she advised. "Don't get so wound up.

It's easy for us to sit around and bellyache, but the fact is, neither of us has any magic wand. We don't make policy, and you gotta realize that."

She picked up a pile of books. "If we had a whole range of options for kids like Callie, without any tags like 'retarded' as the price of admission to the show, we might be able to do business together, you and me. But that's not the way it is at this point." She paused. "We're talking about getting a tutoring kind of program in the regular system in a year or so. Maybe, as we go our separate ways, if the government in its wisdom doesn't cut off funds, we'll be building up things that will eventually go together."

Maggie sat in the office after Abigail left, wondering how many Callies would be bounced around before things eventually came together. Can't wait for that, she decided, not exactly sure what could be done about it.

Walking home in the fading light, Maggie passed along a charming old tree-lined street, cobbled with stone. The town of Davidson, ringed with mountains, was literally built on a hillside, spilling down into the valley. Some of the streets sloped close to thirty degrees.

Maggie wandered onto the playground of Stockdale Elementary School, a huge, fortresslike building with "1921" carved on to a granite slab over the doorway. Two prefab classrooms had been put out behind the school for special ed. In the evening, the adjacent playground was a good place to sit quietly, sometimes to draw or write, sometimes to let the hills still your thoughts, always to get back a feeling of order and natural progression. From that hill in the spring, you could keep track of the way green softly obscured the ridge lines, a little more each day.

Looking down the valley from the high vantage point, you couldn't see Callie's house, but you could almost make out the rock quarry. It had shut down about five years before, putting many people out of work and deeply affecting the area economy.

After she had gotten to know the special ed kids, Maggie was able to locate most of their homes from the hill. It was easy, because they were concentrated geographically — on the mountain behind Stockdale, for instance, in Squirrel Hollow just outside Davidson, and in the town's low-rent district below the hill on which Stockdale stood. No more than five of the children in the program lived in the affluent middle-class section of town. The middle-class children had problems too, but their parents, as a rule, wouldn't allow them to be placed in special ed, as it existed then.

Maggie was feeling around for the calm of the evening. It wasn't there. A few lights came on in the town near her house beside the train station. A little beyond the house, the river wound by Dummy Tech. She threw a rock at Dummy Tech and missed. It was over a mile away.

When Maggie first took the supervisor's job, it had seemed strange that one county (school population 2500) could produce almost 200 retardates. She had speculated about things like malnutrition. But, as soon as she began to spend time with the kids, the theories went out the window and were replaced by a feeling bordering somewhere between anxiety and panic. She kept encountering groups of alert, lively children. The overwhelming majority came from low-income families. Many of them had not developed the vocabulary and basic concepts a child needs to negotiate a rigidly structured middle-class school. Many hadn't had the range of experience a middle-class child takes for granted. No more than fifteen of the children enrolled in special education at that time were severely handicapped, mentally or otherwise. The rest had a wide variety of correctable, frequently minor problems, so many of which, as Abigail had said, also turned up in the regular classroom.

For most people, the words "mentally retarded" summon up a far more serious picture. In Copper County and in most of the United States, retardation in practice is defined as an IQ score below seventy. Only 5 to 10 percent of over one million children classified "retarded" in the schools in the United States in 1975 were severely retarded, according to the President's Committee on Mental Retardation. The other 90 to 95 percent were supposedly "minimally" or "moderately" retarded, whatever that may mean in each school system.

The public and many educators don't make these distinctions. The 90 percent often have to bear the same stigma and aversion commonly and tragically directed in our society toward the severely retarded child. Saddest of all, the so-called retarded children don't make these distinctions either. They don't tell themselves, "Oh, I'm only minimally or moderately retarded." They think, "I'm retarded, I'm different, I'm second-rate." The best academic program in the world couldn't erase the humiliation they feel and often express.

What is retarded? Specialists have been trying to define that category for at least the past century. The problem has been that, like most categories, the definition keeps getting broader and broader to include more and more children. An array of terms has been developed, terms within terms. Ronald W. Conley summed up the debate in his book *The Economics of Mental Retardation.* "Many terms have been used as synonyms for 'mental retardation.' Such an abundance of terminology would be of little consequence if there were general agreement as to the precise meanings of the different terms. Unfortunately, there is not.

"To illustrate, the terms 'mental retardation' and 'mental deficiency' are frequently used interchangeably by modern authors. But the term 'mental deficiency' has also been used to describe the inadequate *social* functioning resulting from 'mental retardation.' More often, the two terms are distinguished by using the term 'mental retardation' to 'refer only to those whose educational and social performance is markedly lower than would be expected from what is known of their intellectual abilities,' and by reserving the term 'mental deficiency' for those conditions 'of mental arrest resulting in a social inadequacy which is not amenable to fundamental improvement through education and experience and any known treatment.' Others have further restricted the term 'mental deficiency' to include only those cases 'with demonstrable neurological damage or pathology.' When a distinction is made between 'mental retardation' and 'mental deficiency,' the term 'mental subnormality' is sometimes used as a general term to cover both cases."

Such an array of opinions about terms is mind-fuzzing, especially since the word "retarded" could be applied to all the children at

Gateway School, as well as to the profoundly retarded child. On the more technical end, the American Association of Mental Deficiency provides a medical classification system for mental retardation that included nine major categories, 55 subclassifications, and over 100 sub-subclassifications.

The two categories used in Copper County were known as EMR and TMR. EMR means "educable mentally retarded." TMR means "trainable mentally retarded." The children so categorized are also referred to as "educables" and "trainables." There are extensive lists of "characteristics of the EMR" and "characteristics of the TMR" in many textbooks. Callie Peale was an EMR. Her characteristics supposedly are there in the textbook, like the characteristics of a car with standard parts.

Reality is much less complex than lists of characteristics. An EMR, according to the regulations of many states, is a person who scores between 70 and 50 on a "properly administered" IQ test. Some states use 75 as the cut-off point. Others use 79. A few states don't have EMRs. They have eliminated the idea. A TMR, in practice, is often a person who scores between 30 and 49 on an IQ test.

The President's Committee on Mental Retardation has added another term to those applied to children considered retarded in the schools. In 1969, they published a jarring report entitled "The Six-Hour Retarded Child." "We now have what may be called a six-hour retarded child," the report began, "retarded from nine to three, five days a week, solely on the basis of an IQ score, without regard to his adaptive behavior, which may be exceptionally adaptive to the situation and community in which he lives."

Most six-hour retarded children are officially classified EMR.

Up on the Stockdale playground, Maggie watched some children playing on the swings and seesaws. When a little girl with flying pigtails swung high in the air, Maggie caught her breath. For a split second, the child seemed to hang suspended between the river and the mountain. She sent Maggie back through the years to her own pigtails and the time of swinging "up so high, you can touch the sky."

Maggie had grown up in a county about fifty miles from Copper

County, so the area was familiar to her. Part of her county was visible from the hilltop above Davidson. There wasn't any special education in her schools back then, and severely handicapped children weren't allowed to come to school. One of her friends got polio in the fourth grade and wasn't allowed to come to school afterward, because her wheelchair wouldn't go up the stairs. It was long before the practice of including ramps in public buildings.

Maggie understood a little of Callie's desire to be "regular" at any price, since she had spent much of her own grade school career praying that the Lord would shrink her about five inches, put some fat on her bones, and make kids stop calling her "beanpole." There were also a few little hexes thrown on teachers who made everybody line up by height.

From an adult point of view, it was easy to see that being tall and skinny are by no means the worst things that ever happened to a kid. And yet the pain of being different had made it possible to identify with Callie. It would still have been hard to belittle the pain of a tall, skinny kid. Or a fat kid. Or an "emotionally disturbed" child. Or a shabbily dressed child. All those pains so often spring from the same source. It isn't the tall and skinny, it's the "being different," when different is made to be bad or shameful. When different is bad, different is painful to a child or to a grownup. Different can even cause further problems under those circumstances.

Different is a funny thing, because it's seen in so many ways. Outside school, people's parents often said, "Why can't you be like everybody else?" so that became very important. It was essential to have a red crinoline and a ponytail, to have a boyfriend, and to make good scores on the Stanford Achievement Test.

It was also important to be up to grade level. There were kids like Callie Peale in Maggie's classrooms. She remembered their confusion when the teacher asked them questions she knew they couldn't answer. She especially remembered one fourth grade girl who stood up reluctantly to answer a question, cleared her throat several times, and finally asked with a very red face if she could go to the bathroom. The whole class laughed at her, and Maggie laughed too. Somebody whispered "dumbo" and the teacher didn't say anything. A weird feeling of collaboration and comradeship shaded the entire incident.

Maggie remembered, because later that day, she got hers. The music teacher made her dance with the shortest boy in the class, who made terrified faces and muttered something about being crushed by a monster. Everybody laughed, including the girl who had run to the bathroom. She had been physically regular, so the roles were suddenly reversed. The look that passed between them stuck very clearly in Maggie's memory. Maggie was as red as the other girl had been and was thinking hard about the bathroom.

That moment taught her something. Something had made both girls ashamed to be themselves, when they didn't really need to be ashamed. The girl had laughed at Maggie, Maggie had laughed at her, both of them trying to improve their own standing by making fun of somebody else. Trying hard to show that they were regular, they laughed whenever somebody else was irregular. And it had just seemed natural to do it.

Regular is a word that gives many people trouble. It has been universally used to describe a child who is *not* in special education. The "regular" children. The implications of the word are enormous.

In Copper County, something that was not regular was irregular. Special education was separate in a bad way, so it was bad to be irregular and good to be regular. People who were irregular were punished by removal, as any kid in the school system knew, whether the grownups intended it that way or not. Callie Peale knew that. Irregular was called special, yet a kid was mortified to be special under such circumstances. Special was equivalent to "dummy" or "crazy" in the average kid's mind. So regular was better.

There were regular children, regular teachers, regular classes, and regular schools. Special children, special teachers, special classes, and a special school. If special was separate in a negative way, special was bad. So nobody wanted to be special.

Regular implies that there are a whole lot of children who fit some standard mold and are therefore more desirable people than the irregulars (who will, they hope, become regular someday). Somehow, the choice of that word doesn't seem to be any accident. It's a rather powerful label in itself.

2. According to Regulations

> "I get very alarmed when I read, talk with colleagues, go to conferences, and so forth, and hear this hue and cry about the increasing percentage of children who are considered handicapped. The question really becomes one of 'where do you cross over the line?' Where is the kid handicapped, and where is the school system handicapped?"
>
> — Andy Andersen, learning resource specialist,
> Regional Resource Center, July 1975

BACK IN THE LATE SIXTIES, about five years before this story takes place, the special education profession went through a major philosophic controversy about the concepts of regular and retarded. The legal groundwork was laid in 1967 by a lawsuit filed by black parents in the District of Columbia against the District's "tracking system," in which children were tested at an early age and sorted into "ability groups." Once there, most children stayed in the same track for the rest of their educational career. The children in the lower tracks typically got a very watered-down program, had a lizard's chance of attending college and a very big chance of dropping out. The aptitude test that was used to sort the children was geared toward white middle-class children. The lower tracks were filled up with black low-income kids, while the top tracks were almost exclusively white. Judge J. Skelly Wright ordered the District's tracking system abolished, saying that "the track system translates ability into educational opportunity. When a student is placed in a lower track, in a very real sense, his future is being decided for him; the kind of education he gets there shapes his future progress not only in school, but in society in general. Certainly, when the school system undertakes this responsibility, it incurs the obligation of living up to its promise to the student that placement in a lower track will not simply be a shunting off from the mainstream of education, but rather will be an effective mechanism for bringing the student up to his true potential."

The same kinds of questions had been cropping up in special education for years, but the controversy really took off in 1968 when Dr. Lloyd Dunn, who had written major textbooks on retardation and had spent his entire career working in and for EMR classes in Appalachia and elsewhere, delivered a speech in which he said that, based on his own experiences and all available research, he had come to the conclusion that, much as EMR classes are intended to help children, they actually damage the lives of many of them in unexpected ways. He was, in effect, questioning the direction of much of his life's work.

"Regular teachers and administrators have felt sincerely," he stated, "that they were doing these pupils a favor by removing them from the pressures of an unrealistic and inappropriate program of studies. Too, special educators have fully believed that the children involved would make greater progress in special schools and classes. However, the overwhelming evidence now is that our present and past practices have their major justification in removing pressures on regular teachers and pupils, at the expense of the socioculturally deprived, slow-learning pupils themselves." Dunn then offered a few models for changing the structure of special education, so that such children could be mainstreamed into regular classes.

Dunn's statement sent out shock waves, and he was soon seconded by many others. A movement to develop alternatives for the otherwise-EMR child began. Many people had the same kind of leery feeling about separate classes for most children labeled emotionally disturbed. The terms "least restrictive alternative" and "mainstreaming" kept turning up to represent the idea that each child should be provided with the most near-to-normal schooling situation possible. A child who would otherwise be in an EMR class, for instance, might spend most of his day in a regular classroom and spend whatever period of time seemed appropriate with a special education resource teacher.

Charts similar to the one on page 19 started appearing in education journals.

Then, in the early seventies, before this point of view was really widely known, the court orders and mandatory legislation ordering the establishment of special programs started coming down on school systems all across the country. During the rapid expansion

The cascade system

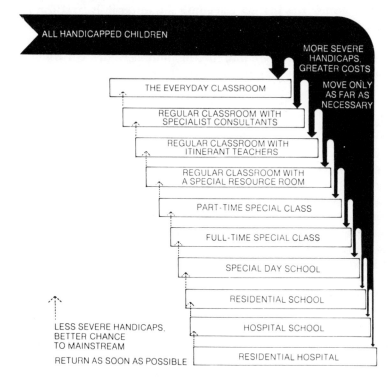

that followed, the objections to levels and isolation of "mildly" and "moderately" handicapped kids frequently got lost in the shuffle.

Under the new laws and court orders, school systems that were ordered to produce special education programs often didn't get a chance to sift through all the pros and cons first. The regulations (which vary widely from state to state) were usually dropped down on the system from above, and most of them required the school system to put labels on children. In all but a few states, the law was written so that it was usually quite easy to put children in self-contained segregated classrooms. Many school systems quite naturally did things the way they had always been done, and so placed the minimally handicapped kids in separate classes.

The upshot was that special education for "mildly handicapped" kids was going in two directions. At the same time some places were moving away from the idea of isolating and labeling any but severely handicapped children the number of self-contained classrooms was increasing dramatically in others.

Maggie had come to Copper County during this period of rapid expansion. She had gone to a teacher-training institution that didn't use categories for "mildly handicapped" children, and she had never had an experience with programs in which such children were largely placed in separate classes. Copper County was located in a state requiring categories. The state mandatory special education law had just been passed a few years before, and many counties in the state were looking for people with special ed training to staff their programs.

Before Maggie went to interview with Copper County, Sam Watkins, an official at the state division of special education, told her that "around the state, we've got a few dynamite programs with everything from self-contained classrooms for severely handicapped kids to support services in the regular classrooms. One county is trying a traveling van that goes between three schools for kids with minimal problems. But mostly, the counties — Copper County included — have ended up with EMR and TMR classes and schools at this point."

"How many of the kids get transferred out of special ed every year — back to the regular classroom?" Maggie asked him.

"We have no way of knowing that at the state level," he replied. "At this point, this office is concerned with keeping track of the children who *are* in special ed, not those who aren't. As short-staffed as we are, we can't do all we'd like to do." He smiled as if it pained him to say that. "I try to be honest," he added. "The pay's too low, and there's too much at stake not to be."

Maggie's first interview with the Copper County superintendent of schools, shortly thereafter, hadn't lessened the size of the question mark. "I must say, I have wondered about the numbers of children in our classes for the retarded," the superintendent said. "We have increased the number of classes from four to thirteen in the past two years, and I shudder to think that any child might be placed in one of those classes when he didn't deserve it." He smiled gently. "If you take this job, I hope you will be able to reassure us on that score.

"Until we have a director of special education," continued the superintendent, "our school board secretary will be handling the necessary paperwork for our program. She's overloaded, and of course we realize that we need a professional person . . ."

The supervisor was to be paid through federal funds, so the superintendent took Maggie to meet the Title I director, a chatty, grandfatherly man named Warner Jenkins.

Title I is one of six "titles" of the Elementary and Secondary Education Act (ESEA) originally passed in 1965. School systems can secure federal grants for "educationally disadvantaged" children under Title I. Therefore, Title I hits a lot of the same children special education does. Title III of that same act can provide school systems with money that can be used for, among other things, "supplementary and innovative programs" for children who might otherwise be considered "minimally handicapped."

As ESEA director, Warner Jenkins' main jobs were to get and then to administer federal funds for the school system. He made an immediate impression on everyone. His short shock of white hair stood out like a tiny Afro around his pink weathered face, and he always looked as though he were ready for some sort of emergency.

Warner wanted to talk about the number of parents who were refusing to allow their children to participate in special ed. "I expect you'll be able to visit these people and convince them otherwise," he said. "If those children *qualify*, it's our *legal* obligation to put them in a program."

Warner made liberal use of hand gestures as he spoke, searching the air in front of him for words when they failed to come. It wasn't hard to imagine him fussing over grandchildren.

After leaving Warner, Maggie went down to a little hamburger joint beside the First National Bank. Main Street was crowded with small businesses of various kinds. Men in overalls were as common as men in ties. A man from the seacoast was selling fish out of the back of his truck. People would wave, whether they knew you or not. There was a sign in the grocery store that said, "Those of you who think you know all the answers are very irritating to those of us who do."

During the first week on the job, Maggie visited the special ed classrooms, asking each teacher, "What can I do for you as a supervisor?" The footprints of the separate system as bottom priority showed up everywhere.

Their answers:

"You could get me some paper and glue! I'm buying my own."

"I need books these kids can read. They're on first and second grade level, most of them are seven, eight years old, and the office gave me a bunch of encyclopedias."

"Could we take field trips? The office said special ed kids can't take field trips."

"Well, this one kid is driving me up the wall."

"Get me out of here!"

This last request was delivered in point-blank fashion by the teacher-principal of Gateway School, who said he'd been recruited at the last minute from a regular classroom. "I'm not qualified to teach these kids," he said. "And I'm honest about it."

One of his kids showed Maggie a long gray blue feather. "It came off of Elvis Presley," he said seriously. He held it up for her to examine. "I made a feeder for him."

"It's beautiful," Maggie said, equally seriously. They looked at each other, and a slow grin spread over both their faces.

"Elvis is a bluejay." He grinned. "Been around our place two years. My dad named him that."

Up at Stockdale School, that stone fortress on the hill, Maggie was ushered around by the principal, Mr. Dillard. The painted wood walls and wide worn staircase suggested generations of Copper County kids. Mr. Dillard, a cheerful, frenetic man, cracked jokes and charged ahead of Maggie into each of the three special ed classrooms, announcing her presence in a loud voice. They went first to the half-day class. "The superintendent's brain child," explained Dillard, wiggling his eyebrows.

"Were the children placed in this half-day class because their problems are less severe?" she asked the teacher. The teacher made a face and said they were probably placed in half-day because they were next on the waiting list. "Some of my children have worse problems than any out back."

By "out back," she meant the full-time portable classrooms erected on the playground to house special education. Mr. Dillard took Maggie out there to watch a spelling test in progress. Jerry Bigelow, the teacher, was the first person who seemed particularly excited about the idea of having a supervisor. "Hey, I hope you aren't going to be sitting in the office all the time." When Dillard disappeared into the adjoining classroom, Mr. Bigelow added quickly, "Listen, they keep dropping kids in with us, you know, when they want to cool them out. Sometimes they stay two days. Some of them haven't left yet."

Mr. Dillard poked his head back into the doorway. "Come on over here, Maggie." He ushered her over to a bustling, friendly, elderly lady named Mrs. Cales. "Mrs. Cales is always fussing over these children," explained Mr. Dillard, peering out the window at the playground.

Mrs. Cales nodded energetically. "They come to school with dirt on their faces, I scrub it off. I've got toothbrushes for every one too. I just got finished scrubbing Donald and Laura."

All the children were listening attentively from their desks. "Donald and Laura," called Mrs. Cales. "Stand up and show this lady how clean you are!" Two children turned red, stood up very slowly, and sat down quickly. "Some of these children have trouble learning, and some of them can't do much, but we do what we can."

Mrs. Cales beamed. All the children were staring at them. "Some of the other teachers think these kids won't amount to anything, but I don't believe it," Mrs. Cales said in a firm, clear voice.

At that point, Mr. Dillard said he wanted to show Maggie the whole picture. He took her back into the main building and introduced her to Mrs. Maslow, the third grade teacher. Then he went out the door. Anita Maslow, a woman about Maggie's age, shook her head as Dillard disappeared around the corner. "Perpetual motion." She turned to Maggie. "Now, what can I tell you?" Looking around at the rug and round tables in the room, Maggie asked her how the children for the special ed classes had been chosen at Stockdale. "You mean *identified*," Anita said with a slow smile. "That's the word Warner Jenkins uses."

"Warner Jenkins? The Title I director?"

"Oh yes. He takes a hand in most everything and anything around here." Most of the special ed kids, Anita explained, came through teacher referral. "But Warner had to identify educationally disadvantaged children for Title I aid. Those who scored below 70 on the Slosson were also put on a list of children 'to be further evaluated' for special education."

The Slosson Intelligence Test is widely used for such purposes in schools all over the country. "Takes about 10–20 minutes to give and to score," according to the front cover of the manual. This chart was printed on the inside cover:

IQ	Classification	School Accomplishment and Placement
140 and up	Very Superior	Gifted classes, college, graduate work
120 – 139	Superior	Gifted classes, college, graduate work
110 – 119	Bright	High school and college
90 – 109	Average	High school, college is dubious
80 – 89	Dull	Slow learner classes
70 – 79	Borderline	Slow learner and retarded classes
(Below 70 —	Feebleminded)	
50 – 69	Moron	Retarded classes (educable)
20 – 49	Imbecile	Retarded classes (trainable)
0 – 19	Idiot	Not in school (not trainable)

"I'm not sure what all this testing is worth," Anita said.

Mr. Dillard stopped back by Anita's room and invited Maggie up to his office, where he told her cheerfully that "special education is getting big in a hurry around here, and there's things happening which don't seem to bear much relation to the children or teachers themselves. Always happens when things get big in a hurry."

Dillard suggested that Maggie eat lunch in the school cafeteria, "so you can see a lot of our children milling around at once." The smell of pinto beans and corn bread had already drifted up the stairs. Following it back down the stairs, Maggie couldn't help thinking about the time when she was a kid in grade school in a nearby county.

The sixth grade teacher was in charge of the Stockdale School cafeteria that day. When Maggie entered, she was taking preventive action against possible uprisings. Watching her brought back a movie Maggie had seen of a sergeant keeping hordes of enemy cowering in their trenches by systematically spraying the air above them with machine-gun fire.

"Danny!" she barked. "KeepyrhandstoyrselfSusiewhatdyathink yrdoing!Whosmakingthatnoiseinthecorderstopthatfoolishness LesterandcleanyrplatesandRebeccaifIhavetospeaktoyouone moretimeJerrygityrfeetbackwhurtheybelongyouveonlygotfive moreminutestofinishupso —"

She spotted Maggie. "Come in! Come in!" she told her, never taking her eyes off the children for a second. After a little diversionary fire — "SamifIhearsomuchasapeepoutofyouandBillyyouremember whathappenedtoyoulastweek" — she abandoned her post long enough to take Maggie into the kitchen and run her by the cook.

When Maggie came out with her plate, the teacher said, "This isMizCallahananshescumtalookatthespecialeducation —" Maggie went over to eat at the longest table. The children watched her closely, so she watched them too. They began to smile and wave.

"Hurryupnfinishyoudonthavealldaywereduentheplayground fiveminutesago —" Finally, the children lined up against the wall and waited until they received permission to leave. One little girl was wearing a sweat shirt that said, "Remember how you felt when you were my age."

After the children filed through the door and disappeared from sight, Maggie sat in the cafeteria, hearing voices. One voice was saying, "Well? What are you going to do about it?" The other voice was saying, "Hey, will you just end up supporting something you felt was bad for children?"

Maybe many teachers hear voices like that, when there's time to hear them. In the middle of passing out and collecting papers, arranging schedules and activities, taking playground duty, a teacher looks around and wonders exactly what's going on. And then the lunch money has to be collected.

The doubts do come back, at night or in the quiet classroom minutes after the children have gone home. The questions go in circles, while teachers try to think of ways to make things meaningful for their kids, sometimes within a structure that works against children and adults. There are always a few moments when a teacher in a situation like Stockdale School's might wonder if the system isn't pointed in the wrong direction. Then it's possible to doubt the doubts. And finally there are times when doubts seem to be the only way to make a difference in unquestioned practices. But the questions do keep coming back to the children. No matter how each person resolves the conflict, the children, after all, will be there the next morning. They have to be. They're required by law to be there.

Cafeteria thoughts: What happens when there's one part of the system that's totally separate and the problems of the whole system can be deposited over there? What happens when the separate part of the system isn't structured or properly equipped to take care of the "problems" by itself? Will lack of progress then be blamed on shortcomings within the children? If a lot of people think the children are in special ed because they can't learn, can special education classes be used to disguise and perpetuate the problems of the whole system? We can say, "They aren't learning because they're retarded or learning disabled," and the system can go on functioning as before.

In this frame of mind, Maggie returned to the superintendent's office. "Now that you've spent time in our classrooms," he said, "I wonder what direction you feel our program should be taking."

"It seems that many of these children shouldn't be isolated in self-contained classrooms," Maggie replied. "There's the self-contained structure already for kids who really do need full-time help, but it would be good to get many of these children mainstreamed into resource-type programs in the regular schools . . ."

The superintendent thought for a moment. "It's been my impression that the mainstreaming type of arrangement takes a highly qualified person. I'm not sure we have many of that type of personnel at this time." That left a question in Maggie's mind as to why highly qualified personnel wouldn't be required for self-contained classrooms also. Maybe because everybody would see what's happening in the resource program, and nobody really knows what happens in a self-contained classroom, she wondered to herself. "Gateway School," she continued hesitantly, "seems like an especially demoralizing situation for these children. If there would be any way to use Gateway as just another school . . ."

"Yes, as a matter of fact," the superintendent said, "I feel that way myself. However, I'm afraid we can't do that. We've tied our hands by erecting Gateway School with Title I money." He folded his hands and nodded sympathetically. "Since Gateway was constructed for special education with Title I funds," he explained, "we are obligated by federal regulations to use it for that purpose. Besides, we have no other classroom space available. So I'm afraid that we're going to have to work within reality. However, I do agree philosophically with the idea."

"We had all these children qualifying for special education," Warner Jenkins told Maggie later, "and no place to put them. There was the new law that said we had to supply the services. Nobody was giving us any real direction about how we were supposed to go about it in the best way, so it seemed like putting up some other building was the most logical way of going about solving the problem. People are saying now that it wasn't the best way, but it's too late. The building's there, and we've got to use it for special ed and make the best of it.

"The government keeps doing things like that to us all the time," he added. "Telling us to fill out five of this, fill out four of that, send them back, and we never did understand what they wanted them for in the first place. Then they come back and tell us we did it wrong. It's a very rare occasion when anybody comes around and explains the ins and outs of the whole thing. If they did, things might run better."

Over at the Stockdale playground that afternoon, Maggie sat in one of the swings. School was out and a few kids were around the playground. One of them was in special ed. He sat down in the next swing and looked at her silently for a few seconds.

"Hey, why does a hummingbird hum?" he asked, brushing the hair from his eyes.

"I dunno."

"Because he doesn't know the words."

They both started swinging, keeping pace together.

All kinds of thoughts were running through Maggie's mind. What's this Title I stuff mean? Funding's no reason for deciding what happens to the kids. It couldn't be. Doesn't make sense. But then, how does anything ever get decided? The two swings were climbing high at exactly the same pace.

Well, on the other hand, the superintendent agrees with me philosophically, and the teachers don't seem too happy about the whole arrangement. I'll bet it could be changed. I know pretty much about curriculum, so maybe . . . but then, there are so many things I don't know . . .

You could see Gateway School from the swing. Maggie's long hair blew into her eyes. Title I regulations? she wondered again. Huh?

3. Facts and Opinions

"Children who are categorized and labeled as different may be permanently stigmatized, rejected by adults and other children, and excluded from opportunities essential for their full and healthy development. *Yet* categorization is necessary to open doors to opportunity; to get help for a child, to write legislation, to appropriate funds, to design service programs, to evaluate outcomes, to conduct research, even to communicate about the problems of the exceptional child.

"Children may be assigned to inferior educational programs for years, deprived of their liberty through commitment to an institution, or even sterilized, on the basis of inadequate diagnostic procedures, with little or no consideration of due process. *Yet* we have the knowledge needed to evaluate children with reasonable accuracy, to provide suitable programs for them, and to guarantee them recognized due-process requirements.

"Large numbers of minority-group children — Chicanos, Puerto Ricans, blacks, Appalachian whites — have been inaccurately classified as mentally retarded on the basis of inappropriate intelligence tests, placed in special classes or programs where stimulation and learning opportunities are inadequate, and stigmatized. *Yet* these children often do need special assistance to manifest and sharpen their unappreciated competences."

> — Nicholas Hobbs, *The Futures of Children,*
> *Categories, Labels, and Their Consequences,* 1975

THE ABILITY to cope with frustrating or complicated questions and ambiguities is a necessary tool for anybody trying to get a feel for special education today. The realization that a question can have many answers comes in very handy too. There are many possible answers and opinions applicable to nearly every child and every question. If Maggie felt confused, it was partly because she had elsewhere seen kids similar to those in the Copper County EMR classes getting along well without the retarded label and the separation. In those cases, the system had adjusted instead of segregating the child. So "retarded" was just another answer, an opinion, not a fact.

Some of the special education labels *are* facts: blindness, deafness, loss of limbs, severe retardation, severe emotional disturbance. The degree of the condition varies within each category, as does the way the individual deals with it. Each individual has a different spirit, and the handicap is only one part of him.

Thanks to the efforts of many special educators, some of the "facts" about handicaps are changing too. Down's syndrome mongolism, for instance, has been thought to be such an unchangeable fact that, until recently, doctors would commonly recommend that mothers institutionalize such children. Yet in 1976, five-year-old kids with Down's syndrome mongolism in an early intervention program at the University of Washington were making developmental gains comparable to other children their age.

Other categories are wide open to opinion: "mild retardation," emotional disturbance, learning disabilities, social maladjustment, hyperactivity, slow learner, culturally disadvantaged, and so on. The category often depends on who's looking at the child and which definition is being used. The definitions of specific categories vary from state to state, as do the means of "identifying" children for those categories. A few states don't even use categories for children considered minimally handicapped.

Many people have expressed the opinion that the category system actually keeps people from looking at the child as a person. "We've been deep into efforts to get teachers to look at each child as an individual for years now," explained James Tucker, the chief consultant to the Texas Education Agency, Division of Special Education in March 1975. "But the plain political reality at this point is that, if you want to get any state or federal funds, you've got to put labels on the children. People are so used to thinking in terms of categories that they think you're not doing anything if you aren't willing to tell them how many of these children are retarded, how many are emotionally disturbed, and so on.

"I'm resigned to it, as an unfortunate fact of life. So we do identify children in Texas with legally qualifying criteria. Once a child meets the criteria for funding purposes, however, those criteria should cease to have any influence whatsoever on his program. Ten children categorized as EMR may have ten totally different needs and need to go in ten different directions.

"Unfortunately, when people hear the term 'EMR,' they automatically want to put all those kids in one place. They think the term tells them what the child's needs are. But each child is an individual. A child who is categorized as 'learning disabled' may have needs which are very similar to those of a child who is labeled 'emotionally disturbed' or those of a child in the regular classroom. The labels say nothing about the child's educational programming needs. If we can't get rid of meaningless labels in Congress at this point, at least we should be able to get rid of them in the teacher-training institutions."

At this point, some teacher-training institutions do teach strict categories, and others are either abandoning or limiting the opinion-based categories, figuring it's a lot less risky just to describe a child in terms of what he can do and what he can't do. Going one step further, some teacher-training institutions are teaching students to look at the system around the child before deciding that the problem is in the child.

Opinions vary even more out in the schools, since most of the questioning of labels and self-contained classrooms has occurred within the past ten years. A teacher who will accept no labels can end up teaching alongside a teacher who learned brain damage and IQs as gospel in college, as well as those teachers who are trained for other fields and are teaching on "emergency." Practices vary from place to place, so that a child who is declared retarded in one school district could easily be learning disabled in the next, emotionally disturbed in a third, or be a member of a multilevel regular classroom in a fourth. A child who is seen as emotionally disturbed in a rigidly structured school system might well be seen as creative and sensitive in another. The child in a self-contained classroom in one system might well be placed in a resource program in another. The children's problems are real, but there's so much room for opinion about their nature and source.

All this division of opinion can and often does create some delicate diplomatic situations in school systems, since people who see things in different ways may all feel that their way of doing things is best for the children. Maggie loved kids and teaching, but she wasn't the best diplomat. From the time she arrived in Copper County, when anybody in the school board office asked her, she'd just tell them she hoped the day would come soon when the re-tarded label and segregation could go. She'd talk about mainstreaming and then tell stories about kids like Callie Peale. From her point of view, she was just being honest. From the other side of the fence, she was bluntly saying, "Hey, you're doing things wrong."

Other school administration employees were much more adept at dealing with delicate human situations than Maggie was. The most striking example was Howard Birdwell, the superintendent of schools. Coming from outside the county, he had been hired for a job a local man had been expecting to get. The school board had been divided into factions by the choice, so Mr. Birdwell could ex-pect flak over anything he undertook. He had a long-term contract but was well aware that anything he wanted to do depended on not antagonizing the wrong people.

"This is a small county, and politics have to find some sort of arena," one of the superintendent's supporters explained later. "The school system's the biggest employer in the county, next to the highway department. Power's the name of the game, and the school system happens to be the football field they're playing on."

Mr. Birdwell had been a superintendent in various school sys-tems for over twenty years. During those twenty-odd years, he had acquired a solid reputation for fair dealing and dedication to his profession. He had also mastered many of the necessary tools of the superintendent's trade, including the fine art of expanding verbal replies to avoid questions he didn't want to answer. A par-ticularly difficult or touchy question was likely to elicit at least a fifteen-minute Birdwell discourse on anything but the question it-self.

That kind of approach seemed to be useful as camouflage. A superintendent sits on top of a whole system that involves a wide variety of services, interests, organizations, transportation, and ma-terial needs, all of which sometimes conflict. The superintendent is expected to be a parent figure of sorts and take care of everybody's interests, so loyalties are divided. This can become complicated if the superintendent also has to juggle several new laws, limited funds, and local politics at the same time.

Mr. Birdwell moved his heavyset frame decisively, as if each movement was powered by thirty years in the driver's seat. His thumb was perpetually hooked through his belt, and he had the appearance of a man capable of making momentous decisions, at any time.

He carried a fine pocket watch on a long gold chain that Maggie admired during their first interview. "Yes. The people in my last school district gave me this," he said solemnly. Then he smiled in a gentle, shy fashion. "I think they appreciated what I did there," he said.

That smile was very endearing. Somehow, a little boy had the habit of peeking through his formal businesslike expression. That smile made Maggie hope that Mr. Birdwell had many chances to go fishing or whatever else he liked to do.

Howard Birdwell had been a little boy, over fifty years before, in one of the railroad towns not far from Copper County. He had gone to work for the railroad when he was fifteen years old and had saved enough money to put himself through college. He learned early that life involves hard work. During the Depression, he had taught in a one-room schoolhouse and later was principal of a small high school well back in the mountains. By 1951, he became superintendent of his first school system. Maggie was in kindergarten at the time.

During their first interview, Maggie asked Mr. Birdwell if there was any possibility of putting some of the children back into the regular classroom at the end of the year. "I've always considered myself an educational pioneer," replied Mr. Birdwell. Again the gentle smile. "I've seen what lack of education can do. There's still room for pioneers these days, you know.

"I've had offers to go to big-city school systems, places much more prestigious than this one," he went on. "But that's not where my heart or my calling is. I've always been content to stay right here in the country. I didn't have it easy as a boy, and I learned early that a boy can't have anything much more valuable than a good education. So I've used my chance to make one for some other boys and girls."

These touching words were delivered in a dry, matter-of-fact fashion.

A picture of his wife, a rather serious-looking lady, sat on a bookshelf filled with school law texts. Mr. Birdwell's home was a hundred miles away. He went there only on weekends. "He stays in a little old apartment over the bank during the week," his secretary told Maggie. "Seems like he'd get lonely, but that's what he does. He thinks it's important for him to be here during the week, even at night."

"What does he do for recreation?"

"He reads and goes to the Lions Club meeting."

"Copper County was in a financial mess when I arrived," Mr. Birdwell told Maggie later. "It hasn't been an easy job to straighten it out, I promise you, young lady." He hooked his thumb under his belt and stuck out his elbow. "No easy job," he repeated thoughtfully.

Abigail Robin commented on Mr. Birdwell's situation. "I admire him," she said. "He's got the right ideas, but sometimes I wonder if there's room for everybody's priorities. He's on a political tightrope, and that means compromises, whether he wants them or not. And when there are compromises, that's when your kids really need somebody to stick up for them, you know." Maggie decided right then and there that there would be none of those politics for her. Straight-out dealing, by golly. Lay the cards on the table. She said something to that effect to Abigail. "You've lost your mind," Abigail answered. "Politics isn't a bad word. It's a fact of life and systems. You've *got* to play politics if you want to get anywhere."

Maggie didn't have much time to sit around and consider the good and bad of politics. Her first assignment, as a paid employee, was to write the state proposal for special ed funds. It had to be done within three days. "Couldn't we get a delay?" she asked. "I don't know anything about the needs of the program yet."

"I'll tell you what to ask for," said Mr. Birdwell. "We want one supervisor's salary, one additional teacher's salary, and one thousand dollars for materials." He handed her a book of forms and a how-to-write-it pamphlet. "I'm sure you'll do a fine job with it, young lady."

"But shouldn't we ask for more money to bring the classroom conditions up to par?"

"We should only ask for what we're sure we can get."

When the superintendent said things like that, he wasn't offering an opinion. He was stating a fact.

Maggie went out to her desk and looked at the state forms. They contained spaces for 319 statistics on the first two pages alone.

Statistics are supposed to be facts of a sort. The left-hand column of each page of the forms listed the various categories eligible for state aid. The adjoining column listed a "prevalence" percentage. According to the prevalence percentage, for instance, 1 percent of the Copper County children were likely to be emotionally disturbed.

Other prevalence percentages ran as follows: educable mentally retarded (2 percent), trainable mentally retarded (.25 percent), physically handicapped (.15 percent), homebound and hospitalized (.50 percent), speech and language (3.5 percent), deaf and hard of hearing (1.6 percent), blind and partially sighted (.10 percent), behavioral disorders/emotionally disturbed or socially maladjusted (1 percent), specific learning disabilities (1 percent), multiple handicapped (.10 percent), gifted (1 percent).

Nobody seemed to know who had made up the original prevalence percentages.

The next column of figures was the only one that bore any relationship to reality: "children served this year." Since all the Copper County children were considered either retarded or homebound, all those other categories didn't apply. But the number of EMR "children served" in Copper County beat the estimate by approximately 1000 percent.

It was baffling. "If they'd call some of them by another name besides retarded, the charts would look a little more balanced," somebody joked. The rest of the chart was mostly fiction. The number of "children unserved" was obtained by subtracting the actual numbers of children from the prevalence estimate. The number of "additional teachers needed" was obtained by dividing the "children unserved" figure by the "recommended teacher-pupil ratio." And so on.

The "additional teachers needed" figures bothered Maggie a lot, so she took them to the school board secretary who had done them the previous year to see if she could help make sense of them. "None of these figures turns out to have anything to do with actual county needs," Maggie said.

"Oh, I should have told you. They use those charts to supply the federal government with statistics. They don't use them on the state level to decide on how many teachers we get or anything like that. Tell you what. Don't beat your brains out over it. Just copy off the figures from last year's proposal. I think that's what we did the year before anyhow."

Maggie did, since the figures were going to be pure fantasy anyway. They were sent to the state division, from which they were sent on to the Bureau of Education for the Handicapped in Washington.

Maggie worked late that evening. So did Mr. Birdwell. She saw him in his office, poring over piles of papers, writing notes on this one, throwing that one in the trash. Winter was coming, and each day darkness fell a little earlier. About six o' clock, she went out in the hall and leaned on the windowsill to watch the leaves falling over the rows of houses clinging to the side of the steep hillside. "There's places in this town where you can go in the front door, walk up three flights, and come out on the ground floor," one of the teachers had told her. Houses piled like pancakes. Leaves falling fast, chasing each other over the rooftops. The church clock sounded. Down below the window, two teen-agers were sitting on a bench holding hands. The streetlight switched on above their heads. They seemed to be telling secrets. They looked happy.

When she got back to her desk, Mr. Birdwell was putting on a big shapeless overcoat. He stopped to stuff a pile of papers into his briefcase. "Don't work too late, young lady," he said formally, adjusting the brim of his felt hat and turning up his overcoat collar. He walked down the long, dark hall, passing beneath one light fixture after another. A tall, heavy figure, taking papers home to dinner, his footsteps echoing through the quiet building.

Maggie chewed her pencil and watched him. He stopped to look out the window and lingered there for several seconds. Fifteen minutes later, Maggie left too. The couple was still sitting beneath the streetlight, leaves falling all around them.

The next morning, Maggie went to Warner Jenkins with a list of basic supplies that would probably be needed for the classrooms. Warner was in high spirits. His niece had sent him a giant salami in the mail. Then he found out about the list. "I take care of the purchasing for the school system," he said, raising a white eyebrow and peering at the paper in Maggie's hand.

"Special education has had more than its share of funds this year," he added. "Purchasing supplies isn't your job. Your first priority at this point is to get those teachers on schedules."

"But the teachers say —"

"I handle the purchasing," Warner repeated. "That's not a part of your job." Then he showed her a little giraffe he had carved, which crooked its neck up and down when it was wiggled. Maggie, while charmed by the giraffe, was taken aback by what Warner had to say and stood there, shifting from foot to foot, exchanging nervous looks with him.

"Have you met any of the children yet?" Warner wanted to know, setting the giraffe on top of the salami.

"A lot of them. And many seem fairly normal. That's why I think we ought to —"

"If they were normal, they wouldn't be there, would they?" Warner said. It was more a statement than a question.

4. Copper County

"Deviance is not a property *inherent* in any particular kind of behavior; it is a property *conferred upon* that behavior by the people who come into direct or indirect contact with it. The only way an observer can tell whether or not a given style of behavior is deviant then, is to learn something about the standards of the audience which responds to it."

— Kai Erickson, sociologist, 1966

"Abusive practices are those which, regardless of intent, separate one group from another in a fashion which demeans one group . . . Socially healthy practices are those which bring people together in mutual recognition of individual differences."

— Seymour Sarason, professor of psychology, 1976

MAGGIE AND ANITA Maslow, the third grade teacher from Stockdale, had moved into a rambling white house near the train station. A snub-nosed, open-faced redhead, Anita was the kind of person who related to children the same way she related to adults — frankly, forthrightly, with great interest. It was not at all unusual to find her eagerly questioning some child about a subject with which she wasn't quite familiar. Anita one day went to buy something from the elderly lady who ran the hardware store, and Maggie found her there an hour later, practicing a quilting stitch and hearing about the wreckage Herbert Hoover had inflicted on the state.

Anita had a habit of saying exactly what she thought. Since her comments were unusually perceptive, her bluntness could be doubly disconcerting; and yet, she didn't offend where another person might have. Somehow, she could take delicate subjects off the shelf and brush away the awkwardness. Her bluntness stemmed from genuine human interest, rather than a desire to intrude, and people could tell. She asked the woman who lived over the hardware store, for instance, how it was to be alone and old. "It isn't often anybody takes an interest in an old person like me," the woman responded as she left. "You come back."

Anita's husband was working in a nearby county, building low-cost housing. He moved around a great deal, and she stayed stationary, getting a little lonesome in her apartment from time to time. So the house worked out well for both Maggie and Anita. It also worked out well for Brown Eye, a scraggly stray dog who had adopted Anita weeks before.

The neighborhood was jam-packed with kids and dogs, and had a bustling feeling about it. From the day they arrived, the house was filled with children, who already liked Mrs. Maslow, and were delighted to have someplace to go. They kept slipping scraps to Brown Eye, and she grew sleeker as the weeks passed. Brown Eye had never had it so good.

The adults in the neighborhood weren't quite so quick to accept them, although Maggie and Anita didn't involve themselves in anything that might have been controversial or political in the community. The job effectiveness of both women, particularly Maggie, would have been hurt if they had begun to get involved in factional matters. Gradually, the initial suspicious reserve developed into a somewhat reserved but warm friendliness. Like most nonnatives, the two young women were still considered outsiders.

"We were thinking maybe you two were hippies," the minister's wife down the street confided apologetically one afternoon. "On account of you being young and sort of different dressing, I guess. But I can see you're both decent hard workers." The minister himself wasn't convinced until they sent his little boy home one day for telling them a flat-out whopper lie. "My dad says you ain't hippies," the boy reported the next day.

In short order, they grew to love a couple of children who lived directly across the street in a rambling old place covered with peeling paint and spotted with broken windowpanes covered with polyethylene sheeting. One kid was in special ed; the other one wasn't. Their names were Pickle and Jenny Krebbs.

Nine-year-old Pickle radiated energy. The first time Maggie ever saw him, he was sitting in a corner of her living room enthralling several other children by demonstrating fancy knot-tying with two pieces of rope. He looked up as she came into the house, shaking snow from her coat. "Bet you can't do this, and you're a teacher!" he challenged, as if he had known her for years.

"You're right about that," she answered. "Who are you?"

"I'm Pickle Krebbs, and you're Miss Callahan, right?"

"How'd you know?"

"Mrs. Maslow told me about you."

Pickle had foiled efforts to place him in special education by scoring quite high on three IQ tests. He was very proud of that. "You're going to work with special ed," he said confidently. "Well, you ain't gonna have me to work with, but you'll have old Jenny here." Old Jenny, his older sister, gave him a good kick and wouldn't look at Maggie. They both had freckles and red hair. His was carrot red, hers auburn. She seemed to be as reserved as he was animated.

"Where'd you get the name Pickle?" Maggie asked him.

"Everybody asks that. My real name is Harold." He grinned in an accommodating fashion. "My mom had three kids before me," he explained. "And when my dad heard that I was coming, he hollered, 'Lord bless, Mary! Now we're in a pickle! We'll have to put this one in the yard!' " Pickle was rolling his eyes and imitating his father's deep voice. He fell backward against the wall with his hand over his heart.

"They certainly don't have any trouble getting him out in the yard," Anita laughed as Maggie dropped her books in the kitchen. "The main problem is to get him to come back inside long enough to sleep and eat."

Pickle was in Anita's third grade class at Stockdale. "He's already legendary up there," she said. "Mr. Dillard is forever announcing his latest plans for wearing out the seat of Pickle's pants."

"Seems like a really bright kid."

"Yeah, but you know what? He can only read on a first grade level. Jenny's only a year older than he is, and she's in special ed. But she can read a third grade book."

"Why can't he read?"

Anita frowned. "I'm not sure. It sure isn't because he doesn't want to."

"How're you teaching him?"

"Well, he relates to printed words in a weird sort of way," she said, tapping her fingers on the counter. "I can't quite figure it out.

think, in his way, Pickle needs special ed more than Jenny does. But not the kind we have here. Anyhow, so far, he's learning best through stories he makes up and dictates to the aide. The aide practically lives with him. We do a lot of basic stuff too, like phonics, but that doesn't seem to be Pickle's style."

Anita was making meat loaf. Jenny came to the door of the kitchen and stood there quietly, hugging the door frame, looking at them. "Come on in, Jenny," said Anita. "Have a seat."

Jenny blushed slightly, then sat down awkwardly at the kitchen table. "Do you need any help?" she said softly.

"With what?" replied Anita.

"Oh, I dunno. With anything," said Jenny, blushing again. Anita put her to work chopping onions. Though she didn't talk much more, Jenny was obviously pleased to be included.

She was a very pretty girl, dressed in patched-up jeans and a too-big wool shirt. Her auburn hair curled and tangled down her back, and splashes of red fingernail polish decorated her broken nails.

Jenny wouldn't look at Maggie for at least a week. But after she stopped thinking of her as "the special ed lady," she opened up like a flower and let Maggie see her peculiarly poetic way of looking at the world.

Maggie and Jenny sat on the front steps one evening with Pickle watching the sun set. "When the sun goes behind the mountain, somebody can go back there and steal it," explained Jenny. "Only it'd be so hot, they'd have to drop it."

She was full of questions about what she had read. She read every book she could get her hands on. Since her special ed class didn't have any library, Anita lent her books like *Sounder, Charlotte's Web*, and junior biographies of Mary, Queen of Scots, and Helen Keller.

Jenny didn't know why she had been put in special ed. "Two men came and asked my mother to sign a paper, and she did," she murmured, shrugging her shoulders. "But I don't like it. Special ed is a bad thing in my head. It teases me when I think about it."

Special ed wasn't the only bad thing in Jenny's head. A lot of loud noises came out of the Krebbs house at night sometimes. Mr.

Krebbs was looking for work and not having much luck. He'd been out of steady work for two years and was making ends meet by making deliveries for a hardware store ten miles away. With four kids, the family had been forced to go on welfare. Mr. Krebbs got paid in cash at the hardware store, since the welfare rules didn't allow him to work. He was a proud man, and that kind of arrangement ate away at him. Late at night, crashing, yelling, and breaking noises sometimes came out of the house after he'd been home a while.

Those kinds of noises had double meaning for Anita. "Every time that happens, Pickle comes in the next day, wound up tighter than a corkscrew, and is hell on wheels in the classroom. If I didn't live across the street from him, God knows what I'd think about his behavior."

During the day, Pickle and Jenny's mother rarely spoke. Mrs. Krebbs would stand for hours in her doorway, staring out into the street when it was filled with children, staring at the street when it was empty. At first Maggie thought she might be waiting for something. But she wasn't. She was waiting for anything.

When Maggie first noticed Mrs. Krebbs' staring, it reminded her of rows of people manning the apartment windows in her old neighborhood in the city, looking and looking. Within weeks, Maggie found herself gravitating to her own screen door, staring into the street after a particularly frustrating day. Once, lost in some sort of limbo between whatever might happen in the street and whatever was going on in her life, Maggie looked up and saw Mrs. Krebbs staring through her own screen door. We're not just staring at the street, Maggie realized. We're also turning our backs on what we don't want to see or think about.

It wasn't hard to understand why Mrs. Krebbs would "sign a paper" from the school without a fuss. Like many people in the neighborhood, she had a lot to turn her back on. Davidson was an economically depressed town. When the neighborhood people expressed resentment against hippies, they were thinking about people who didn't value what they had, who didn't contribute anything to the community, who were suspected of encouraging young people to be shiftless and maybe even use drugs.

This resentment didn't include all the outside people coming into the county. "I used to think all those people with long hair were no-goods," Mr. Krebbs told Maggie, "but you know, it's not that way at all. I'm all in favor of some of these long-hairs." He was talking about a few families who had moved nearby a few years before and had gradually established themselves as decent, friendly, hardworking people who took care of their farms, helped their neighbors, and generally contributed something to the quality of life in the county. "Those people are good neighbors, I hear," Mr. Krebbs said firmly. "So you have to judge each long-hair by what he's doing, I guess."

"Well, it's kind of interesting to see how some of these new people are doing things we gave up a long time ago," declared the woman next door.

"Why, there's a man I hear of, up on Bald Mountain, has got enough money to buy himself ten indoor toilets if he wanted them, and still uses a crapper a hundred yards from his house. Now, we had a celebration at *my* house when we got indoor plumbing."

A deaf mute named Jesse lived in the neighborhood. He slept on a cot on a neighbor's closed-in porch down at the end of the street. These people were fairly well to do for that area. They kept Jesse warm and fed him, and he did odd jobs for them.

Jesse got up very early in the morning to walk around the town. You might see him on the bridge, you might see him beside the river, or he might be sitting on the steps of the funeral parlor. Wherever he was, he was usually standing very still, wrapped in layers of stiffened garments, staring out impassively at whatever passed from behind a dingy gray woolen hood.

Maggie always thought of Jesse as the town oracle, telling everyone, including herself, something they didn't want to hear. There was no way of knowing how old he was. His hands looked young, his hair was brown, but his beard was gray. Like so many people in his position, he had to put up with children who teased him and even threw rocks at him. Mothers used him as a boogieman: "If you stay out past dark, Jesse'll get ya."

Pickle and Jenny felt an odd kind of sympathy for Jesse — odd, because it wasn't usual for the children in the neighborhood to have this kind of feeling. Jenny was too timid to go up to him without Pickle, but she agreed that he was "nice as all."

From time to time, Pickle would sit and talk with Jesse. They'd just talk about whatever he'd seen: a fire in another part of town, a fight that took place on the playground. One day, Maggie watched him sitting with Jesse on the curb in front of their house. After they'd been sitting for several minutes, Pickle took a piece of cake out of his pocket, started eating it and then absent-mindedly split it with Jesse and kept on talking. It wasn't charity. Maggie never saw Pickle give Jesse anything without bothering to talk to him. He was Jesse's friend.

There was a woman named Lucy in the neighborhood. She lived next door to Maggie, and on warmer days she and Maggie spent a lot of time in her porch swing, talking about the children, corrupt politicians, the way life is, and the way life used to be. Lucy, who had about fifty years on Maggie, had concluded that Davidson and the whole county had reached an all-time low in self-serving government. She predicted that "Some day, that whole pack of politicians is going to ignite — just catch on fire — from pure wickedness. You wonder why they haven't burnt up already."

Of all the stories Lucy told, one particular conversation kept coming back whenever Maggie thought of her. "Old people like me, we're pretty much stuck in our houses, you know," she said one day. "I can go downtown, but there's no place I can go sit down and have a pleasant conversation, pass the time of day. Those are little human things that don't seem to be on our city council's priority list.

"When I was your age, things like that never bothered me. My husband was alive, we could get a lot of pleasure from a simple walk in the sunshine. Now he's gone, and there doesn't seem to be anything useful I can do. That's bad, because there's just hundreds of old nuisances like me in these parts, sitting around getting in the way." Maggie told her she wasn't an old nuisance, and Lucy said that Maggie was a young nuisance who wouldn't know what she was talking about until she was an old one.

"There's only one time I can remember when it wasn't that way for old people in this county," she continued, swinging vigorously. "That was back when they had the WPA. They'd taken the whole floor over top the five-and ten-cent store and made it into a sewing cooperative. They paid minimum wage, and whole bunches of us would go down there and work." She laughed. "We'd make the clothes, and we'd sell them cheap, so it was good for everybody. And, oh, we'd have a pleasant time of it while we worked, visiting back and forth. They gave us coffee and it seemed like the time flew."

Lucy loved Franklin Roosevelt. "The government understood a lot more about people back then than it does now. Roosevelt knew that people needed self-respect. If people were out of work, why the government gave them work that was worth something. Those bridges over the river were built while WPA was on too.

"These days, the government doesn't bother about making a poor man feel useful or giving him a job he can respect. No. They set it up so a man like Krebbs over there feels like a criminal if he manages to get an odd job." Her eyes were angry, and she nodded her head slowly before turning abruptly to look at Maggie. "You know, that sewing cooperative even made *money*." She sighed, running her hand over her white hair. "But they shut that project down, and none of us ever knew why.

"And I'm going to tell you something, Maggie." She spoke slowly, with a sharp edge to her soft voice. "It wasn't making the money that I missed the most, though the good Lord knows that money helped. But it was just being useful and being together with other people that made me glad to get up in the morning. It's hard on people to be isolated.

"It would have hurt anybody's heart to see how many of those people died during the two or three years after that project shut down. People who hadn't been sick for years were coming down with all kinds of ailments. Maybe they didn't have the will to fight the sickness, when all they had to look forward to was being lonesome and useless."

They died of separation, Maggie thought. The project report wouldn't have included that.

*

Maggie and Lucy's neighborhood represented only one face of Davidson. The county also had its Lions Clubs, country club, Methodist Church, and housing developments where well-dressed children played on manicured lawns and in parks donated by the Garden Club. It had its lovely, expensive, well-kept farms.

"There's lot of Episcopalians living over there in that section of town," Lucy said somewhat disdainfully. Lucy was a Baptist. Episcopalian was a label with characteristics all its own.

The goals and life-styles of the economically comfortable people inevitably differed drastically from those of the average family in Maggie's neighborhood. Their concerns weren't so immediate. They took Dale Carnegie courses, watched soap operas, organized spaghetti dinners, and took group trips to football games. These were, in general, the people who controlled the schools, and, to a large extent, local politics. Their values more or less determined the values of the schools.

In Maggie's dealings with them, she found them friendly, decent people. They were always sincerely glad to know that something was being done to help "those poor retarded children who haven't had the advantages ours have." If they were quick to protest any suggestions that their own children be put in the classes, most didn't see the implications of their double standard.

If life wasn't easy for many people living in Copper County, they were still blessed and surrounded by the kind of natural splendor that exists only in dreams for millions of city dwellers. When the weather was warm, a kid could fish from the river and ramble around in the mountains. The stars were brilliant at night, and, as Lucy put it, "the goodness of this land gets to running in your veins."

"Sometimes all that beauty makes a pain in my heart," Mrs. Krebbs told Maggie in a rare moment of confidence. "And it's going to make my heart hurt more if we have to move somewhere else. You can love it, but you can't eat it."

The town of Davidson itself retained a timeless quality. Old men sat in front of the courthouse and complained about high prices and said the world was going to hell. Freight trains never stopped coming through, and children never stopped telling themselves that someday they'd go where those trains were going. Then, when they'd finally do it and then come back, they'd tell everyone that they'd never realized what a blessing Copper County was until they left it.

Environment and living space always seemed to have a big effect on the emotions and thinking. Lucy used to say, "If I could live up on that mountain, I would. It frees the mind and the spirit." When Maggie went up there, she always felt that too. Just the expanse of space could melt away so many of the considerations that seemed so important in the crowded town.

Most of the people who lived on Bald Mountain had farms of one description or another. There were a few families living up there who had, over the years, collected a great deal of political clout. It was said that the man who ran the grocery store and post office could pick up the phone and get anyone a driver's license or on the welfare rolls. The county had paved one of the back roads right up to his driveway.

The land was very important to almost all the older people who had some, a feeling they tried hard to convey to their children. A surprising number had deeded away their property to their grand-children, "so that son of mine can't sell it to some speculator. He hasn't got any sense now, but, by the time the land can be sold, maybe they'll know the worth of what they've got." Land prices were rising steadily. "There's even people from Canada buying land around here," one old man told Maggie. "If I deed this land over to my grandson, I guess that's protection against my own weak minutes too."

People really can't be divided into groups, and it goes without saying that the Copper County population was complex. And yet, because the special education program is a product of the whole school system and the schools are a reflection of the society sur-rounding them, Maggie recorded a few observations, not as a sociologist, but as a teacher who knew the area from childhood, lived in Davidson for a short while, and tried to keep her eyes open.

All groups overlapped, but there seemed to be at least one major separation. It could be seen in the way the grocery store clerk looked at the person who offered food stamps in payment for groceries. A large percentage of the county population received public assistance, especially after the quarry shut down. If there was any real dividing line among groups of people, that seemed to be it. The way some people said the word "welfare," it sounded like a character defect. Racial prejudice was no joke in Copper County, but it seemed to be completely overshadowed by prejudice against "the welfare."

Cars around town carried bumper stickers reading, "I fight poverty. I work." The fear of poverty was very real throughout the county. The people who expressed prejudice against people on welfare most openly and with the greatest bitterness were often themselves on the lower edge of the middle economic group. That seemed odd at first, since, if people were barely able to keep their own noses above water, one would expect that they would have more sympathy with the problems of people who couldn't make it on their own.

Maggie said something like that to a group of teachers once and was told, "That's just the point. Some people are willing to do it for themselves, others aren't. There's people just lying around having more kids so they can get more welfare. Each kid means more government money, and they're making more money off the government than others that work and never accept a penny otherwise."

"Well, it's not the people so much as it is the system," reflected another teacher. "The way it's set up, they can't work or take odd jobs if they want to, especially when they've got a lot of kids to feed. So the system's done a real bad thing to a lot of people where it was supposed to be helping them out, if you ask me."

Another woman wondered why there wasn't a good nutrition program in the area. "Day care, Head Start, and all those things might prevent these children's problems in the first place," she said. Everyone agreed, but the thought got lost in the next comment.

"Just look at those Watkins kids from up Squirrel Hollow," complained another teacher. "Lord knows how many of them there are. You could have all the programs you want, and they'll probably all do the same when they grow up anyhow."

So the children from the welfare families were a constant irritant to those who resented the way the welfare system operated. Sometimes people seemed to want to put as much distance as they could between themselves and people on welfare. Maggie began to feel that there was a connection between that attitude and the fact that so many of the welfare kids were referred to the retarded classes soon after they got to school.

The idea that the problems of poor people are located inside them isn't limited to Copper County. According to a survey of a cross section of more than one thousand Americans, "A majority of Americans, in 1969, held poor people themselves responsible for poverty and were correspondingly reluctant to support new programs aimed at eradicating poverty."

An eighteen-month Office of Economic Opportunity research project concluded just the opposite. They found that the "labor-force participation of the poor is determined primarily by factors over which the poor have no control: racial, class, and occupational discrimination, poor training, poor health, restrictive and regressive welfare programs which penalize recipients for work, inadequate transportation to and from work places, and so on . . .

"Their apparent apathy is not the cause of their status, rather it is a response to an inability to fulfill important goals, an adaptation to the experience of failure. As one sociologist notes, 'We are still apt to visualize deviant behavior as the product of a deep-seated characterological strain in the person who enacts it, rather than as the product of the situation in which it took place, and we are still apt to treat that person as if his whole being was somehow implicated.' This statement could describe the plight of the handicapped as well as that of the poor and ethnically different."

5. Referrals: From the Regular System to the Special System

"Most teachers of the 'normal' children have been trained with certain assumptions, and expect to face a certain kind of behavior from normal children. They don't expect to find the kind of behavior that they have been taught to attribute to the other ten percent. The implication in teacher-training has been that any kind of abnormal behavior is something that requires special training and special understanding.

"Now, the fact is . . . the world isn't organized into 90 percent and 10 percent, or whatever percentages you want to divide handicapped and non-handicapped into. Children don't really distribute themselves into those two groups neatly. So, what regular teachers classically find is that they have a lot of children in their classes who show learning styles, behavior styles, all kinds of differences which puzzle them. So they often feel that those kids shouldn't be there, and they should be in special education, since that was the implication of teacher-training.

"Now, this and many other factors have led to an increased push for larger special education, which means expanding the definition of handicapped. Philosophically, I'm opposed to it. Practically, there can be a great deal of logic to it. So there's going to be a real clash here between philosophy and what seems logical on the surface."

— Edwin Martin, director, U.S. Bureau of Education
for the Handicapped, July 1975

THE TERM "ecological system" is sometimes used in textbooks to express the idea that a person's behavior or problems are often caused primarily by events and circumstances around him rather than being entirely located inside him. It's an odd, stiff term for such a warm, human idea. In a 1974 letter to Senator Jacob Javits, the directors of the Mississippi Head Start Program applied the idea to their work:

"A child who wakes up to the weather coming in on his bed is not emotionally disturbed if he is hostile, nor is a child emotionally disturbed if he is withdrawn after awakening to find that one of his three siblings who sleep in the same bed has wet during the night.

These children are normal in their response to life. It is life that is abnormal.

"A child from a family that can afford no books, few toys, and inadequate food may test out (*if* we were to give him one) below what is normal for middle class children, but he is not retarded."

Anita was saying the same thing when she said, "If I didn't live across the street from him, God knows what I'd think about his behavior."

Each person has an ecological system that affects and sometimes determines his behavior. Many education textbooks deal with the fact that when a child is subjected to undue pressures, when he feels inadequate, when the system imposes insane demands on him — he may act out or become apathetic, or perhaps turn into a "behavior problem." He finds ways to release the pressure. Grownups do the same thing. Outside school, each person finds his own way to let off steam. Inside school, a high-pressure system can make people of all ages become behavior problems for others or act out in ways they ordinarily wouldn't.

In a nine-year study entitled *Labeling the Mentally Retarded*, published in 1973, sociologist Jane Mercer surveyed the public schools, medical facilities, law enforcement agencies, departments of mental hygiene and public welfare, religious organizations, and private organizations for retardation in Riverside, California. She found that the public schools labeled far and away more people "retarded" than any other agency. A very high percentage of the children labeled retarded by schools in this large urban area turned out to be black or Chicano. In Copper County, the predominant local prejudice was welfare.

Mercer also found that elementary teachers did most of the referring. "What are the standards which the elementary teacher applies when she decides that a child is sufficiently deviant to be referred for psychological evaluation?" Mercer asked. "What teacher expectations does the child violate who eventually achieves the status of mental retardate?"

Whatever the answers are, they have their own odd twists in each individual case: divorces, pressure from the administration, personal biases, noise level, faulty air conditioners — all the things that affect the way human beings react to other humans in such situations. Occasionally, referral is even out of the teacher's control. In Copper County, for instance, many of the "retardates" had been "identified" to begin with, when all the children in the county were given a Slosson IQ test to find out how much money the county schools would get under Title I.

Then there is always the pressure from the system or the particular school. In Copper County, teachers were expected to do at least two things: cover the grade-level textbooks and preserve law and order. Covering the textbook meant go through the fourth grade books assigned to the fourth grade. Law and order meant variations on stay in your seat, keep quiet, and ask when you want to go to the bathroom.

That kind of pressure can make grownups do funny things. The year before Maggie came, a regular classroom teacher had gotten locked into the principal's office accidentally when she sneaked in after hours to get a copy of the achievement test. She knew her own performance would be judged by the kids' scores, and so she had wanted to prep her kids. From all reports, she wasn't the only one. She just happened to be the one to get locked into the office.

The way the teachers were viewed also depended on who was looking at them. Anita Maslow, operating her third grade classroom at Stockdale, would have been considered a successful teacher in a less rigid environment. In that school, she was a deviant, and therefore in some people's eyes bad. "I knew those children weren't going to be taught right as soon as I saw those round tables in her room," sniffed the first grade teacher. "There's no way to hold these children in line if they haven't got assigned seats."

Pressure on teachers to conform to rigid standards, along with other factors, has its effect on special education referrals. In their December 1974 report, *Children out of School in America*, the Children's Defense Fund documented the nationwide tendency to misuse special education as what many call a "dumping ground."

. . . special education classes [commented a Cambridge, Massachusetts, school official] consist of kids that don't react normally to regular classroom situations rather than strictly retarded or emotionally disturbed kids. A Davenport [Iowa] official said, "Teachers who feel 'low functioning' kids are too much trouble wish that special education would take them all away. Especially at the junior and senior high school level, the staff has often made a decision about placing a child in special education or kicking him out of school." In Davenport, the Director of Special Education said they have made good progress in keeping special education from becoming a dumping ground for children teachers don't want to handle. He added, however, that a teacher trying to differentiate among the 70+ IQs says, "I can handle the one who says 'good morning,' 'goodbye' and erases the blackboards, but not the hellion." A Springfield, Massachusetts, counselor pointed out that, "there is a big difference between a 'disturbed' child and a 'disturbing' child . . . as a result learning disabilities classes become another dumping ground."

A Portland, Maine, community worker complained that the children placed in classes for emotionally disturbed children are not those with really severe problems, that these children either are suspended or they drop out. She charged school officials with misclassification of educationally disadvantaged children as mentally retarded. "The kids grow up thinking they are mentally retarded when they are intelligent." The D.C. assistant superintendent for Special Education said, "One out of ten [of the referrals from teachers for special education evaluation] are legitimate special education referrals." A retired school teacher in a Georgia county said she did not think misclassification was a major problem, but commented, "there are many teachers who are quick to brand any slow learner retarded and try to place him in special education."

There were approximately eighty teachers in the Copper County system, and the group, like most, contained all kinds of people. There were teachers who took their kids hiking or skating after hours, and there were teachers who would paddle a kid if she looked cross-eyed. There were teachers who got there early and worked late, and those who came to school totally unprepared.

There was a teacher who organized an environmental club that met during his lunch hour, and there were teachers who complained if they had to fill out an extra piece of paper. Some were teaching because they wanted to, others because they needed a job.

These differing individuals reacted in differing ways, of course, to children who were having problems. Special education and regular education as two separate systems seemed at times to create further divisions among some teachers and administrators. The special education personnel could get trapped into a stand-off with some general education personnel over the question of responsibility for the child who differs from normal but can't be considered handicapped by traditional definition. In such cases, the special education teacher would often accuse the regular classroom teacher of trying to get rid of children who weren't handicapped. The regular classroom teacher would often see the special education teacher as lazy and perceive no reason why special education shouldn't take the child, since the classes were smaller. Each would see the problem in the other.

In Copper County, dozens of written referrals started coming into the office within weeks of Maggie's arrival. The odd thing was, they all came from approximately fifteen out of the eighty teachers, some of whom listed "behavior" like "low mental ability," "doesn't catch on," "incapable of behaving in a proper manner," or "disrespectful." Most of these came from schools that were either overcrowded or very concerned with children being up to grade level. There were only two referrals from Little Creek, for instance, but twenty-three from Roosevelt School.

Part of Maggie's job was to investigate these referrals. The investigating process was called "screening," a term that always brought up a mental picture of running children through a net. A description of one screening day provides a peek into a system where all the little insanities and rigidities, all the way up the line, don't leave much room for certain children.

Waking up to a screening day wasn't so much fun for Maggie under the circumstances. As soon as the day's mission came into consciousness, she would scoot farther down under the covers. On this particular day, one of the neighborhood kids banged on the door at about 7:05. It was Cheryl: "Can I come in and get my sweater?" She didn't really want her sweater. By the time Maggie got to the bathroom, Cheryl was at the typewriter, finishing a letter to a friend in Connecticut. Cheryl was eight, and she was a state-certified EMR. She also had visual and muscular problems, so she had less difficulty with a typewriter than with a pencil.

What do I do if I run into another Cheryl today? Maggie wondered. I wouldn't worry so much if we had several alternatives to offer.

8:30 Maggie stopped off at Stockdale Elementary to deliver some number sticks to one of the teachers. Mrs. Cales grabbed her in the hall. Mr. Dillard, the principal, had deposited a "discipline problem" in her class the day before.

"This boy's sixteen years old!" the teacher ranted, gray hair almost steaming. "He and Johnny got into a fight, all the other kids won't go near him, and we still can't get a thing done. And Mr. Dillard says he's going to leave him with us because none of the regular teachers will take him. How come they keep using us as baby sitters?"

Children as tennis balls. Maggie went up and knocked on Mr. Dillard's door. "You kids get out of here!" he yelled. Mr. Dillard was a paper tiger, and his make-believe fierceness was part of his sense of humor. Maggie didn't move. Realizing that the body hadn't gone away, he threatened it with his ruler before he looked up and saw her. "Why, Miss Callahan! What do you want me to agree to today?"

Before she could open her mouth, he tipped back and threw up his hands. "Wait! Don't say a word! I know. You want to tell me that special education isn't a dumping ground for behavior problems. You want me to make Frank Bishop disappear from Mrs. Cales's class." He peered at her and winked.

"It's a beautiful day." She winked back and looked up at the ceiling.

"O.K., I surrender," said Dillard. "I'm too weak to argue with you this morning. I'm saving all my energy for the battle with the cafeteria help. I'll take him out, and he'll be happy as the dickens.

He told me he was going to cause trouble if he got put in there. Well, I don't know where I'll put him now. The sixth grade teacher is pretty high-strung, you know. She just might quit if I try to put him back in there. Being a principal is an awful job. You have to be crazy to work here. Have a good morning, Miss Callahan. I'll see you this afternoon when you come back to check up on me."

What about Frank Bishop? Maggie thought with a pang on her way down the stairs. Then Frank was crowded out of her mind by other thoughts.

9:00 Pickle waved to Maggie from Anita's classroom. Down the hall, the second grade teacher was patting and comforting a crying child who had broken a little string of plastic beads. Across the hall, the first grade teacher was upbraiding a child who had colored a kitten green. "Haven't you ever seen a cat?" she sneered. "Maybe we need to teach you to see."

9:15 Many of the old men around town were out jawing on the sidewalk in front of the post office. It seemed they got there as soon as it opened. The Dollar Store was across the street (cotton petticoats 99¢) and next door to the post office was the Copper County Court House, yellow brick turrets popping out all around it. Maggie called it the Yellow Castle. The board of education offices were on the second floor.

Just about every time Maggie went into the Yellow Castle, she got set for a nasal archaeological dig. Old courthouse smell. You could smell that green paint right off. Sawdust, too, official documents, soap, and the men's room. Maggie always tried to figure the total smell out a little more, adding to her list as she walked through. Perfume, tobacco, and empty Pepsi bottles. Sheriff's uniforms.

Upstairs, her office smelled like a Xerox machine. That morning, a note on her desk told her that Mr. Schwartz wanted to take his kid out of Gateway. When she called him, he said he was tired of his boy coming home with the same book, that his boy was no slow learner, and that he figured there was some slow teaching going on. After she hung up, Maggie spent about ten minutes looking for the boy's records, hoping there would be something on his specific problems. In the middle of this, Warner Jenkins told her he wanted her to get the serial numbers on all the televisions in the special education classrooms.

10:10   Harry, at the Instructional Materials Center, where all the textbooks were housed, called Maggie to tell her that Mrs. Legg, one of the special education teachers, had ordered fifteen sixth grade science texts for her fifteen multilevel kids, in response to some prodding. "Seriously, here's my question," said Harry. "Can those kids *read* those books? Mrs. Legg said she'd just order all on the same level to make things easy for me, and Miss Adkins said I'd better tell you about it."

"Stall Mrs. Legg off till I can reason with her."

"O.K. I'm just a happy delivery boy."

Sometime thereafter, Maggie was wallowing in catalogues, working on a skinny state-funds equipment budget for the following year, when Craig Bailey, the school system's business administrator, peered over her shoulder and said, "You'd better cut that down. The superintendent told me to order a refrigerator-freezer out of that account. For Miss Adkins' classroom. Costs three hundred and fifty dollars."

Maggie scratched her head. It was an occasion for wonder. Peggy Adkins had said something about asking for a refrigerator the previous fall when school opened, but now she was talking about paperback books. There wasn't any food to put in a refrigerator anyhow. What had brought the refrigerator into the picture on that particular day?

Mr. Birdwell was getting ready for a tussle with the school board over finances for the new vocational school. Maggie went in to talk with him. Her goal for the day was screening. Mr. Birdwell was tied up with the vocational school. And here was this refrigerator.

Mr. Birdwell said that Warner Jenkins had reminded him of the refrigerator, and to cancel it if it wasn't needed. Maggie asked him what was happening with the school board. He sat silently for a few seconds. "Politics get in the way of children's interests sometimes," he said finally.

*

12:00   On her way to assess the intelligence of her fellow human beings, Maggie stopped off at Gateway to reason with Mrs. Legg about the science texts and ran into Mr. Morris, who was just leaving. "Are you the director of transportation or the truant officer today?" she asked him.

He chuckled. "I think I'm the boogieman," he said, puffing away on his pipe. "One of the little girls, Priscilla, flew off the handle."

"Everything O.K.?"

"Sure, she was fine when I got here. One of the aides had said something she didn't like. She started hollering, sassing the aide. Told her she couldn't teach anything."

"How come they called you? She's only ten years old."

He chuckled wryly. "Guess they wanted to scare her. Here's the little girl now." Priscilla came running up.

"Why'd you yell at the aide?" Maggie asked her.

"She told me I was stupid," said Priscilla, coloring strongly. Priscilla had a severe hearing loss in one ear, but she hadn't missed that one.

Maggie talked to Mrs. Legg about getting textbooks the kids could read. "If you say so," Mrs. Legg said. Then Maggie went next door to tell Miss Adkins that she'd been done out of a refrigerator, hoping to prevent misunderstanding, since the afternoon edition of the grapevine was undoubtably carrying the story. Miss Adkins took the news with a smile and was much more interested in telling Maggie about the progress one of her boys was making.

1:15   Maggie was off to Franklin D. Roosevelt Elementary School, IQ tests under her arm. Roosevelt School served Davidson's "wealthy" district, plus a couple of outlying areas. From what people said about the school, most of the classrooms could easily have passed military academy inspection. As it happened, Roosevelt had sent more kids to Gateway than any other school. Mrs. Bradley, the fourth grade teacher, had referred one fourth of her class to special education, so that's where Maggie was going. Mrs. Bradley's referral sheets said that most of her candidates were either emotionally upset or crying a lot. (Different teachers seemed to see different things. Another Roosevelt teacher had handed in four referrals, all mentioning "slow reaction time.")

When Maggie came into the building, two kids were sitting outside the principal's office, giggling and poking each other. A little red-headed girl whacked the boy next to her and whispered, "Wait'll Miss Burgess gets hold of *you*. Girls don't get paddled."

He didn't seem to even notice her for a few seconds, then he turned around and smiled sweetly. "Girl," he said solemnly, "you do that one more time, and you'll never grow up to be a woman."

Upstairs, the principal was telling Mrs. Bradley that she had to hand in a list of all the children's brothers and sisters, complete with birthdays, that her children were being too rowdy in the lunchroom, and that the office said there wasn't enough money for those books she needed.

Mrs. Bradley watched the principal go back down the stairs before telling Maggie, with a harassed air, that she had already planned what she wanted to do while Maggie was there, but she had forgotten which children she had referred. Maggie made a list for her. It turned out later that one of the kids had been left off, but Mrs. Bradley didn't notice.

"We're going to have reading while you're here," she said to Maggie. "Want to make sure you have a chance to hear the other children, so you'll know what *these*" — she waved the list — "are being compared to." Thirty books of thirty people were opened to the same story about the goose that laid a golden egg. The story covered only five pages, and so they went through it four times. Towering over the rows of desks, Mrs. Bradley interrupted her special education candidates frequently to ask them the meaning of words, asking them to rephrase sentences, and correcting their pronunciation. If they hesitated for more than ten silent seconds, she would call on one of the other kids. The other children's hands shot up like vultures as soon as the hesitation occurred.

Afterward, Mrs. Bradley called Maggie aside to say how much she was worried about the children she had referred. "All of them seem to be reading near third grade level," Maggie commented.

"Yes," Mrs. Bradley replied, "but they just can't seem to make it up to grade level, and they all have other problems too. They deserve to be in special education. I just don't have time to get them all up to where they're supposed to be."

Supposed to be? Maggie wondered about the pressure that was

being put on Mrs. Bradley and the definition of normal at Roosevelt School.

While each child was out of the room with Maggie, she checked his math concepts and work-decoding skills, did a survey of perceptual abilities, and checked to make sure the child was understanding the words Mrs. Bradley was using. Most important, she would just talk with the children.

The vehicle for breaking the ice: the Peabody Picture Vocabulary Test. Each page features four pictures. The examiner says a word, and the child shows which picture goes with that word. This process gives information about the child's test shyness, reaction time, willingness to venture a guess, extent of vocabulary, familiarity with common objects and concepts. It also invariably turns up a good conversational topic, although that isn't really in the scope of the test itself. Harry stared at a picture of a pony, and Maggie told him she had always wished she had a pony to ride. "I have a pony at home," ventured Harry. "It got a rock in its foot yesterday . . ."

The Peabody also turns up an IQ score, no minor arrogance on that small amount of information. And this is the first item many teachers ask for.

None of the Bradley eight passed on to stage two. That was Maggie's opinion. Stage two would have been the psychologist and the "official" IQ test. It was always important to remember the realities of the situation. In other systems, some of the kids would have benefited a lot from working with a special education resource teacher or reading specialist who could then in turn work with Mrs. Bradley. But, under the circumstances, if they were "qualified" for special education, that meant they would be transferred to Dummy Tech.

Six of the eight children came from low-income families living in the outlying areas. Shy, soft-spoken Vicky had been the most disturbing member of that group. She stared at Maggie's mouth as Maggie spoke. When they got to the Peabody, she pointed to a picture before Maggie got the word out of her mouth. A couple of times she didn't even look at the page. After six such occurrences,

Maggie moved her mouth without making a sound and Vicky pointed to a picture of a submarine.

Maggie asked her to turn her head and raise her hand when she heard her voice. Maggie began whispering "ice cream and cookies" and escalated in volume until Vicky raised her hand, at loud-normal pitch. But Vicky didn't know what had been said. Clapping and finger-snapping produced similar results.

"Vicky, do you always understand what Mrs. Bradley is saying?" Maggie asked her.

"Lots of times I don't."

"Do you tell her you don't understand?"

Vicky looked at her shoes and shook her head. "She gets mad if I do." Vicky had apparently learned to perform so that nobody would get mad at her. Unless an examiner noticed her problem, Vicky would flunk the Peabody or any other individual IQ test flat. School must have been meaningless, at best, for her.

"How'd they do?" asked Mrs. Bradley, after the last child had come back. She and Maggie had gone into the cloakroom to talk.

"None of them should be transferred to special education," Maggie began. Mrs. Bradley registered such skepticism that Maggie added, "None of these children is retarded." The word "retarded" threw Mrs. Bradley back a little.

For the sake of the children in that situation, it would have been good to erase the word "retarded" from the dictionary. It was odd, Maggie thought, that you almost never heard the word mentioned until the kids were actually in the classes. After the kids were there, she heard it a lot.

Mrs. Bradley seemed to be under the impression that all children below grade level should be removed to special education, so the word "retarded" served in that case as a reminder of the reality of that particular system. Maggie told her that her children were coming along much too well to be uprooted. Mrs. Bradley seemed to feel complimented and slightly encouraged.

Maggie gave her several suggestions, then said, studying her notes, "Vicky seems to have a significant hearing loss." Mrs. Bradley looked as though she could have been knocked over with a sugar spoon. Vicky had been in her class for seven months. Maggie described the testing session while Mrs. Bradley fussed with a gold-starred chart labeled "Work Completed."

"Well, you know," Mrs. Bradley began finally, "I wonder why her parents didn't tell me about this . . ."

"They probably didn't know," Maggie said. "Sometimes people just don't think of things like that."

Mrs. Bradley brightened and launched into a brief tirade on Vicky's home conditions. The guilt had shifted and freed her up.

"You know," she said energetically, "just the other day, that little girl was standing beside me at the board, and she caught on to everything I said. I remember complimenting her . . ."

"I'll send the school nurse up right away to confirm it." Maggie smiled. "Maybe you could move her desk up near yours . . ."

"I'll do it first thing after school . . . this probably explains all that hand-raising she's been doing. She's always raising her hand to answer a question, and then says, 'I can't remember' when I call on her . . ."

"The aide could keep checking with her to make sure she understands . . . try to give her written directions . . ."

". . . oh, the poor little thing . . ."

"Yes."

4:20   When Maggie got back to the office, the assistant superintendent called her into his office. "I just want to tell you," he said, "that that refrigerator for Miss Adkins is already on its way over to Gateway." He looked so pleased that Maggie didn't have the heart to make any noise while she choked.

Down the hall in the business office, Craig Bailey threw up his hands and said, "I know, I know. Mr. Birdwell told me to cancel the order, but he didn't tell the assistant superintendent. It's just lack of communication."

A little later, the school nurse phoned Maggie to say that she'd checked Vicky and confirmed the hearing loss. "It's pretty bad," she said. "I'm going to see about a hearing aid for her."

Abigail and Maggie sat around and talked about how outrageous the referrals from Roosevelt School were and how those teachers had better shape up. The principal from Roosevelt called the school board office the next day and told Mr. Birdwell, "The new special education director isn't doing her job. She was of no help to us whatsoever."

There just wasn't any "appropriate alternative" yet to telling Mrs. Bradley that the kids were her responsibility and leaving her and the children with the same pressures and feelings of inadequacy they had been facing before.

School systems all over the country are having to face questions about children who might "qualify" as retarded or emotionally disturbed by system standards, but who are normal by their own standards, or whose problems are actually aggravated by labeling or segregation. In July 1975, for instance, the Washington *Star* carried an article called "Aiding Minority Problem Pupils and What Should Be the Limit?" which stated the basic dilemma fairly well:

> In Montgomery County [Maryland], you might say, education achievement is next to godliness. Consultants recently found that if a child in the county does not fit "an undesignated, but ever-present achievement norm," it can be pretty rough sledding. Especially if the kid is black and low-income.
>
> But the time has come when the Montgomery County schools, recognized as some of the finest in the nation, are going to have to consider bending a little to accommodate all their children.
>
> "We can't continue to operate on the upper middle class standards that Montgomery County has always operated on," said Harriet Bernstein, school board vice president, at a board meeting last night. "Yet there have to be limits."
>
> What prompted her comment was a consultant's report investigating allegations that low-income, minority students end up in special education classes when they do not belong there. Such classes are designed for mentally retarded, emotionally or physically handicapped children . . .
>
> How much of white middle class standards are beyond the pale (for minority and low-income acceptance) . . . and what accommodations can a white middle class achievement-oriented society reasonably expect from low-income children? . . .
>
> Staff [the consultants reported], particularly teachers, experi-

ence considerable pressure to get children to perform academically and conform behaviorally or to "get them out." For instance, certain norms about noise level, learning patterns and communications styles seemingly have become imposed on all children and when any variance occurs, special education placement (removal from regular education) is considered.

Sometimes a student is removed from a class and put in a special education class simply because he is so far behind academically that extra resources are needed to catch him up and they're unavailable except in the separate special education class, the consultants found.

They urged that resources be made available so that these children are not placed in special classes — for the mildly retarded, for instance — where they risk being stigmatized throughout their educational career.

6. Dummy Tech

"Not one person dared admit he couldn't see anything, because if he did, it would mean he was either stupid or unfit for his job."

— Hans Christian Andersen,
"The Emperor's New Clothes"

"There is definitely a mystical quality about special education. Experienced educators can walk into a really bad situation and not say anything. Because they really don't know anything about special education, and they're afraid there's some sort of hidden purpose to what they're seeing, and they don't want to say they don't see anything. Under these kinds of conditions, outrageous situations can keep going on for years and years, for the simple reason that the people who are supporting these efforts don't really know what they're supporting. And they don't like to admit it."

— Robert Jackson, chairman, Division of Special Education,
University of Massachusetts, February 1974

ACCORDING TO school system policy, the children from Roosevelt would have to be sent to Gateway School because of the bus schedule. Maggie had begun to notice an odd difference between what was sometimes assumed to be at Gateway and what was actually there. Sometimes people would talk as if the children had been sent to a diagnostic clinic staffed with trained specialists. Reality kept getting lost. Maybe that's why the word "retarded" threw Mrs. Bradley back.

Anita didn't think that was surprising. "People really do want to think they're sending the kids where they can get the help they need," she told Maggie. "But then, it could also be due to compartmentalized thinking: my job is to refer and your job is to supply the program. And you've got to remember that this is the way things have traditionally been done. Most people can think of instances where special classes have done children a lot of good, so in all good faith, you just hope that these will too. Or maybe people don't really take all the side effects into account. Out of sight, out of mind? Who knows?"

The side effects could definitely be seen throughout the system. For instance, the regular children were learning a disastrous sort of lesson: namely, people who have problems or who are different should be removed.

A freckled-faced fourth grader at Stockdale School solemnly informed Maggie that "there are a lot of kids in our room who ought to be taken out of there because they don't keep up." A neighboring child told Maggie that she was afraid to ask her teacher for much help, "because she'll think I'm dumb, and I might have to go to the retarded class."

Besides the physical separation, the retarded label also seemed to be convincing people that it wasn't particularly important to have a good academic program for children who "couldn't learn anyhow." Maggie was primed on that subject by the reading she had been doing. "As long as a category of mental retardation exists, it will be used as a convenient 'dumping ground,' " she read in an article entitled "Mentally Retarded or Culturally Different?" "Some of the consequences of locating the school learning difficulties within the minds of these children," the authors wrote, "are to limit efforts on their behalf, as well as to persuade the children and some of their parents and peers that they are 'dumb,' rather than different. In addition, such a classification tends to relieve educators and others of some feelings of responsibility for intervention on behalf of these children, since their problems are viewed as 'mental' and 'genetic,' and therefore as essentially irreversible. In effect, besides adding the insult of stigmatization to the injury resulting from poverty and minority group status, we limit our confidence in our ability to effect change as well as diminish our interests in attempting change. Thus, within these terms, many of these children are viewed patronizingly as 'educable,' meaning that they have little capacity to learn as middle-class children may be expected to learn, given their experiences and values."

The authors' comments seemed to fit so many of the Copper County special education kids. A very high percentage had truly been far less lucky in terms of advantages than those who were born into the middle-class homes. Their school situation, as much as it was originally intended to help them, was actually making sure they wouldn't have those advantages. Every day, the doors closed a little more on social standing, self-respect, and a right to an education at least as good as that of other kids.

It wasn't a noisy tragedy. It was a quiet, respectable one.

Maggie had decided that a supervisor's first priority ought to be helping the teachers. On her first visit to Gateway as supervisor, she and Mr. McCreedy, the principal and teacher, stood in the morning mist as the school buses came in, watching the kids pile off, some quiet, some chasing around:

"Hey, look, I got this worm here. Look how far it stretches out!"

"There's this old dog keeps getting into our trash. Next time I see him, I'm going to blast his rear with my dad's gun."

"You see that cowboy movie on TV last night? Sheriff really stomped this old guy that threw him in a well." Running around, faking karate chops on every kid in reach.

"Leave me be, Johnny Bragg! I threw up last night!"

Mr. McCreedy started telling Maggie about a boy who would "never settle down to his work." She suggested that they get together to plan a program for him. "You know what?" Mr. McCreedy answered. "It snowed up on the mountain this morning. I had to wear my boots."

Maggie's neighbor, Jenny Krebbs, got off the bus and waved shyly as she passed. When they got back to the subject of the restless boy, Mr. McCreedy said, "Well, the truth is, I was kind of expecting you were going to come in and take care of kids like these. Special education's not my field, so you could do a lot better than I could." Mr. McCreedy was always very up-front. "I'd be glad if you would teach my whole class," he said, grinning candidly. "Now that's what I'd call help."

An elderly lady named Mrs. Quigley taught in the classroom adjoining Mr. McCreedy's. A few years away from retirement, she had taught high school chemistry before she'd been replaced and transferred to the elementary school as a science resource teacher. In the elementary school, parents had become concerned about her ability to maintain "class control," so the superintendent had decided to transfer her to special education.

She was a proud person with a very formal manner, who, like her children, deserved more respectful treatment than she had received. It wasn't surprising to find her feeling somewhat bitter, but it was hard to see that bitterness directed at times toward the children, whom she periodically called "my dummies."

Mrs. Quigley did try to keep an academic program going, even though she was out of her element. When Maggie came into the room, a girl with fluffy brown bangs leaped up and nearly tackled her. "Wanna see what I'm doing?" It wasn't really a question. Maggie took the waving white paper from her hand in self-defense. The paper turned out to be a much-mauled mimeographed list of the multiplication tables. "My name's Brenda, I've seen you before, and I'm learning my times!" exclaimed the child, hugging her waist.

Mrs. Quigley steered Brenda aside and began to explain the markings on the paper. "They study it, and when they think they know one of the tables, they may recite it to me," she murmured, handing Brenda over to the aide. "If they know it, I write my initials on that table." She squinted at the paper. "You see, Brenda already knows her two's and five's." Mrs. Quigley's initials were printed across the two's and five's.

"We're having reading now," she explained. "My reading program is individualized. The other children study their multiplication tables while I work with one child at a time." As each child read to Mrs. Quigley, the other children, seated in rows, were studying an object that looked like a plastic car, staring at Maggie, or looking out the window. One boy was poking everybody within reach, and a couple of kids were looking at the white paper.

Most of the kids were quite shy of strangers, but when recess was announced, a few kids drifted up to Maggie out of curiosity, asking things like "Want to see my loose tooth?"

A large pink-cheeked boy wanted to know if she'd been turkey hunting. He'd been the poker-during-individualized-reading.

"What's your name?" Maggie asked.

"Preston," he replied evenly and firmly, meeting her eyes directly. Then he told how "me and my dad were laying under a big pile of brush for hours, not moving an eyeball, except to call for turkey every now and then, until this old gobbler sneaked right up on us, and called right behind our heads." He paused for dramatic effect. "By the time we got the gun swung around, old turkey was gone. Off somewhere, laughing at us."

Preston plunked down and demonstrated considerable skill with multiplication before telling Maggie about his house, his favorite black dog, and his reasons for hating school. With both elbows planted firmly on Mrs. Quigley's desk, he announced that he was too smart for that place. "Aren't I, Mrs. Quigley?"

Mrs. Quigley didn't answer. Within minutes, all the children filtered out onto the playground, leaving the two women alone. They made small talk for a few minutes; then Maggie asked, "How did Preston come to this school?"

The older woman blinked her eyes and frowned. "Why, he's retarded," she answered rather formally. "Why do you ask?"

She offered to show Maggie Preston's test scores. "You know," Maggie continued, declining the offer, "he's so quick in conversation. And he was off and running with multiplication by sets before I'd even finished showing him what I was doing . . ."

"Yes," said Mrs. Quigley, fingering some neatly colored mimeographed ducks on her desk. "You don't have to show him twice. But his behavior isn't always what it should be." She frowned and picked up one of the ducks to examine it.

"That doesn't sound like a retarded child . . ." Maggie ventured.

Mrs. Quigley stiffened. "Oh, he's well behind in his work! And, like I said, he's going to have to show a lot of improvement in his behavior."

"How long has he been in special education?" Maggie wondered.

"I can't tell you offhand," said Mrs. Quigley. "At least two years. All those Bennetts are in special education, you know."

All those Bennetts? When did "Bennett" get to be a handicapping category? Maggie walked across the playground to the "junior high" section of Gateway and opened the door to Miss Adkins' classroom. And there was Preston Bennett, squirting water all over one of the girls. It looked like Preston — same quick smile, same mischievous brown eyes. But it turned out to be Eric, one of "those Bennetts" in Miss Adkins' class. She calmly removed him from the water faucet.

Miss Adkins had an affectionate relationship with her students. They laughed and kidded each other, and students like Eric usually responded without resentment to her directions. The kids called her "Big Red." Her home economics background and lack of experience put her behind the eight ball. When Maggie asked her about her reading program the week before, she had laid it on the line.

"Frankly I'm just groping in the dark." She told Maggie somewhat nervously that she more or less let the kids read whatever textbook stories they wanted. "I took the two summer courses to qualify for this position, as Mr. Birdwell asked me to," she continued. "But I still feel I need a lot more experience."

Six hours in summer school is standard emergency preparation for special education teachers in many states. Peggy Adkins' courses had not prepared her for her sixteen teen-age students, who ran the whole gamut, from good readers like Jenny, through those students with a whole range of difficulties, some correctable in school, some tied to home situations, to Louise, a genuinely retarded fourteen-year-old. Louise's vocabulary, concept development, and motor control were roughly comparable to that of a four-year-old. Although she was the only severely retarded student in that class, her presence appeared to have a tremendous, though subtle effect on the other students.

A large pleasant girl, Louise seemed to serve as a mirror to the other students. Her limitations reflected back their worst fears about themselves. For, as much as they would have liked to, these students couldn't totally reject the judgment that had been passed on them by the school system, and, consequently, by their peers and neighbors. Louise was undoubtably retarded, and they were Louise's classmates, sent to Gateway for ostensibly the same reasons. They saw her and seemed to fear that they saw themselves. "Louise doesn't come here all day. She doesn't really belong here," one girl told Maggie pointedly.

"Do you think I could ever get a chance to talk with a child psychologist about the kids?" asked Miss Adkins. "That's probably like asking for a hippo in a playpen, I know, but as I said, this whole situation is affecting the kids and I feel helpless."

Miss Adkins was thinking mostly about the older kids' futures. Most of them were within two years, or even a few months, of sixteen, the crop-out age. Academic instruction sometimes seemed beside the point in comparison with their other needs. It wouldn't be long before they would be looking for jobs, getting married, and having kids of their own. Although they were nearing adult responsibilities, very few had been exposed to much beyond Davidson. To several, even downtown Davidson was an intimidating mystery. Yet nearly all had been exposed to some form of violence or misery. In terms of school, they were old enough to be bitter — or to have given up on themselves. Cynicism existed side by side with naiveté in these children-adults.

Gateway School was especially hard on them, since they had begun the year at the regular high school. The construction of the Gateway classrooms wasn't completed until two months after school opened. At that time, the truant officer and a couple of other people from the administration building went to the high school, picked up the occupants for the new rooms, and took them to Gateway. "They came to get them out of the blue," reported the high school principal. "Arrived with a list, got a dozen or so kids out of their classes, piled them in cars, and took them down to Gateway." Nobody had warned the students that they were to be transferred. Their parents had signed the paper, and that was enough.

The high school principal was dismayed by the whole incident. "I don't know how those particular students got picked," he said. "We sent a couple dozen names over to the school board office when they asked us, and never heard any more about it until they came to pick some of them up. I guess somebody thinks those kids don't have any feelings."

The high school students had been assigned to Miss Adkins and Mrs. Legg. During the afternoon "vocational period," Mrs. Legg was to teach crafts while Miss Adkins taught home ec. Both had responsibility for the students' total program.

Mrs. Legg had come to special education from high school social studies. A fast-talking, fiftyish, red-faced woman, she was quick to complain. She didn't have enough materials to teach crafts, her salary was too low, the office ignored her requests, the other teachers didn't care about the children, her back hurt, her hair was falling out, and she didn't know how to teach kids to read, since she'd been trained for high school. She had started working on her master's degree in special education, however, "so I can be sure and have a job." She was also openly maneuvering for the principal's position at Gateway and asked Maggie if a supervisor made more money than a principal.

Miss Adkins, with her two training courses, was making a sincere effort to teach her students academically as well as she could, mainly through total group instruction. Mrs. Legg was apparently feeling so discouraged that she had given up on any kind of academic program, other than copying problems from the board, handwriting, and silent reading. Although their outlooks differed greatly, neither teacher was sure how to determine reading level or locate individual problems. Maggie quickly offered to do a reading inventory on all the students the next day. "So it will be easier to get at their problems," she explained. Miss Adkins said guardedly that she'd be interested "if you'll show me what to do with it." Mrs. Legg frowned and said, "Think you can get me some wool?"

Recess was in progress as Maggie left. Preston threw a toy football. "Think fast!" Some of Miss Adkins' girls were swinging, long legs dangling. They sang as they swung. "Even if we ain't got money . . . I'm so in love with ya honeeeeee . . ."

When Maggie got home, she headed straight for the TV, hoping to find Perry Mason, an old movie, or something else with a well tied up plot and a happy ending. Nothing confusing, unresolved, or irrational. "The Case of the Moth-Eaten Mink" was on. Unbelievably enough, during one of the commercial breaks, Julie Eisenhower came on the screen, advertising special education. She had taped the ad as part of an HEW information-dissemination campaign. Julie explained that *special education* means "highly skilled teachers using the most advanced equipment and techniques to give the problemmed child the help he or she needs."

Anita was watching TV with Maggie. "Boy, that's really a different situation, isn't it?" she commented.

"Yeah, it's really confusing the way programs vary so from place to place."

Anita agreed. "That program she's talking about is help, apparently, and, at least for now, the program here has turned out to be punishment for not being what you're supposed to be. Nobody consciously intended it to be that way, but, if you look at it honestly, that's what's happened."

Help or punishment? Over a bowl of ice cream, Maggie thought for a while about the use of the word "deserve." Mr. Birdwell used it: "I shudder to think that any child might be placed in one of those classes when he didn't deserve it."

Mrs. Bradley used it: "They deserve to be in special education. I just don't have time to get them all up to where they're supposed to be."

A substitute teacher had used it: "You ask me, several of these deserve to be out back."

Even some special education teachers used it when they said that "a lot of these kids don't deserve to be here."

Deserve seemed to be another one of those odd words that can be approached from several directions. If you deserve ice cream, she thought, that's different than if you deserve a spanking. If you deserve Dummy Tech, that's punishment sure enough, only the person who says deserve might not mean it that way, because he or she might be visualizing Julie Eisenhower's special education, and in that case, deserves is good.

Round and round. All in the way you see it. All in what it really is.

Maggie took Brown Eye and went next door to talk to Lucy about all the ambiguities. "Well," Lucy said thoughtfully, "Jesus said, 'Inasmuch as you do it unto the least of these my brethren, you do it unto me.' We set up so many things in this country of ours intended to help people. But my guess is, we've just got to keep checking up to make sure that what we're doing unto them is what we think it is."

Lucy had put her finger on a tendency that affects many programs designed to help people who are considered different. As

Dr. Joe Cunningham, who trains special education teachers at Peabody College in Nashville, put it: "Particularly in those social programs dealing with people who are regarded in our society as 'less productive' and therefore less valuable, the original goals of the program are set out one way by the people who start the program. Then, over time, as systems and social priorities have their effect, what's really going on becomes something very different. The new reality is usually something that serves the purposes of the 'advantaged' group rather than the actual people for whom the program was created to help. But the fact that the program was set up to help can actually keep people from seeing what's really happening.

"Almost any original statement of goals for any institution for the retarded, for instance, says that one of the prime functions of the institution is to give the inmates the best possible care and get them back into the community as soon as possible. Yet, as all the recent uproar over miserable conditions in many such institutions has shown, the real function of the institutions has turned out to be what some writers call 'social sanitation' — providing a poorly funded warehouse in which to store certain groups, adults and children, that our society would rather not see or deal with. (Have you read *One Flew over the Cuckoo's Nest* by Ken Kesey?) This is why you'll find much concern these days in many states about getting people out of institutions, into foster homes and group homes.

"The main point to see here is that the recent concern and action about the practice of labeling and isolating certain groups of children in special education just fits into a growing overall social and human concern about what effect institutions have on the people they are supposedly helping."

There can be many reasons why it could be difficult to tell what effect an institution is having. An article Maggie read in the *National Observer* helped her clarify her thoughts on the subject. Entitled "Catch 22 in Mental Hospitals," the article described an experiment dreamed up by David L. Rosenhan, a Stanford University professor of law and psychology. Rosenhan's thesis was "We cannot distinguish the sane from the insane in psychiatric hospitals."

"Essentially, it's a Catch 22 thing," commented Rosenhan.

"You're in the hospital because you're mentally ill; you're mentally ill because you're in the hospital." To launch the experiment, Rosenhan and seven other persons, described as "clearly without what we technically call mental defects," went to a dozen psychiatric hospitals in five states on the East and West coasts, between 1969 and 1972. They told the admissions crews that they were hearing voices saying "empty," "hollow," and "thud." Seven of them were diagnosed as schizophrenic and one was reported to have a "manic-depressive psychosis."

After they were admitted, the subjects dropped all faking, never mentioned the voices again, and behaved in their normal manner. "Except at the private hospital," reported the *Observer*, "none of the pseudo patients received much psychotherapy. But, when they did, they talked about their real situations, their job anxieties, their family relationships, their deepest feelings. When asked, they said they felt fine."

None of them were reevaluated and pronounced sane. Eventually, they were discharged with diagnoses of "illness in remission," left "against medical advice," or else got grounds privileges and escaped.

This was the unnerving part of it all. It was a demonstration, Rosenhan said, of how context can actually determine what a person sees. "The easy example that comes to mind," observed Rosenhan, "is the book that looks very respectable on your shelf but like refuse in the garbage can. It was a simple extension of this, that one could take a man from his ordinary environment and put him in a psychiatric hospital, and he just wouldn't look the same.

"We saw the misinterpretation of things, the tendency to attribute everything [the patient did] to craziness and nothing at all to stimuli which exist in the hospital . . . the business where you're pacing the corridor and a nurse very kindly turns to you and asks, 'Nervous?' And you turn to her equally frankly and say, 'No. Bored.' It never dawns on you that patients would be anything but nervous and upset. The tendency to misattribute the source of the disorder occurs very often in a psychiatric hospital . . ."

During the whole course of the experiment, the only people who spotted Rosenhan and the others in the experiment as fakers were fellow hospital patients. "A typical comment was 'You're not crazy. You're a journalist or a professor. You're checking up on the hospital.'

"The fact that the patients often recognized normality when staff did not raises important questions," Rosenhan concluded.

"Rosenhan does not criticize hospital workers," the *Observer* reported. "He says in his [*Science* magazine] article, 'It would be a mistake and a very unfortunate one, to consider that what happened to us derives from malice or stupidity on the part of the staffs. Quite the contrary . . . when they failed, as sometimes they did painfully, it would be more accurate to attribute those failures to the environment in which they too found themselves, than to personal callousness.'" Rosenhan added, "There's no question that I could have made the same error, and there's no question that I probably have. I don't have the slightest doubt about it, because one treats patients as patients, rather than as people."

7. "Johnny's Such a Bright Boy . . ."

"The traditional categories of exceptionality yield too little information to plan a course of action for a child. To say that a child is mentally retarded is to tell a parent or teacher or physician very little about what should be done to help him. The imprecision of the category lets popular and stereotyped conceptions of mental retardation influence reactions to the child . . . To say further that a child is educable adds only a modicum of information about his specific assets and liabilities. (Does he need glasses? Is he good at caring for children? Can he read?) . . . Schools should strive to defeat the limiting predictions of tests, and good teachers recognize this as an explicit goal. However, schools too often work, unintentionally, to confirm test predictions and validate established categories. The handicapped child can get locked into a category, unable to extricate himself from the conceptual box into which psychologists, psychiatrists, pediatricians, teachers, and parents put him. He becomes more and more like what his label requires him to be."

— Nicholas Hobbs, *The Futures of Children,*
Categories, Labels and Their Consequences, 1975

"We must stop using special education as a means of warehousing children. In the past, a great deal of this warehousing has been caused by the idea that every Friday afternoon at 3:00, every fourth grader should have learned the same information and be at the same place."

— Charles Meisgeier, coordinator, Center for
Human Resources and Education Research, Houston
Independent Schools, October 1974

WHEN PEOPLE SEE that an institution or a program is having a reverse effect on the people it is intended to help, the first reaction often is to blame the employees rather than to question the system itself. During her first few weeks, Maggie heard several remarks about how "apathetic most of those teachers at Gateway are," and she made a few herself, without really stopping to put herself in the teachers' shoes. When children are punished by being sent somewhere, when they are at the bottom of the system's priorities, the special education teachers usually are punished too. If the system writes the children off, their teachers, whomever they turn out to be, don't get a fair share either. A California researcher, for instance, states that "in many school districts, assignment as a special education teacher is regarded as a punishment. 'Next year,' the principal promises, 'we'll give you a regular class.' Certain teachers, the researcher notes 'weren't good enough to teach normal kids, but for special kids, they were just fine.' As a result, 'many special classes function only as mass babysitters.' "

So much seems to depend on the priority the individual system gives special education children. Systems that value the children give their teachers a lot of materials to work with. In those systems that don't, personnel shortage problems can be compounded when the system gives the teachers leftovers or even puts the special education resources somewhere else. In a California district, for example, after a special education teacher's protest caused an audit of the school books, special education materials budgets increased over five times. This kind of situation also occurs in other programs dealing with disadvantaged children, as documented by the Lawyers' Committee for Civil Rights Under Law (Washington, D.C.), organized to help people deal with situations in which Title I funds are not used for disadvantaged or handicapped children.

Teachers lose motivation under such circumstances, just like kids, no matter what their training is. In Copper County, all but five of the fifteen special education teachers were teaching on emergency certificates. Six teachers had backgrounds in such high school subjects as accounting and chemistry. Five were in their first year of teaching. A lot of support and assistance seemed to be called for.

Jenny Krebbs came by Maggie's house in the early morning when Maggie was getting ready to go back to Gateway to do a reading inventory for Miss Adkins and Mrs. Legg. Jenny had had a piece of toast for breakfast and ate some cereal with Maggie and Anita.

Jenny had a heartache. She was in love with one of the fifth grade boys at Stockdale School, and he didn't know she existed. "I'd be in his class if I was going to Stockdale," she said, wiping milk from her mouth and blushing as usual. "I'd see him all the time. Now, I just see him after school . . ." She chewed another mouthful before adding, "I don't mean I *see* him like we're boyfriend and girlfriend or nothing. He's never even talked to me. It's more like I see him, but he doesn't see me. He knows I go to Gateway, and he probably thinks I'm dumb or something." Her blue eyes were full of feeling.

That idea seemed so ludicrous that Anita started to laugh, until she saw Jenny's blush deepen to the point of tears. "Oh, sweetheart!" she exclaimed. "I wasn't laughing at what you said. That's very serious. It just seemed like such a silly idea for *anybody* to think *you're* dumb!"

It was bitter cold that morning, so Maggie gave Jenny a ride to Gateway. As soon as the kids settled down, Maggie began the reading inventory with Mrs. Legg's kids. As far as reliable content goes, it wasn't much. It involved checking the kids' phonic mastery and basic vocabulary and established rough oral reading levels and comprehension levels by working upward through a basal series. Some kids dictated paragraphs and read them back. The inventory turned up some useful information, but most important, for Maggie, was getting to know the kids. Within this group of students, patterns emerged that would be repeated again and again in other classes, in children of all ages.

For some kids, school just wasn't important. There was Billy Tate, rapidly approaching six feet and sixteen, stocky, pleasant, and low-key. Billy's parents didn't have any use for school since it took him away from work that he could have been doing at home on their small farm. He had more or less adopted their attitude. Why not? Maggie told him she had seen him in the back of a pickup truck the other day, and Billy said it was his brother's truck. "Lots of nights, he rides me around, and we get drunk up by the cemetery," he added.

Billy's eyes lit up when he talked about his pony. "He comes when I whistle to him." He hoped he could get a farm someday: "maybe on some of that level ground downriver, but I'd go back to my home place for hunting."

Billy read on an early third grade level, but he responded to phonics like a dry plant to water, like a lot of other kids. His reading ability could have been vastly improved within months. It would make the difference between struggling with a newspaper and reading most printed matter with relative ease.

A couple of kids were faking. Mrs. Legg warned Maggie before she began, "Joe Mullins will probably put you on. He plays dumb so he can stay down here." Sure enough, Joe, a heavyset, athletic boy, didn't have much to say. But, at fifteen, he read easily on a sixth grade level, with good comprehension. Both Mrs. Legg and Miss Adkins were convinced that he deliberately messed up on the IQ test so he could get out of the "hard work" at the high school. Maggie looked in his folder and found two IQ tests. For what it was worth, the first full-scale test score was thirty-two points higher than the second one, which had sent Joe to Gateway.

Many kids were handicapped mainly by limited experience. Elizabeth, a shy, delicate person, seemed, at thirteen, to have both the untouched freshness of a six-year-old and the worn appearance of a middle-aged woman. "I want to show you what I'm reading." She smiled, picking up the sixth grade book with a naturally gracious manner. "It's my story." Elizabeth read with great expression the story of a young journalist's trip on a ferryboat among the skyscrapers and office buildings in turn-of-the-century New York.

"What's a journalist?" Maggie asked when she finished. Elizabeth said she didn't know, maybe it was a man. She had a very vague idea about the purpose of newspapers. She had no idea at all what a ferry might be. As Maggie explained, her eyes became very wide. "You mean they could put a big car on a boat?" She recalled seeing people fishing from rowboats. "Skyscrapers" and "offices" mystified her. The entire concept of a large city was so far beyond her experience that she found it impossible to imagine it. Elizabeth had learned that fluid pronunciation is all there is to reading. She read from five other stories in the same book with expression, ease, and very little comprehension. Her conversation showed her to be sensitive and alert. She simply had not been introduced to many things others take for granted.

Elizabeth came from a mountain family of religious fundamentalists, gentle, withdrawn people. She and Jenny Krebbs were special friends. Maggie had seen her every Saturday with her family, when they walked down into town to shop and visit the minister. The family always gave everyone a warm feeling.

Several children suffered from definite disabilities, varying in severity. Anybody who watched Karen for five minutes would notice her muscular control difficulties. Her gross-motor problems made her very awkward. In the fine-motor department, Karen had trouble even holding a pencil. Writing was a fearsome task for her. A chubby fourteen-year-old with a mass of curls and thick glasses, she had a lost and confused but doggedly hopeful look about her. Her poor muscular control made her reluctant to play kickball or participate in crafts and every other activity involving coordination. She was receiving no help with her motor problems, not because anybody wanted to ignore them but because her teacher, Mrs. Legg, wasn't familiar with methods of working with muscular problems. Karen had a compulsive need to touch everybody within arm's range. She had been transferred into Mrs. Legg's class because her touching "frightened" a younger teacher.

There were also unusually alert children with emotional problems. Johnny was full of questions as soon as he sat down beside Maggie: "What do you want to know, I'll tell you." "What's your job?" "Will you be here very often?" Maggie found no ceiling either on his reading ability or his comprehension. As they read a story about walruses, he supplied additional information and theories about aquatic animals. He firmly opposed the killing of these animals and wanted to know Maggie's opinion on zoo confinement. Maggie told him what she had read about the St. Louis zoo, which he concluded might be all right. As he related various incidents in his school history, Maggie noticed a confusion about time. "I think I came here a couple of years ago," he said. He had actually arrived in November, three months before.

Johnny's teacher and aide said that Johnny, like so many Gateway children, had witnessed extreme physical violence between his parents, who had divorced and moved away, leaving him with his aging grandparents. He believed that neither of his parents wanted him. From all reports, he was probably right.

It seemed that Johnny's attention in school had begun to lapse for long periods of time about the time his parents split up. He was then at Roosevelt School. At that point, he was referred to special education as a discipline-academic problem. "And even now, he's so often far away," mused the aide.

Johnny's psychological report made one want to look again, to make sure that some other child's report hadn't ended up in Johnny's folder. But it was he, John Fitzgerald Bragg. The psychologist had found, during an hour-long session at Roosevelt School, that Johnny was "below average in ability to form and relate concepts" and "mildly deficient in analysis and reproduction of designs and learning new skills." In all other areas, including reading, he had found Johnny "within the average range" or "above average." On this evidence, the examiner had somehow concluded that "Johnny will find learning in a normal classroom situation difficult, will need more intensive help in a special class. He may obtain a sixth grade level of competence by his late teens." At thirteen, Johnny's "level of competence" in all areas but math already exceeded "sixth grade level," if there is such a thing. (The list of EMR characteristics says that an EMR will not exceed sixth grade competence.)

Maggie expressed her amazement at this report to Mrs. Legg.

"Well, I'll be honest with you," she said. "I've never understood why that kid's down here." She checked Maggie's expression before continuing. "I mean, I know something must be wrong, his IQ turned out pretty low and all . . . I'm just not familiar with this sort of thing and I just don't know what to do with him. He catches on to just about everything I show him, and he reads nearly everything he picks up without a hitch. Good with his hands too. But he's not learning much down here, he's so bored . . ." She stopped herself at that point and examined her fingers.

The aide spoke up. "Mrs. Legg's right about Johnny, and there's others like him too. I know a lot of bad things have happened with him and his family, but, other than that, I can't see what his problem is . . . there must be something . . ."

She and Mrs. Legg exchanged nods. "We'd really like to help him out," said Mrs. Legg. "Johnny's such a bright boy." She reflected a few seconds. "Johnny's such a bright boy. What a shame he's retarded."

Billy needed a phonetically based, high-interest reading program. Other kids needed counseling; others needed to be taken all over town and exposed to a multitude of words, sounds, sights, smells. Karen needed highly specialized perceptual-motor training. Johnny needed love and a stable home — or lacking that, some constant emotional support. And so on and so on, and none of these children could get what they needed. They all needed to get away from the stigma of going to the retarded school. Miss Adkins asked Maggie what they needed, and Maggie told her what she thought, in abbreviated form.

"Help!" Miss Adkins said.

Maggie felt like yelling "Help!" herself. All her frantic feelings were coming back, and she didn't know which direction to point them in.

During recess Jenny and some of the kids came over to talk with Maggie, a few of them hanging back several feet. Others played country music records, starting and stopping the record while they memorized the lyrics.

"I wish I was a teddy bear . . . Not livin' nor lovin', nor going nowhere . . ."

It had started raining outside, and everybody seemed to be feeling pretty sluggish. Johnny spotted a *Bluegrass Songbook* in Maggie's pile of papers and pounced on it.

"Hey! My grandfather has one of these at home!" he exclaimed quizzing her in the same breath on where she got it.

"Hey, would you get your guitar, so we can sing?" Jenny asked the aide.

Several others started saying "Yeah! Yeah!" so the aide, getting wet, ran across the playground for the guitar. It was worth it. The record player went off immediately, and bodies piled onto the surrounding desks, more enthusiastic than Maggie had yet seen them. Sluggishness gone.

"I Walk the Line!"

"Wildwood Flower!"

"Gospel Ship!"

Most everybody knew the tune to those songs, and most everybody knew at least a smattering of the lyrics. Within fifteen minutes, they had gone through four or five songs. The volume, at least, was impressive. In between, everybody wanted to tell about his cousin who played the banjo or about the guitar at home that needed a D-string.

The aide found "I'll Fly Away" in the songbook and spread it out where everybody could see. Johnny pushed Luke Bennett off the desk because he was blocking his view.

About that time, the door opened, and in came Mrs. Pearl, the music teacher, struggling bravely under several cartons. "O.K., everybody, time for music!" called Mrs. Legg. The children spread out to their desks. While Mrs. Pearl unpacked a bunch of tambourines and other rhythm instruments, Jenny slid the guitar into the closet and Maggie sat in a corner chair.

"We're going to march today!" announced Mrs. Pearl with a big smile. She passed out song sheets containing "God Bless America," "It's a Grand Old Flag," and several others. "Joe, would you like to play the tambourine today? Here's one for you, Luke. You haven't had a turn in a long time. All right, everybody ready to march? Let's stand up!" They all lumbered to their feet.

"Remember, left foot first! Everybody ready with their left foot?" The needle touched down.

It was like watching a Fellini movie. The laughing, jostling people of minutes before had turned into clumsy, wooden caricatures. Faces into masks, aggressiveness into lifelessness. Joe, hulking, would-be football star; Billy, drunk in the cemetery; Jerry, the school's motor-scooter stud; eager, curious Johnny; poetic, shy Jenny — all marching to "God Bless America," all lifting their left foot first. Their faces were blank. They didn't protest. None of the snickers or clowning around you might expect even from seven-year-olds. Conditioning? Resignation? Maggie slipped quietly from the room.

As Maggie drove up the winding road to the school board office at the Yellow Castle, Johnny, Jenny, Preston, and so many others walked through her mind. Did any of the children ever get out of special education? It was frighteningly easy to wake up and find yourself at Gateway. How hard was it to go back to being a regular kid?

Up at the office, Maggie had a question for the school board secretary, who had handled all special education paperwork in addition to her own duties before Maggie arrived. "Were any kids transferred out of special ed last year?"

"I'm not sure." She was typing, preoccupied.

"Well, do we have a list of those kids?"

"No. Every child who has ever been in special education has a folder in those files." She pointed to a gray monster in the corner.

"Is there something in the files that tells if the child has been transferred?"

"No, the only way I could tell would be to compare last year's class lists with this year's list."

"Oh."

Maggie was leaving the office when the secretary called after her, "There's no official record at all."

Copper County was not alone at all. As reported in *Children Out of School in America*, the Children's Defense Fund found children "dead-ended" in programs in every state they surveyed. "Once misclassified," they wrote, "children are often segregated in inferior programs which stigmatize and cut them off from their peers; once placed, they are trapped indefinitely, sometimes permanently, with negligible benefit . . ."

This situation, so opposite from the intent of everybody involved, has led to renewed questions about labeled and segregated classes for children who aren't severely handicapped. Following reports from the early seventies that 90 percent of the children enrolled in EMR classes, nationwide, never return to the regular classroom, the new federal regulations and the regulations of several states have been redesigned to try to keep special classes from becoming a dead-end street and to encourage systems to use special classes only where it can be proven that the children need and benefit from the specific situation.

8. Beautiful Teachers in Not-so-Beautiful Situations

"I've heard school systems speak proudly of the fact that they're taking care of their minority kids by putting them in classes for the mentally retarded. Somehow, they don't seem to see what they're doing."

— Dr. Lloyd R. Henderson, director of the Elementary and Secondary Education Division, Office for Civil Rights, February 1975

AFTER REALIZING that there was no record of any transfers, Maggie sat at her desk and wrote random thoughts in a notebook. Why are the classrooms so poorly equipped compared with the regular classrooms? How do we know what's happening? Trying to see what's going on is like trying to put a cloud into a bag.

A copy of the Title I proposal for Copper County was on the desk in front of her. There was a section in that budget for special education, so she looked at it again, hoping to find some answers. According to the budget, federal money alone for special education added up to $75,284. "And that's not even counting state money," Maggie told herself. Thirty-two thousand dollars of that money had gone to remodel Gateway School. The building, the aides, the special ed music teacher, and Maggie's salary knocked off slightly over $68,000, leaving about $11,000 by Maggie's calculations. She began to feel hopeful.

Abigail stopped by her desk at that point and told her that Warner was in a twit because he hadn't been invited to the special education teachers' meeting. "How come?" asked Maggie. "All we're going to do is make out lists for how many rolls of masking tape we need and things like that."

"Warner's used to being in charge of expenditures," Abigail said. "He doesn't like to feel left out or that he hasn't been consulted about what's going on."

"Well, that's preposterous." Maggie frowned. "I have my job

after all, and he has his. We just have to get the roles straight, is all."

"You'd better stop that 'my job, your job' stuff right now," Abigail told Maggie. "That might sound right logically, and maybe you want to get things done as fast as possible, but, when you get down to it, it's going to hurt you more than it helps you when there are problems to be worked out."

Maggie didn't answer. Instead, she asked Abigail what the special ed classes at Goshen School were like. "Got some good teachers out there," Abigail replied. "Beyond that, I'll let you judge the situation for yourself."

Like the classes at Stockdale School, the Goshen classes were attached to a "regular school." As nearly as Maggie could make out, special ed children were sent to Goshen, Gateway, or Stockdale, primarily on the basis of the bus schedule, Goshen School in particular being twelve miles away from Davidson.

The road to Goshen passed a cast-iron statue of an early woodsman. That day, when Maggie drove past it, a bald man was taking a picture of it. He had set his little boy on the woodsman's foot. The frontiersman scowled down at his rifle. The child, laughing up at him, stretched upward to close his fingers around the gun barrel. His stomach showed under his jacket.

The special education classes at Stockdale had been located behind the school. At Goshen, one of them was located in the basement, one was upstairs, and one was in the cafeteria. A thirtyish fellow named Harry Blankenship was teaching the class in the cafeteria.

A former manager for the power company, Mr. Blankenship was likable on sight, low key and unpretentious under his blue baseball cap. Nobody was doing much in Mr. Blankenship's class. They were waiting to be run out of the cafeteria. "Sixth grade coming, in about ten minutes," drawled a redheaded boy. The students, seated randomly at the long cafeteria tables, were dwarfed by the size of the room. Pots and pans banged behind them. The smell of spinach filled the air. Other kids kept cutting through the room.

"It's a little confusing at times, but we make out. The way I see it," Mr. Blankenship said, "I'd rather use my energy doing something for these kids than hollering and complaining."

That's an unusual song, Maggie thought. "Can I get you anything?" she asked. "How about some shelves? And some things to put on them?"

Mr. Blankenship explained that he couldn't have shelves because of the lunch lines. "And I can't have a bunch of materials. They have a way of walking off during lunch."

He introduced Maggie to his kids.

"Mr. Blankenship's got a new baby at home," announced the red-haired boy.

"He's got a new home to put the baby in too," added another boy.

"But he still drives around in a green heap of junk," added a third.

Blankenship blushed slightly. "Guess the pickup comes last, boys. A man's got to have priorities."

"I'll give you ten bucks and a dead possum for it," offered the first boy.

Blankenship smiled and turned back to Maggie. "Since we don't have room for many books and things, we mostly make up our material out of our heads." He relaxed against the table and pushed up his sweater sleeves. "We sort of arrived at that arrangement by necessity, but it's turned out to be a good one. You wouldn't believe how much they've learned, just from writing about themselves. And I've learned at least as much as they have."

"Aw, what've you learned, Mr. Blankenship?" a pink-cheeked boy wanted to know.

"I've learned that I have a lot to learn. Just like you," Blankenship shot back.

"I hope I'll get to know the kids well enough to give you some decent help, if you want it . . ." Maggie began.

"Well, if you'd really like to get to know these kids," he cut in, "here's how you can get started . . ." He dragged a big cardboard box out from under one of the tables and gave it to her. "Here. I'll give you one of our shelves."

The box was full of notebook paper and mimeographed sheets. "It's a lot of things the students have written. If you read these, you'll know something about their lives."

Blankenship lowered his voice. "You've got to understand about their lives if you want to do anything," he said. "Some of these boys have so much anger and resentment stored up inside them . . .

seems like nobody's ever let them come out and say what they think before. They've got everybody saying, 'Don't do this, don't do that' on every side of their existence. So I let them write whatever they want. They can even take a poke at me if it helps them express how they feel about life.

"Some of these boys seem to feel that they've got to compete with every man they see," he continued. "They've learned that at home. A few of them kept wanting me to fight with them at first, still do every now and then. I don't squash them down. We work it off in the gym, basketball or something . . ."

Most of the students were teen-age boys. "These are all farm kids," said Blankenship. "And some of them have it pretty darn tough at home. They deserve better than what they're getting. I'll be honest with you. I know the academic program we've got going here leaves a whole lot to be desired. And I don't see why they have to be in the cafeteria . . ."

In the middle of all the boys sat a determined-looking little towheaded girl. "That's Trudy," explained Blankenship, shaking his head. "We just got her a week or so ago. If you want to help me, you can tell me what to do with her. She can't even read at all, and she doesn't know a lot of her letters. She used to be down with the primary group, but they moved her up here. Since my whole program has depended on the students being able to read, I just don't know what to do with her . . ."

"How come they moved her?"

Blankenship scratched the back of his head. "Her other teacher hollered often and loud because he had to carry her back and forth up the stairs to the bathroom. You can't see her braces, the way she's sitting, but she's crippled. Her parents kept her out of school until this year . . ."

"Now, don't get me wrong," Blankenship added quickly, adjusting his baseball cap. "I'm not criticizing. Everybody does what they think is best. Anyhow, Trudy's been put up here. It's probably more convenient for us to get her to the bathroom. I'm not sure what we can do for her otherwise, but I don't believe in hollering."

The meek shall inherit the cafeteria, Maggie thought.

*

At that point, the sixth grade came charging in, hollering and whooping. Mr. Blankenship and Maggie talked for a few more minutes, then she left, lugging the box and an already growing respect for Harry Blankenship.

The principal's office was located down the hall. He was standing in the doorway and invited Maggie into his office. She noticed that his bookshelves covered a wide variety of subjects touching on education: curriculum, philosophy, methods, the law. "Could we talk a little about Mr. Blankenship's class?" she asked him. "He deserves to get . . ."

"I'll bet you want to know when we can move them out of the cafeteria," he said, spreading his fingers in front of him. "It's simple. We've got space for them in the addition, same as we've had all year. Any time the superintendent picks up the phone and tells me I can move them, I'll move them. You can't get much more cooperative than that. I don't know why he hasn't given me the go-ahead before this."

He eyed Maggie with what amounted to suspicion and said that there was nothing he could do about Trudy's placement. "That one was an administrative order."

"Stop back by before you leave," he called as she went out the door.

The special class in the basement was discouraging too: small room, very few materials, a willing but confused and untrained teacher, and a very interesting group of students. These older children read well, cracked complicated jokes, and, in general, seemed confident and full of energy. A couple of them impressed Maggie immediately with their unusually perceptive comments. Only one boy seemed to be having serious difficulty.

The teacher, trained for high school English, shook her head when Maggie commented on her students. "You know," she said, "a lot of these boys used to come by the room at the first of school and ask me when 'that test' was going to be given. They'd say they were going to take it and mess up so they could get in here. Somebody had told them that you wouldn't have to do any work in here.

"Well, they're here," she said. "And now that they're here,

they're beginning to realize that they aren't going to get credit for seventh grade math or English, whichever. So now they want out. I've told the office, but they say they're ineligible for regular classes because of the test scores."

She shrugged. "It's a mess, I knew it as soon as I saw their names on my list." She looked at Maggie's face and tried to repress a smile. "I know it's awful to laugh, but after a while, it gets so crazy, it's funny.

"The saddest part about it is, I know there must be more kids who really do need help." She looked toward the boy who seemed to have severe problems. "He's improved a lot. I can't believe there aren't other kids who really need the same kind of help."

Maggie asked her if she had been well supplied with materials. She said she was buying them herself. "The third time I called Warner Jenkins he got mad and yelled at me that there was no more money. After that, I was afraid to ask."

The third class at Goshen met in a spacious room on the second floor. The room assignment reflected the status of the teacher. "If all my teachers were like Mrs. Coleman," Mr. Birdwell said, "I wouldn't worry about the welfare of a single child in our schools."

Mrs. Sarah Coleman had been at Goshen for over twenty years, almost as long as the gigantic evergreens on the lawn. Her classroom looked out over the mountains. "Mrs. Coleman's a real teacher," the school board secretary told Maggie. "All the kids nobody else wants to fool with — she wants them."

Maggie opened her door a crack and peeked in. Mrs. Coleman was in the back of the room at a small table with two children. The other children, working at desks, spotted the crack as soon as it appeared. "Somebody's here!" they caroled.

Mrs. Coleman, a sweet-faced, frail lady, urged Maggie to come in and make herself at home. After introducing her to the children, she went back to her table. Maggie looked around.

The children were very glad to talk and proud to show what they were doing. After several children explained their projects, it became apparent that every child knew exactly what he was doing and why he was doing it. Instant admiration for Mrs. Colemen.

Wandering around the various areas and cubbyholes in the room, Maggie was astounded not only by the variety of materials, but also by the fact that everything seemed to be appropriate for the children involved. Shelves of educational games and toys, cabinets full of mimeographed puzzles and exercises, pictures and children's books everywhere. Artwork prominently displayed, Peabody kits and other perceptual build-up materials in easy access. A little bed behind a partition. Record player and a good variety of Alpha One well-worn records. And, in one corner, an Alpha One kit for beginning readers. Its use was made obvious by the homemade devices, games, and knickknacks in front of it.

"Whenever part of the kit turns out to be inappropriate or insufficient for these children," explained Mrs. Coleman, "why, we just make up our own. That way, we can use it just fine, and the children get a lot more out of it."

In short, everything in the room seemed to fit the children. "How did you manage to get such a collection of materials?" Maggie asked her later.

"Honey, I begged, borrowed, and hoarded. And I made more than a few. I've been at this a while, you know." The best part was, Mrs. Coleman served as a willing resource for the other teachers. She'd lend them materials, give them advice, and pat them on the back when they needed it.

Local legends are sometimes a letdown in person. Not this lady. Mrs. Coleman's gentle, firm, intuitive direction of the children's activities was a joy to watch. Her aide was constantly active with one child or another. She was one of two aides in the entire special education program who seemed to have her own schedule of activities. She never sat idle or seemed unsure of her next move.

The room was so well structured, and the adults so well organized, that the children were able to proceed easily with a sense of natural progression, and — more important to these children — security. In spite of Mrs. Coleman's and Maggie's shared doubts about the totally self-contained structure, these children were definitely getting something special inside the classroom. "It's just the teasing they get outside that worries me," Mrs. Coleman said. She showed Maggie the children's work and talked of their progress with great pride. "Here's a child they said couldn't do anything," she whispered, showing Maggie the folder of a pale, shy brown-haired girl. "Why there was even some doubt about whether Becky should attend school . . ." The initial papers showed aimless scribbles. The latest efforts were clear, coherent sentences.

"She's coming along all right. If you could see what she has to put up with at home, you'd be surprised that she could do anything when she got here. Her parents have been known to go off and leave her with some canned food for a day or so at a time.

"You know, it was Mr. Birdwell who finally got the child welfare people on to the case and made sure the child had warm clothes and enough to eat." The little girl looked up at one of her classmates without smiling and brushed the hair out of her eyes. "You'd be surprised how many children come to school looking like somebody might have been beating on them."

Mrs. Coleman showed Maggie a couple of voice-of-doom psychological reports on other children in the class. "They say these children will never do anything. I don't believe them, because I know better. I know that it's the job of psychologists to be able to tell such things, but don't you think they can be wrong sometimes?"

Maggie watched Mrs. Coleman carefully. Her pride was obvious, but it seemed to be pride in the children's accomplishments rather than her own. She obviously cared for the children as individual souls. Perhaps that was her greatest asset. The children couldn't help but feel her concern and expand in its warmth.

Outside Mrs. Coleman's room, a teacher stopped Maggie. "You're the new special education supervisor, aren't you? I've got a boy I've been wanting to transfer into Sarah Coleman's room for months and haven't been able to get anybody to do anything about him. Will you come test him? He misbehaves so badly, I think maybe he's hyperactive. He belongs in special education."

The principal had a pile of papers waiting on his desk for Maggie. "I could talk about the classes, but you've seen 'em," he said. "The thing that burns me up the most about special education is this so-called evaluation system this county has going for itself. I've just been sitting here thinking about it. So sit down, and let me talk it out.

"Now, I don't know what your philosophy is," he began, "but if you have any sense, this should concern you. And you should hear it from somebody who's been in a position to watch it."

He sat down behind his desk. "O.K. I'm principal of a school that has three of these classes. I've only been here a year, and I don't have enough clout yet to say what goes on or doesn't go on in my school. That's not the way it should be, but that's the way it is. I'm informed of new programs more often than I'm consulted. I don't approve of the way this program is handled, so I've been keeping a close eye on it. And I'll tell you one thing." He paused for a few seconds. "The way they hustle these kids into special education, half of them never should've been there in the first place. Others that are crying for help turn out to be ineligible."

He snorted in obvious frustration. "And then they put the eligibles in a cafeteria. And act like we're doing them a favor! Even Mrs. Coleman's kids get a rough time from the other kids at times. She does beautiful things with those kids, but you wonder about the basic setup . . ."

He started pushing papers in front of Maggie as he talked. "These are so-called psychological reports," he said. "There's one child declared brain-damaged, apparently because he had poor fine-motor control and can't pronounce his r's right. I asked the guy who does the testing about him, and he said these are some of the symptoms of brain damage."

He snorted again and pushed another report across the desk. "I sat right here and listened to him test this girl. They were in this little room adjoining my office. Why, that little girl would barely talk! And yet, look here, there's a verbal score, no mention of shyness, and a comment about the kid's poor vocabulary mastery. And, if you'll look, this kid's also supposedly brain-damaged."

The principal leaned back in his chair. His face was getting a little red. "Now, the testing session doesn't last but about forty-five minutes, an hour or so at the most. I'd like to know where anybody gets off making judgments on these children on that amount of exposure. I'm not naive," he went on. "I know that that's the way they do it in more places than you and I could think of. State after state. Railroading children is nothing new. I also know that it's perfectly legal to classify a child by one IQ test."

He stopped and drummed his fingers. "And while I'm talking about it," he resumed, "I might as well dump the whole load on you. I always considered the term brain-damaged one of the most horrifying and irresponsible labels we educators lay on children when they don't do well in our schools."

He began to flip through a large sheaf of reports. "If you go through these reports, you'll see that maybe three out of five kids get labeled brain-damaged.

"Here we go: 'probable brain damage,' 'brain damage is likely' . . ."

The papers came sailing across the desk, landing in a pile in front of Maggie.

" 'The possibility of brain damage,' 'organic brain damage is indicated,' 'scattered scores point to brain damage,' 'suggest brain damage' . . .

"Baloney!" he exclaimed. "And the subject requires a much stronger word!" He settled back to look at her. "Now, maybe you think I'm nitpicking. But if one of those reports was on your own child or on you, it wouldn't be any nitpicking matter. Burns me up! I go down to the school board office, and everybody there thinks the county's doing such a great job with special education, maybe because the reports go in on time. Well, that may be true in a couple of classrooms, but they don't have to walk into the school cafeteria every day and see a perfectly bright ten-year-old who's going to be nowhere in six years and is being pushed around now."

He looked at Maggie. "O.K. It's up to you to do something about it."

Maggie suddenly felt like a little peanut caught in a big flood.

The road from Goshen to Davidson curved around the base of the mountains, now close to the river, now high above the rapids. The mist was constantly moving. It curled in the valley, it spiraled to incredible heights between the hills, making formations in the air, creeping magically through the bare trees. Maggie didn't notice it. She was totally preoccupied and feeling disoriented. A teacher can get absorbed in her classroom and forget about what's going on elsewhere. An administrator who never or rarely sees the children can assume that they are mostly severely handicapped or that things are indeed special. A supervisor's job doesn't leave much time for fooling yourself, unless you stay in the office. With her overview, the only way for Maggie to be optimistic was to think about one thing at a time, without relating it to everything else. As soon as Mr. Blankenship would inspire her, the sight of the cafeteria would remind her of what was really going on. As soon as Mrs. Coleman lifted her spirits, a teacher stopped her in the hall to find out how soon she could get rid of one of her overactive kids.

The supervisor's view also gave Maggie an uncomfortable feel for the fact that constructive improvement depends on a lot of factors that don't seem to be related to the children. Back at the Yellow Castle, a talk with Mr. Birdwell didn't ease her frustration. He folded his hands, said that he always wanted his staff to keep him informed of the problems arising within the school system, then answered one question after another.

Could training workshops be arranged for the teachers? "The law puts us in a difficult position there," he said. "We are only allowed X number of free days, and those days are frequently absorbed by snow, so we may have to wait to see how much snow we're going to get."

She told him what the Goshen principal had said about the available room for Mr. Blankenship's class. Mr. Birdwell agreed that the cafeteria placement was awful but added that one certainly had to admire Mr. Blankenship's spirit. "If all of my teachers had that kind of attitude, I'd never worry about any of the children in the school system. But they don't. I can tell you, that kind of attitude is extremely rare these days. I have a teacher right now who . . ." Finally, in a businesslike way he said that he was aware that the room was vacant and explained that the situation was more complicated than it seemed, since the agricultural reference library was housed in one end of that room. "There are ticklish diplomatic problems here, and the law does require us to maintain that library in an area with free access, so my hands are tied unless we can find another area to house those books and charts."

Maggie said as gingerly as possible that the law also required at least equal facilities for the special education children. He agreed that it was a tricky problem and promised to take it under advisement. "I am not in a position at this time to do things as rapidly as I would like," he said. Maggie wiggled around in her seat impatiently.

Could something be done about the class full of boys who had deliberately messed up on the IQ tests? He said he'd never heard of such a thing happening and that he didn't know if the class arrangement could be changed, since it was funded on the basis of those names. He asked her to look into it further. "And we certainly want to keep that teacher busy, so don't be too hasty."

What about the way a lot of the teachers were buying supplies out of their own salaries? "Yes, that's not right. That's not right at all. I suggest, young lady, that you consult with Warner Jenkins and make arrangements to correct that situation." He was trying to tell Maggie something important, but she wasn't hearing it.

"I've already tried, without much success . . ."

"I'm sure, if you present the problem to Mr. Jenkins in the proper manner, he'll be responsible. We all want to work cooperatively here. We're all interested in the same thing, after all. This kind of problem arises again and again in school systems. I've encountered it many times in my experience. I well remember one time over in Christiansen County, we had a situation . . ."

Mr. Birdwell obviously had other problems on his mind. They were getting nowhere. It occurred to Maggie that Mr. Birdwell might wish that she would disappear from his office. She did.

Maggie had to phone the state special education division about some other matters. Sam Watkins asked her how things were in Copper County, and she told him about the cafeteria. "How come the state funds classes like that?"

"If we do," Sam answered, "we always assume it will be a temporary situation. It's the responsibility of the local school system to make sure those children have suitable classroom space."

Before Maggie left for the afternoon, the secretary remarked that Mr. Birdwell had been swamped all day with complicated paperwork. "It's about the new vocational school." She shook her head. "That's his dream, you know," she said. "It's all he can do to keep up with the planning and everything else too." Maggie nodded absently.

The secretary stared after Maggie as she left the office. "How come she always has to be so uptight?" she asked another secretary. "You'd think special education was the only thing in the school system. And you'd think we were all personally responsible for anything that's wrong."

Maggie was totally unaware of the effect her uptight manner was having. Driving home, she thought about Mr. Birdwell and his dream. A wonderful dream that could improve life in the county for many people. It would mean much-needed training for young people. Evening classes could bring new interests and a social life to the hundreds of older people isolated in their homes with little to do and no real means of getting together.

When she pulled up beside the house, at least eight neighborhood children jumped off the porch and ran to the car. "Oh, hello, we've been waiting for you and Mrs. Maslow!" they exclaimed, bouncing up and down. "Can we come in?" No other place for them to go.

Drema, dangling a skinny leg over the railing, blowing big pink bubbles. Pickle in his baseball cap. The superintendent's dream could mean a lot to them. In comparison with the vocational project, the needs of the special education program may not have seemed to be the most pressing issue in the county. But everything is interrelated, Maggie thought, and this program does involve 183 children, 183 lives.

"There but for fortune, and all that," said Anita. "Just one life is all the world, when it's yours."

We have so darn many realities to choose from, Maggie thought. While the children painted with water colors, Maggie turned on the television and learned that the Pentagon had stepped up its B–52 bomber raids on Laos by 100 strikes per day. Before that increase, the U.S. forces had averaged only 280 strikes per day. Who can understand those numbers? she wondered. One strike could wipe out Davidson, children, Mr. Birdwell, me, and the new vocational school. I'll bet the money behind two jets could pay for several vocational schools.

At that moment, Drema and Jenny interrupted Maggie to ask if they could make popcorn. When Maggie got back from the kitchen, a man in a business suit had appeared on the screen. He asked if there could be anything worse than feeling your dentures slip.

Before going to bed that night, Maggie reached into Mr. Blankenship's file box and pulled out a few papers. Brown Eye settled down at the base of the couch. An hour later, Maggie was still sitting on the edge of the sofa beside a cup of cold coffee and a sleeping dog, pulling out paper after paper and wondering about the young people who had written them.

She had always tended to be dogmatic and say, without exception, "Self-contained classrooms for these kids are bad." But obviously, Mr. Blankenship's and Mrs. Coleman's classes were doing the kids a lot of good in many ways. Questions like "But do they have to be labeled and segregated to get that kind of sympathetic support?" kept going around in her head, without any answer, until she finally fell asleep.

About the same time, in another part of the country, two college professors were doing a two-year study to find out whether an intensive year in a self-contained class could help children make the adjustment from their former EMR program back into the "mainstream" (the regular system). For the study, they chose forty-eight elementary students, average age, ten, classified as mentally retarded and living in an economically depressed area.

The children were divided up into four classroom groups. Two classrooms were given an intensive, highly organized program. They were called the experimental groups. The other two groups were merely observed throughout the year. They were called the control groups. The teachers in the experimental classes developed a highly detailed program and kept careful track of each child's daily progress. Each child in the experimental group got a really souped-up program, using basic, common materials available to most schools.

At the end of an eight-month period, the experimental group had made an average gain of thirteen and a half months in their reading level and sixteen months in math. During the same time, the control group averaged only four and a half months' reading gain and a little less than five months' math gain.

By the following fall, thirteen of the twenty-four experimental group students were considered ready to be transferred back to the regular classrooms. By the same standards, none of the control group students was considered ready. Follow-up showed that the experimental group students made successful social adjustments and kept learning at a high rate, sometimes even without any kind of resource help. By the time the whole experiment was written up, eighteen of the experimental students had returned successfully to the regular classroom. Only three of the children from the control group had gone back.

9. Title I and Office Politics

"It happens to be my feeling that we have much better cooperation from people if they're included in the initial steps of any operation or any kind of planning, than if we superimpose it on them and say, 'This is what we're going to do. Is this all right with you?' None of us, I feel, like to be treated that way.

"This is also true for the regular classroom teacher who is told by the special teacher, for example, 'This is what's going to happen, and we expect you to cooperate.' It likewise applies to administrators, parents, and children. They may not have the time, the knowledge, or the desire to give specific input, but, when they are included in the process using an approach with which they are comfortable, they are likely to express or feel much less resistance to change."

— Dr. Sara James, director, National Association
of School Psychologists, July 1975

"All too often, you get this incredible turfsmanship that keeps things from happening. If you can only find people who are more concerned with getting the job done than in protecting their agency's turf or in being uptight or being defensive about what hasn't already been done . . . that kind of thing's been such a problem, almost a defeating problem.

"It seems so very important for the people involved to get acquainted as people, and that's not always easy to do, especially if they've got professional interests which seem, on the surface, to conflict."

— Jane DeWeerd, Bureau of Education for the
Handicapped, July 1975

MAGGIE HAD DECIDED that Warner Jenkins was the key to unraveling any of the problems of the special education program and that she should deal with him directly. Though the two of them had already had a few run-ins, Warner had turned out to be a very interesting man. He and Maggie had had a peaceful period during her first week or so in the Yellow Castle, when he gave her advice in a fatherly fashion. She usually ended up at his office in the early

morning, and they would chat while he went through the periodi-
cals and advertisements that had arrived in the mail.

This was one of the duties Warner had assigned himself. He used
a red pen to underline items of interest from *U.S. News & World
Report*, equipment catalogues, or anything else that caught his
fancy. Then he would cut these items out, put them in envelopes,
and stick them into various mailboxes. During that first week, he
gave her two advertisements for cure-all, couldn't-fail reading programs, an article about physical activities for mongoloid children,
and an ad for an electronic brain-scan service that would come into
a school system and perform EEGs for a fat price.

Talking with Warner was enjoyable for several reasons. He told
interesting stories and supplied a lot of information. It was fun to
watch him talk — and he loved to talk. He was small in stature, but
he involved his whole body in the process. His hands were constantly in motion, and he shifted his body around in constant enthusiastic dramatization of the conversation.

Besides being a red-pen underliner, Warner was a verbal underliner. Sometimes when he wanted to make a point, he would bear
down on the important words. "If you want to get something *going*,
you have to *push* it!"

Warner talked about a lot of things during the morning chats.
He talked about the small farm where he grew up with eight
brothers and sisters, about the Depression, when he worked for
thirty cents a day, taking care of the children of a woman who was
working for a dollar a day. He told Maggie charming stories about
the days when Davidson had been a booming railroad center, when
there were always lots of well-dressed strangers walking around
town and saloons had prospered over the objections of the
preachers. "I was just a boy then, but I still remember it *clearly*."

He talked about going deer hunting and singing in the Presbyterian church choir. He showed Maggie pictures of his grandnieces
and grandnephews. "I was married for a while, but she died before
we had any children," he said, the usual urgent tone dying out of
his voice. "But these children are just like my own grandchildren,"
he continued, smiling again. "I make them little presents and have
a lot of fun with them." Out of his desk drawer he pulled a charm-

ing little hippo he had whittled. "This is for my four-year-old," he said proudly.

Warner was a thoughtful person in many ways. He was always making little presents for somebody. A little stool for the lady down the block. A letter opener for a friend. "It passes the time of an evening," he commented. He sent off birthday cards and clearly regarded the clippings he placed in the mailboxes as little gifts.

Warner had taught American history at the high school before he became the Title I administrator. When the Johnson administration announced plans for the War on Poverty, Warner told Maggie, the Copper County officials hadn't paid much attention at first. Then neighboring McCormick County had received one of the first economic blasts of the war. "They got almost a *million* dollars!" Warner recalled, eyes widening. "Well, I can tell you all of us in this county sat up straight! We got our ducks in a row, real quick, and went into the proposal-writing business. I was hired as the ESEA Title I director, and here I am, still here!

"I learned how to cope with the federal government while I did it," he said. "I never had much money myself, and I still have to stop and shake my head when I realize that I'm handling hundreds of thousands of *dollars*."

Warner's desk top was always covered with piles of papers. Even the plants in the window were sometimes buried under catalogues and papers. A file cabinet beside his desk was stuffed full. "I've got a record in there of everything that's been bought, with serial numbers for all the equipment!" he said proudly. "This paperwork keeps me so busy that I never have a chance to go see if the equipment's where it's supposed to be," he added with a worried expression.

Since Warner was largely confined to the office, the world of education, for him, had evolved to the printed page. "I try to keep up with the latest developments in education. I'm *always* reaching out!" He demonstrated by a sweeping arm gesture. "You've *got* to reach out if you want to get something going!" He sighed and sat back. "But there's so much to keep up with that it gets hard sometimes."

By the time Maggie arrived as special ed supervisor, the school system in Copper County was heavily dependent on Title I. And, since Warner was the only person who knew his way around that mass of papers, records, and serial numbers, the school system was heavily dependent on him.

Federal funds were essential to keep the Copper County school system floating, since state funding for education didn't come close to meeting the basic needs of the school system. That's not true in every state. Where state funding is higher, federal funds are used in different ways. "We use our federal money to fill in the cracks for the different things the state money doesn't do," reports Dr. Landis Stetler, director of special education for Florida. "If you see things that need to be done, you can use the federal money to encourage school systems to go in that direction. So federal money acts to get things started.

"For instance, if you wanted to set up a regional program for deaf children, you get school systems to go together and equip classrooms and purchase buses, and you fund the total program for one hundred thousand dollars for two years with federal money, transfer it over to state money, then move the federal money over and start something else. But, as to federal money being a massive part of our total program . . . well, in this state, it just isn't."

In Copper County, Warner showed a generalized federal budget at regular intervals to the school board for approval. A typical item might be "Reading materials — $15,000." The school board would approve the budget, but then Warner would decide single-handedly, for the most part, how that $15,000 should be spent and on whom it should be spent. This fact was well known to the constant stream of sales representatives and teachers who visited and telephoned his office.

"Sometimes it gets to be more than a body can take," said Warner, "but I keep on plugging. You can learn a lot about reading programs from some of these salesmen."

Warner's office isolation had allowed him to develop a distorted picture of what the special education children were like. He knew that they were classified retarded. And retarded, to him, as to many people, meant, generally, "incapable of learning."

"Do you really think," he asked Maggie one morning, "that the amount those children are going to be able to accomplish justifies the amount of money we have to spend on this program? I mean, in view of all the other things we need for the regular children?"

Maggie told the reading supervisor what Warner had said. "Watch out," Abigail warned. "He decides who's getting the goodies and who isn't."

So Warner and Maggie were friendly until the Title I money came into the picture. Then the war began. Despite the shortages Maggie had seen in the classrooms, Warner kept insisting that great piles of materials were stored away in closets and drawers in the classrooms. When they failed to materialize, Maggie would come back and insist they weren't there, and ring-around-a-rosy would start all over again.

"Since you only get a certain amount of money from the government per year," Maggie asked Warner one morning, "what happens if an emergency comes up and you've already spent your money for that year?"

Warner shook his head vigorously. "That just doesn't happen," he explained. "That just *doesn't* happen. I don't spend it *all*," he added. "I still have money left from several years' grants. I have sixty thousand dollars left from this year alone!"

That conversation was the beginning of real trouble. There was something Maggie didn't understand: the teachers were not supposed to know how much of the federal money was left. Apparently, they weren't supposed to know that there was any money left at all. It was an administrative secret.

Maggie asked several teachers to make a list of the items they felt their classrooms needed. "Miss Callahan," Mrs. Legg said pointedly, "we've already been asked twice this year to make out lists. I've spent hours doing it, and am still buying my own paper towels and writing paper. I think somebody up there must be eating those lists."

"Oh, no," Maggie told her. "There's still plenty of money, sixty thousand dollars, left from this year's federal money alone."

"Well, we've been told there isn't any," she said glumly.

Two days later, Warner called Maggie into his office. He didn't greet her in any fatherly fashion. Several of the teachers had phoned him to put in their shopping lists. He was outraged. "Why, one of them even told me how much *money* was left!" he sputtered.

That wasn't all. Mr. Birdwell had given Maggie permission to assemble an order for badly needed math materials. When this had been completed, Mr. Birdwell had run it by the regional special education supervisor, who O.K.'d it. Mr. Birdwell initialed it and gave it back to Maggie a few days after Warner jumped her for talking about the money.

The math materials had to be bought with Title I money. By that time, it was obvious that Warner felt very protective of that money. So Maggie gave him the list with well-justified apprehension. He looked at it, saw Mr. Birdwell's initials, and shot her the kind of look reserved for burglars or cattle rustlers. End of honeymoon.

Warner stuck the math list under a big pile of papers on his desk. "I want you to get those teachers on schedules," he said curtly.

Abigail came by Maggie's desk a little later in the day. "Thought you were going to avoid politics," she said, tapping Maggie on the head. "Warner's practically got steam coming out his ears."

"I'm *not* playing politics," Maggie told Abigail. "The teachers really need that stuff, and it's my job to try to get them what they need. Birdwell O.K.'d it and so did the regional supervisor. So why should Warner mind?"

Abigail shook her head slowly. "My Lord, a disastrous innocent is at large in the school system. Look, Maggie honey, politics are going to happen, whether you want them to or not. So you've got two choices: you can use them in a good way to the advantage of others, or you can use them in a bad way. Use them in a good way. Otherwise, you're going to back yourself into a corner." She paused, relenting a little. "But I know what you mean. The problem with some kinds of politics in the school system is that the kids keep getting left out of it — especially if you're up in an office where you don't see them."

10. The Influence of Dollars

"The problems of identifying children for the purpose of a [funding] formula such as that contained in S. 6 [federal special education legislation] has other dimensions that must concern us. The procedures in this bill would tend to encourage undesirable 'labeling' of children requiring additional special education services as handicapped, and maintain the number at the highest possible level. This could increase the risk that labeling children as handicapped will itself cause harm. For those children labeled as mildly or moderately handicapped, particularly as emotionally disturbed or mentally retarded, the social stigma of the label can have catastrophic effects on the child's affective and cognitive development, effects often outweighing the special educational services they may receive. There are numerous reports of widespread mislabeling of disadvantaged and bilingual children, identifying them as mentally retarded or emotionally disturbed . . . The thorny intricacies of achieving appropriate identification without unnecessary labeling should not be taken lightly."

— Frank C. Carlucci, undersecretary of HEW,
testifying before the Senate Subcommittee
on the Handicapped, June 1974

FROM AN ADMINISTRATION point of view, "programs" can become mostly budgets, materials orders, reports, and so forth, while the point of view of the people involved can be very different. When you walk out of Dummy Tech, if you look up, the first thing you see is the mountains. Look behind you, and you see the river. Go up on the mountain, and you can look down at some points and see Gateway School.

The juxtaposition of those mountains and Dummy Tech could bring a lump to your throat. Sure, in the most awesome surroundings, there has always been ugliness — poverty, cruelty, hunger, violence. But this program supposedly had been created to *help*. And yet, the bureaucracy of the setup actually seemed to preclude more logical arrangements.

There were so many needs throughout the school system, and,

ironically, a large percentage of the regular children shared the need for intensive vocabulary and concept development. It would have made excellent sense for the school system to set up a solid language and concept development program in all the county elementary schools, to serve any children who needed it, on a resource basis, without labels. In many county schools, it would probably have saved time to identify the children who *didn't* need that kind of help rather than those who did.

Day after day, as Maggie got to know the children better and to appreciate them more, one question kept growing bigger and bigger: *How did all these children, with their varied types and degrees of problems, end up thrown together in a bag marked "retarded"?*

Naturally, everybody involved had a theory: "The regular teachers don't want to fool with children who are extra work, no matter what their problem is. The program exists for the benefit of the regular teachers." "State law requires the county to do something it isn't ready to do." "There is prejudice against mountain children and poor children." "If you've got to have special education teachers, retarded teachers are the easiest to come by." "Evaluation procedures I wouldn't use on a groundhog."

Then, to tie everything together, there was Craig Bailey's theory. As school board business administrator, Craig had a different perspective on the school system than most people did. Since he had shown a real interest in special education, Maggie ended up one day reeling off the various theories for him.

"After you finish talking about people's attitudes and the need for training," Craig offered, swiveling around in his leather chair, "I'll tell you about dollars and cents. First of all, this county gets twice as much money from the state for a special education kid as it gets for a regular kid. And I don't use the words 'this county gets' for nothing. After the money comes in, there's no way of telling where it goes." He knew how to grab Maggie's full attention.

"See, when the double-funding law was passed, the legislature neglected to stipulate the money as an earmarked fund under the state-aid formula. Since it's not earmarked for special education, the county can spend the money any way they damn well please."

"Well, what was it spent for this year?" Maggie asked.

"Who knows? It became a part of a whole series of accounts. We just bought that property up by Stockdale School for nineteen thousand dollars. Maybe a part of that was the special education money. Who knows? And you get a lot of money for special education from the federal government too. Not that it's not needed, but from what I can tell, we've got the wrong kids or the right kids in the wrong place . . . something like that . . ."

Maggie was gaping at him, and he laughed. "Well, don't be so pie-eyed naive," he said. "Things are really tight for schools now, and we're getting a lot of pressure from the community besides. This double-weight law is — in most cases — just an incentive to financially strapped systems to put as many kids into special education as possible. Now, what that means for the kids in each place is hard to say."

Maggie couldn't stop gaping. "Well, didn't the legislature realize that this could happen?"

"As a matter of fact," Craig continued, "if you read the record of the proceedings, you'll see where some delegate pointed out that very possibility while they were debating the bill. He mentioned one administrator by name, and said that well-known idiots like this one would have half the state in special education before they were finished if they could get paid for it."

"So what happened?"

"Well, they all got a good laugh out of it, and another delegate stood up and said that if this administrator was such a well-known idiot, then he must be worth twice as much money. But they still didn't earmark the funds.

"I'll tell you," added Craig abruptly. "I'm sick of judging a child on a financial basis. Since that double-weight funding law was passed, without sufficient regulations, the number of children in retarded classes multiplied several times. This county went after it like a fish after a worm.

"I don't know how you judge motivation. People want to do something for kids with problems, after all. There's also the fact that, in an overcrowded school system, it's great to have the government build facilities to house some of the children. It relieves the load in the regular classes and keeps taxes down too.

"And then we've got a couple dozen people employed in the program, many at state or federal expense . . . It's not that all these things aren't needed in general, and I know that special education money's badly needed for really handicapped kids, but . . . I don't know . . . Why is it," he said finally, "that education in general gets funded at such a miserably low rate that the options end up being decided by where the money is? If we had funds available for all kinds of things . . ." He threw up his hands and went out to get a cup of coffee. "The whole subject makes me inarticulate," he concluded, going out the door.

Craig's Copper County observations apply to all parts of the country. "Funding formulas definitely do encourage certain sorts of practices," says Martin Kaufman of the U.S. Bureau of Education for the Handicapped. "Funding formulas vary from state to state, and make a big difference when people start talking about alternative program structures. The funding formulas will either encourage or discourage them. So, legislative and state education agency personnel must consider the implications of state support for special education and related services, not only from the perspective of the amount of money to be allocated, but also in view of the way each funding formula will affect program structure."

A few examples of funding formulas, taken from existing 1975 situations, suggest the complexity:

• New Mexico funded special education classes in 1975 on the basis of a specific number of children identified for certain categories. Regular programs get their money on the basis of a set number of children per classroom. The funding is higher for special education, and, if the child is transferred to a regular classroom for part of the day, none of the extra funds go to the regular classroom with her. As a result, most of the children labeled retarded stay in their self-contained classrooms, because that's where the money has to stay.

• In Texas and Georgia, if Jenny Krebbs spent more than 51 percent of her time in a "regular" classroom, she would be included in both the general and special education funding formulas. If she spent her whole day in special education, the funds would stay only in special education. There is much more financial freedom to find the structure that suits the child. Money doesn't work to keep special and regular education separate.

• Florida distributes money by "weighted equivalency." Each category has a set cost that is multiplied by the percentage of time the child spends in special education. The more time Jenny spends in the regular classroom, the more money the system loses.

• State laws vary widely in specifics. Some states make special provision for out-of-state tuition, which may be good or bad, depending on how the state uses it. Colorado pays 100 percent of the maintenance costs for children placed in licensed foster homes. South Carolina pays for home-school telephones. Minnesota reimburses for depreciation on the school bus fleet.

• Most states now fund by categories. However, a nationwide survey of state special education directors showed that most directors would rather have the funding based on program structure. Massachusetts has adopted this program structure funding arrangement, combined with detailed checks and balances for deciding which structure (self-contained, resource, etc.) is most suitable for each child's needs.

• Minnesota funds special education by personnel salaries rather than by categories or program structure. Maynard Reynolds, University of Minnesota professor, explains why this seemed to work in his state: "School districts were no longer constrained; it became possible for them to institute a variety of administrative arrangements to improve the programs for exceptional children. In other words, it became possible for the school systems in Minnesota to break out of what might be called the 'two-box' theory of special classes, in which children are categorized and allocated according to rigid criteria and financial formulas."

• A national project on the classification of children recommended that funding for children in need of temporary assistance be based on a flat percentage (15 percent recommended) of the total funding available for all children, because "the [present] predominant pattern for funding works to encourage school boards to maximize the number of children classified as handicapped and to keep them so classified." The money for special education, the project report emphasized, should be added on to the total school budget, not taken away from some other part of the school budget.

Realizing that funding arrangements are often crucial in decision-making processes, the government is using money requirements in other ways to bring handicapped people out of their traditional isolation in our society. Federal law now requires that 10 percent of the children included in Head Start programs be handicapped children. The same is true for vocational education. Ed Martin, director of the Bureau of Education for the Handicapped, strongly supports this way of using funds. "When people have said to me, 'Look, instead of making this ten percent set-aside requirement for Title III, vocational education, or Head Start, why don't we just take the forty million dollars and give it to you, and you can administer it from the Bureau of Education for the Handicapped?' I've said no. I'm more interested in seeing the total system redesigned to include the handicapped than I am in having the money in our separate compartment."

Partially because the 10 percent money isn't "added on" to existing funds, there have been some problems. "There's a real reluctance to include the handicapped, unless it really touches you in some personal way," commented a special education professor at the University of Maryland. The Government Accounting Office report released in 1975 showed that a majority of the states were not complying with the set-aside. The level of compliance averaged out to about 6 percent. It varied, from full compliance to almost zero percent, and then you wonder about some of the evidence that was presented as compliance.

"I've had superintendents of schools say to me, 'I can't worry about that small bunch of handicapped kids. I've got to think about the total program out there.' So, as long as minorities are the last to get their share of available resources, somebody is going to have to be on top of the situation. Passing a law doesn't mean it's going to happen."

The effect of funding patterns should never be underestimated.

They also can have a direct effect on teacher referrals. Teachers from districts that receive additional funds for children in special education have reported increased administrative pressure to refer more kids. The reverse can happen in states where the school system has to pay for special education first, then wait for state payback, which may or may not come.

"We've got situations here in this state," reported Frederick Andelman of the Massachusetts Teachers Association in 1975, "in which nontenured teachers are actually fearful of making referrals, because of political reprisals, because the word has come down that, if they make referrals, those referrals end up expressing themselves as dollars and cents that the local community has to spend. The schools themselves are under political pressure from the community not to spend money."

Recognition of the effect of funding formulas is growing. The federal special education law (Public Law 94–142) that goes into effect in 1978, for instance, contains a complicated so-much-money-per-child funding formula. Basically, each school system receives a certain amount of money for each child, age five through seventeen, who is enrolled in a special education program. Congress rarely appropriates the amount of funds called for by the law for education programs, but, if it does, the per-child amount for special education will increase each year until 1982, under the law. The state and local systems will be required to match the funds in percentages that increase for the local system over the years.

It is solidly agreed that such financial support for handicapped children is very long overdue and badly needed. Knowing, however, that this kind of formula could also encourage systems to put children inappropriately into special education programs, the people who wrote the law stipulated that no school system or state can receive these funds for more than 12 percent of its school-age children. Priority goes to children without programs and severely handicapped children, and limitations have been placed on the number of children to be funded in the "learning disabilities" category.

"It's such a delicate thing," commented one of the staff members of the Senate Subcommittee for the Handicapped. "We would like to make it more open and wish all those strings didn't have to be attached, but, on one hand, you have to make the funding terms definite enough that the money can't be diverted to general system use. The money has to reach those children. On the other hand, you don't want to encourage labeling and packing of special education classes. That also, by the way, has the effect of taking funds away from truly handicapped children. Sometimes, I sit back and wonder why we, as a society, have to guard against such possibilities. It's perverse. But I also recognize plain evidence that we must."

11. School Psychologist

"There has to be something else going for school psychologists than just meeting regulations; otherwise, you are asking them to abrogate responsibility, and putting them down as real people when you say, 'Fulfill a requirement for me,' especially when that requirement is tied primarily to money considerations."

— Dr. Sara James, director, National Association
of School Psychologists, June 1975

"Clearly, both psychologist and teacher view the child against a criterion of what they consider 'normal.' What is labeled abnormal must be a function of that which is considered normal.

". . . I would define our major task as that of helping the normal group increase its capacity to include, rather than exclude, to cope with rather than to reject an ever-broadening range of individual differences.

". . . I suggest that, as school psychologists, we consider shifting ground, i.e., that we conceptualize our roles as shifting from that of working with deviants to that of working with the group's capacity to cope with its membership."

— Dr. Rachel M. Lauer, chief school psychologist,
New York City Board of Education, 1967

THE INFLUENCE of funding formulas can cause children like Jenny to be inappropriately placed. Inappropriate placement can also occur as a result of bureaucracy, a situation in which the school personnel are functioning in such a disconnected way that nobody has a total picture of what's happening with a given child. The minister who lived on Maggie's block, a man whose varied experiences had left him both cynical and gentle, had something to say about this kind of process.

"I've spent fifty-nine years doing a lot of different things in a lot of different places," he told Maggie one day. "So there's been plenty of chance to watch people and how they do. I've been involved in labor organizations, health programs, drug abuse programs, and even a few business operations. And I've noticed one thing that would have made all those operations a lot more productive: people need to cooperate and let each other know what's going on. They need to talk to each other.

"I've seen a lot of worthwhile projects die or turn into something they weren't intended to be because the right hand didn't know what the left hand was doing, even though both were supposed to be working on the same thing. People get their own routine going and forget the big picture they're helping to make. Or else they get mad because they think someone's cutting them out."

In Copper County, the people associated with the special education program were mostly functioning in their own separate compartments. A few days after Maggie visited Goshen School, for instance, Buzz Murphy came into the office and stopped off to introduce himself and shoot the breeze. Buzz had administered most of the IQ tests that legalized the children's placement. Maggie asked him how the children from more isolated homes reacted to IQ testing. He said that many of them had some interesting misconceptions. "I couldn't tell you, for instance, how many of them say that George Wallace discovered America. That's a question on the 'information' section of the IQ test. Of course, they don't get any credit for an answer like that."

Buzz was a talkative, likable guy of about twenty-five, very much into double carburetors and always telling stories. He worked for the regional mental health office, which had contracted with the board of education to do the psychological evaluations for special education. While he worked, he was commuting to a nearby college to finish his master's degree in clinical psychology. His title, as it appeared on his reports, was "psychological assistant."

Many of Buzz's actions showed that he held strong convictions about human rights. The school system grapevine had it, for instance, that Buzz had caused a minor uproar at one of the local federal prisons when he informed some prisoners that their rights were being violated. And yet, curiously enough, Buzz didn't seem to see the outcome of his own work within the school system. Giving tests was just one of seven or eight functions he was expected to fulfill for the mental health office. Testing was what he was trained to do. His job stopped with the test. So he kept on recommending special education placement if the numbers turned out right, without really knowing the child or the situation into which the child would be going. This whole approach puzzled Maggie since Buzz went into the classrooms from time to time and even expressed concern about some of them.

Buzz told her a story that helped her understand his predicament a little better. "When I first came," he said, "I wrote a bunch of reports which said things like 'Don't put this child in an EMR class. He mainly needs tutoring in reading' — or whatever. Well, they'd come back to me, demanding that I authorize a special ed label. 'We understand your point,' they'd say, 'but we don't have funds for the kind of thing you're recommending right now. All we have funds for is special ed, and if you won't say this child belongs in special ed, he just won't get any help.'" Buzz shrugged. "So what do you do when somebody says something like that? I guess you just cross your fingers and sign the paper."

People in Buzz's position, Maggie reflected, can have a giant impact on a child's future. As sociologist Jane Mercer observed, "Persons with these skills now form a corps of professional diagnosticians who have official sanction to label deviants by using appropriate diagnostic instruments. In the capacity of legitimate labelers, they control who may enter many programs and statuses in American society."

There are many sensitive, competent psychologists working in the schools today, but there are serious weaknesses in this part of the system too. Testifying before the Senate Subcommittee on the Handicapped, Dr. Lewis Klebanoff of the Massachusetts Department of Mental Health complained that "state standards for school psychologists, counselors, and social workers are often shockingly below generally accepted professional standards, and even then are often ignored.

"It is very possible in a great many states for school teachers to take cafeteria courses in the afternoon and summertime, and, after a number of years, you collect thirty credits for a master's degree and suddenly become a psychologist . . ." adding pointedly that "without solidly prepared, well-supervised and experienced clinical personnel or well-prepared school psychologists with internships and close supervision, the whole system may turn out to fall far short of its worthy goals."

Although Buzz wasn't a psychologist yet, his reports were considered legal by the state division of special education because they were countersigned by a psychologist at the regional mental health office in the next county. This fellow, an older man, assumed final responsibility for the accuracy of the "evaluations," although, with rare exceptions, he never laid eyes on the children involved.

Maggie had never met Buzz's boss, but they did communicate occasionally, mostly through Buzz. One day, for instance, Maggie had suggested to Buzz that it was unfair to evaluate the learning capacity of children who are notoriously shy around strangers with a test that depends on the child's ability to communicate verbally. Buzz relayed her remarks to his boss. The reply came back the next day. "He said to tell you that we're not trying to find out how these children will perform back in the hollow, but how they'll manage in the modern world, in a city like New York, for instance."

Buzz hastily reminded Maggie that all psychologists don't think that way. "We're all different, even if we are in the same category," he said.

The word "appropriate" is very noticeable in just about all the new special education laws: "right to an appropriate education," "least restrictive alternative appropriate," and so on. Written into a law, it sounds like something you could measure, but "appropriate" is a matter of opinion too. Maggie, Buzz, the principal of Roosevelt School, and Pickle, for instance, would be likely to have four different opinions about what's appropriate for Jenny.

So who decides what's appropriate? Dr. Sara James, the director of the National Association of School Psychologists in 1975, says that many school psychologists feel frustrated when the whole burden is placed on them. "Generally, school psychologists as a professional group seem to have evolved with special education legislation, since in many states, as well as in the programs generated through the federal government, someone was required to make decisions about placement of children. Somehow or other, the idea occurred that psychologists should be able to do this by themselves.

Unfortunately, we often ignored the native ability of those who were teaching the children, but we are moving back to the point where we're truly involving teachers in screening and evaluation efforts too."

In 1975, HEW encouraged each state to include in its "five-year plan" for special education a requirement that each school system conduct its evaluation and placement through an "evaluation-placement team." "The team should be composed of all persons who directly or indirectly are involved in or influence the child's education success. This might include the parents and their community representative or advocate, various professional persons in the school, including the regular teacher, special teacher, psychologist, communication/speech therapist, counselor, and nurse. In addition, community-related personnel, including the social worker, minister, and family physician, might also be appropriate."

One important function of such a team is to bring together representatives of the program into which the child might be going and of the program in which she is already placed. Many systems are already using placement teams, and a few systems are going one step further. One grade school in Minneapolis, for instance, uses what they call a Student Support Team for placement in their resource room program. The membership of the team changes, depending on which child is being discussed. Permanent members are the special education teachers, the principal, the social worker, and the regional psychologist. If Harry Jones is being discussed, Harry's regular teacher and his parents also participate. "We knew it was essential to get everybody involved, but we've been frankly amazed at the importance this team has taken on," commented the program's director. "It has served as a fantastic reinforcer for the regular teachers and has broken down barriers between special education and regular teachers. It's an added protection for the children against our errors."

Taken one step further, if the team thinks placement in the resource program is appropriate for Harry Jones, Harry does a trial run in the resource program before any final decision is made. He visits the resource room for a half-hour every day for two to three weeks. The resource teachers work with him, try to evaluate the nature and degree of his difficulties, and then bring a report to the next Student Support Team meeting. The regular teacher brings a report too, and the whole team discusses the child and his program. If he does get assigned to the resource program, the regular and special teachers write a program for him that involves both classrooms.

Many practical problems have to get ironed out before such a project can work in a school. There are questions like Who's going to cover the classroom while the meeting's going on? and What if the parents can't come? And each school has to set up a decision-making process that suits the people and circumstances involved.

"Human beings differ," remarked a representative of the Massachusetts Office for Children, "and so do school systems. I've attended group placement meetings where everybody had done their homework and really showed a strong sense of the significance of the decision on the child's life. They'd look at the program itself, not just at the test scores. But then, there are other team evaluation meetings that are nothing more than a rubber stamp for an IQ score, where nobody knows too much about the child in question . . . No placement structure's going to guarantee a kid a fair shake. It's people who do that."

School records also play an important part in most placement processes. After she'd been there a month or so, Maggie figured it was time to read through the folders in the file cabinet in the corner of the school board office. Digging into the gray monster was a real experience. It apparently contained a folder on all the children who ever had been tested for special education, whether or not they had ever been actually placed. There was a folder on Pickle, as well as one on Jenny. There were files on kids who had left the school system years before.

A typical file contained a "psychological report" and a parental permission slip. The psychological report is written after the child takes an IQ test and whatever other tests might be administered. The permission slip must be signed by one parent before the child can be given an individual IQ test. A few files contained agency or medical reports.

Another set of records was kept by the teachers. Typically, the teachers' folders contained a copy of the "psychological," complete with IQ scores and a permanent record card. Sometimes there was a copy of the additional reports.

When Maggie had finished going through these folders, she had come no closer to answering questions like "Who are these children?" "Why are they here?" and the most disturbing, "What makes them so different from any other child that they have to be sent to a separate place?"

The files did *not* include the following information:

The number of years each child had spent in special education. (This could sometimes be deduced from the permanent record cards, when they had been filled in. The teachers and children often didn't know.)

The exact nature of each child's problem and why that child had been placed in special education.

What each child had been doing during his years in special education. His program. The objectives of his program. What kind of progress each child had made in the special education program. Whether it had helped him.

The file *did* include some frighteningly final judgments on individual children. Too many were two- or three-paragraph assessments of a child's human potential, usually based on one IQ test, written by people who saw each child only during that testing session.

Here are just three assessment samples:

• "———— is a small blond girl who was afraid of the testing. She entered the session sucking her finger to show her regression in the stressful situation. Slowly she began to smile at the examiner as she became less afraid of the situation. She had a bad cold at the time and breathed loudly through her mouth. Her speech was defective, but intelligible. She often asked the examiner to repeat a question, but this was not felt to be a passive-aggressive maneuver.

"[Her] Stanford-Binet is 7 yrs. 9 mos., MA 5 yrs, 2 mos., for an IQ of 64 which is educable mentally defective functioning. Her visual-motor level is on the 6-yr. level and shows signs of organic brain-damage. [She is unable to copy angles, has poor fine-motor control, and poor spatial judgement.]

"RECOMMENDATIONS: It is recommended that [she] be placed in special education class. Because of her brain-damage, she should be in an organized atmosphere where she will know what to do now and what to expect."

• "———— is a shy cleanly dressed girl who looks her age. Much effort was spent by the examiner trying to get [her] to perform. When she felt the task to be difficult, she was very reluctant to try, probably because she expected to fail.

"[Her] Stanford-Binet CA is 7 yrs. 9 mos., MA 5 yrs. 2 mos., for an IQ of 64 which is educable mentally defective functioning. Her writing level is on the 6-yr. level. [She] perseveres and shows poor fine-motor control which may be indicative of brain-damage.

"RECOMMENDATIONS: [She] should be placed in a special education class."

• "———— is a small brunet whose hair and total appearance was unkempt. He spoke little but expressed approval and fear vividly with his eyes. His behavior is typical of children about 5 or 6 years of age. His speech seemed immature, but not defective. [His] speech is intelligible.

"[His] Stanford-Binet CA is 8 yrs. 7 mos., MA 6 yrs. 6 mos. for an IQ of 73 which is borderline intellectual functioning. There are no signs of organic brain damage nor severe emotional problems.

"RECOMMENDATIONS: [He] should be placed in a special education classroom."

Many people everywhere take the numbers on such reports extremely seriously. Too often, if the Lord in person had poked a giant finger down through the clouds, laid it on a child's head, and boomed, "This boy is a 68," it would scarcely be more believable. The test was regarded as so infallible an instrument that children who were achieving at higher levels than the test predicted were said to be "overachieving."

Special education children like Jenny Krebbs and Callie Peale are particularly vulnerable to this kind of irrational record-keeping because they are children, and many adults don't believe that children have a right to privacy. The records also put various opinions about the child's problems and defects into "official" form, which, up till now, could follow a person into adulthood.

Contributors to the HEW-funded study, *The Futures of Children*, make the dangers clear. "Whether or not the 'exceptional' child is seen as responsible for his condition or acts, there is always the risk that records created for use by service and control agencies will serve to perpetuate misleading and injurious characterizations of the child's difficulties, treatment, or abilities." A routinely written opinion, composed in the space of ten or fifteen minutes, can limit a person's opportunities well into adult life.

And yet, certain types of information are essential to productive operation of any educational program. It's not unusual to see all sorts of speculation about a child's "defects" preserved for posterity; but information about the school system's methods of dealing with these defects is often very hard to come by. In a situation like this, children can be buried in special education. If Jenny has been inappropriately placed, and nobody takes a personal interest in her, she is simply submerged, at least on paper. Nothing in her file indicates that anything is amiss.

The kinds of information that would have made meaningful records in Copper County were not available. Since no record existed of the children's capacities upon entering special education or of their program since that time, there was no way of determining the extent, if any, of their progress. There was no way of assessing objectives for each child. Some of the teachers didn't plan daily activities for the whole class, much less individual children.

After she checked through the files, Maggie began to compile some basic information. She asked for the names of brothers and sisters, to begin with, because she had already heard people saying things like, "Those Bennett children all belong in special education." And all the Bennett children had indeed been put in special education. It seemed like a good idea to find out how widespread the practice was.

As nearly as Maggie could determine, the practice of family referral had developed into a custom. Four families had five or more children in special education. And more than half of the children had a brother, sister, or cousin in another special education class. There were people who insisted that this proved that poverty is synonymous with lack of intelligence. As far as Maggie could tell, in that particular situation anyhow, it proved mainly that children were frequently referred to special education on the basis of their name.

Information-gathering is an increasingly touchy subject in anybody's book. In some parts of the country, even the collecting of children's names and addresses has come under justifiable fire, when that information passes beyond the local level and is used in a stigmatizing fashion.

The picture for school record-keeping changed drastically when the Family Educational Rights and Privacy Act went into effect in 1974. The effects of that act are just beginning to be felt in 1976. Under the Buckley Amendment to that act, parents have a right to inspect all records relating to their child that are available to school employees (excluding notes for personal use) and can challenge any inaccurate or misleading materials. School systems are required to do away with all personally identifiable data on handicapped children within five years after the end of educational service, giving the child and her parents a chance to see them first. Before the school officials can supply any information to the police, social workers, employees, or other parties outside official educational channels, they must have written permission from the parents. Failure to comply fully can result in loss of all the system's federal funds.

Like other such laws, the effectiveness of the Buckley Amendment will depend on the extent to which the public is aware of its existence, the extent to which the individual parent is able and willing to use his or her rights, the attitude of the school system employees, and the extent to which the parent can assess the adequacy of reports found in their local system files.

12. IQ Tests and Testing

"Placement devices, and even the concept of separate placement, are increasingly under challenge. The primary device used for screening and placing children in special classes is the so-called standardized individual intelligence test. Respected school officials and psychologists admit that the IQ tests are inappropriate to measure the intellectual capacity of many minority children.

"A child diagnosed by these tests as having limited capacity frequently is treated as retarded for the rest of his often abbreviated education. Part of the tragedy of such labeling is that teachers who believe a child to be of limited educability tend to lower their expectations of the child accordingly. Then the student usually acts out the label by performing at or below the expected level, even if he is able to do better.

"The label of retardation can have serious, debilitating, and life-long effects on the labeled person. A labeled person becomes subject to special discrimination. He becomes a person (or nonperson) who is not heard, or, if heard, not listened to, or, if listened to, not heeded. He often internalizes society's judgment in shame, guilt, timidity, and unusual acquiescence to authority."

— *Silent Minority*, 1973 Report, The President's
Committee on Mental Retardation

WHEN A CHILD is in danger of being declared EMR, those placement meetings that are "a rubber stamp for an IQ score" are especially frightening. Writing in 1973, Dr. Oliver Hurley of the University of Georgia commented on the use of the IQ test in the "evaluation" process. "[The] four step process — referral, evaluation, case meeting to certify or not certify the child as MR, committee meeting to make a placement decision — is what happens in a system with some degree of good leadership in special education and a realization of the serious impact of their decisions on the child's future. These are a minority of our systems. More often, the team consists solely of a psychologist who is required only to administer one test. Whether he observes the child in natural settings or administers diagnostic instruments is up to him. In effect, in most cases, the classification decision is the psychologist's. Operationally, this is so, even in those states which vest such authority in a local advisory council or case study committee. But worse, the decision may be based on a single sample of a child's behavior and the teacher's referral report. In fact, it has been this writer's experience that even in those systems which have a fairly sophisticated evaluation procedure and some attempt is made to develop a complete case study, prognostication and decision-making is based primarily on the child's performance on the intelligence test, with little regard for contradictory observational or achievement data. After all, state laws define MR in terms of an IQ test score. This problem is exacerbated in those systems which hire part-time psychologists to administer a Binet (IQ test) or WISC at the rate of five or six a day. In spite of all that has been written lately about the pitfalls of this system, the pattern of routine testing, labeling, and placement of children persists; in the vast majority of cases, the adaptive behavior of the children in settings other than the classroom is never evaluated. These so-called 'six-hour' retarded children who function normally outside of school are inappropriately stigmatized and inappropriately educated. This discrimination against minority or poor youth has led to a questioning of the basic structure of special education and to litigation in the courts."*

In Copper County, Craig Bailey got to talking about the IQ test in the business office one day. "It wouldn't be possible, as I understand it," he said, "to put these kids into classes if they didn't score below a certain point on the IQ scale. Now, I don't know much about IQ tests, but how come all those children slid in below seventy, if they aren't retarded?"

"Could be lots of reasons," Maggie told him. "For one, these tests depend heavily on a child's ability or willingness to talk to the person who's giving the test. These aren't group IQ tests, where the whole class sits down and writes in little books. They're individual tests kids don't write. They have to talk, put together puzzles, remember number sequences, answer questions, things like that. If a child doesn't feel like talking when he takes the test, he can forget it."

Craig got a good frown out of that one, knowing how shy many

*See pp. 339–41 for examples and details of some of the lawsuits that have been filed on behalf of "six-hour retarded children."

local children could be around adults. Still, it had been an inadequate answer to one more very complicated question. Somebody with a bunch of professional papers would have told Craig that Dr. Henry S. Dyer, a former vice president of the Educational Testing Service, has called IQ tests "psychological and statistical monstrosities . . . probably the most convenient devices ever invented to lead people into misinterpretation" of children's learning abilities. Craig could have heard that research psychologist Dr. Robert Coles has called IQ testing "an incredibly naive and simple-minded way of looking at human beings."

Or even that Alfred Binet, the creator of what has become the Stanford-Binet IQ test, said in the early 1900s that "some recent philosophers appear to have given their moral support to the deplorable verdict that the intelligence of an individual is a fixed quantity, a quantity which cannot be augmented. We must protest and act against this brutal pessimism. We shall endeavor to show that it has no foundation whatsoever . . ."

But, apparently, it doesn't matter who frowns on them, IQ scores are still the nuts and bolts of special ed placement in most school systems, particularly in retarded classes, perhaps because they are convenient, economical, and usually required by law.

Most of the Copper County special ed children were placed by means of the most widely used individual intelligence test in the nation, the Wechsler Intelligence Scale for Children (WISC). Other tests were sometimes used, but the WISC was definitely the big gun.

Danny, one of the special ed kids at Stockdale School, reminded Maggie that she ought to take another good look at the test itself, instead of just fussing about *who* was going to do the evaluation. Danny had gone to visit Buzz Murphy a few days before. Maggie asked him what he did there.

"Played with puzzles, and he asked me a bunch of dumb questions," Danny said matter-of-factly.

"Like what?"

"Like would I beat up a little kid," he recalled.

That afternoon, Maggie visited the Copper County Mental Health office to ask Buzz if she could borrow the kit labeled "Wechsler Intelligence Scale for Children." When she got home and began digging into it, the process by which all those children had been declared retarded became a lot clearer.

An hour or so later, Maggie decided that the Wechsler must be one of the most carefully guarded secrets of the educational world. Otherwise, she didn't understand how it could be used to declare thousands of children retarded every year. It seemed to her that some parts of it read like science fiction. "You know what?" she asked Anita. "If somebody read this thing aloud on prime time television, it would be the educational equivalent of the release of the Pentagon Papers."

Buzz hadn't asked Danny if he would beat up a little kid. He had asked him what he would do if a child "much smaller than yourself" started beating on him. Then Danny's answer was rated from zero to two points, according to a list of "acceptable responses." Knowing Danny, he probably said he'd knock the kid flat. For that response, he would have received zero points. If he had said he would ask somebody to pull the kid off, he would have received one point. To achieve full credit, he would have had to say that he was going to reason with the kid, or something along that line.

That question appears in the "General Comprehension" section of the Wechsler. The entire test contains ten sections, five of which are intended to assess the child's "verbal" ability, five of which supposedly assess his "performance" ability. The "General Comprehension" section is "verbal."

"What is the thing to do if you lose one of your friends' balls (dolls)?" reads another of the Comprehension questions. A child who says he would look for the toy only receives half-credit for understanding the question. A child who tells his friend that he is sorry gets no credit for comprehension. If a child tells the test examiner that he would replace the toy, he gets full credit.

"What should you do if you were sent to buy a loaf of bread and the grocer said he did not have any more?" reads a third question. A child who says he would forget about it receives no credit for understanding the question. If the child says he would get biscuits instead, he gets full credit.

And then there is the one about what to do when you see a train approaching a broken track. "Run like hell" shows no comprehension, while sticking around to warn the engineer gets two points.

The first five questions are judged by the degree of "responsibility" the child is willing to assume. In effect, he is judged by his willingness to conform or pay lip service to "nice behavior," as defined by the author of the test.

For each of the nine questions that rounds out this part of the test, the child must supply two answers to achieve full credit. These questions include such items as "Why is it better to build a house of brick than of wood?" "Why should women and children be saved first in a shipwreck?" "Why is it better to pay bills by check than by cash?" and, Maggie's favorite, "Why is it generally better to give money to an organized charity than to a street beggar?" One of the "unacceptable" responses to this last question is that beggars are prone to keep the money for themselves.

A second verbal section of the WISC, entitled "Similarities," is equally interesting. The general format of this section requires the child to tell the examiner how two pairs of objects are "alike." Again, responses are scored from zero to two points.

To begin with, the child is asked how a plum and a peach are alike. If he says they are good for you, he receives no credit. If he points out that they both have pits and skins, he receives one point. Only if he says that they are both fruits does he receive two points. The examiner is allowed at that point to encourage him to say "fruits." Although the questions are phrased in such a way that limitless responses could be correct, the bright child supposedly will understand that only one answer is right. Creative or unusual answers receive no credit or half credit, though they may be technically correct.

A child who points out the fact that beer and wine both produce dizziness receives only one point. The child who says they can both be bought in bottles receives no credit for perceiving similarities. To receive two points, he must classify them as alcoholic beverages. Along the same lines, a piano and a violin cannot merely have strings for two points. That response is only worth one point, as is saying that they both produce music. For full credit, the child must point out the fact that both of these are musical instruments.

Though perceiving similarities is definitely an intellectual achievement, many educators have objected to this and other sections, pointing out the fact that children can be taught, sometimes within days, to classify objects in the manner required by the "similarities" section. Once again, lack of experience can handicap some kids, and it cannot be assumed that this section measures innate ability.

Several sections within the test are questionable in terms of the wording of the questions themselves. In a study under the direction of Dr. Janet Hardy, the Child Growth and Development Center at John Hopkins University examined the Wechsler protocols of poor black children and found that "many children were failing questions because they did not comprehend the syntax of the questions, the pronunciation of words, or the intention of the questions. Their answers were reasonable, but they received no credit."

Jerome Kagan, professor of developmental psychology at Harvard, charges that "if the Wechsler were translated into Spanish, Swahili, and Chinese and given to every ten-year-old in Latin American, East Africa, or China, the majority would obtain IQ scores in the mentally retarded range. It seems intuitively incorrect to conclude that most of the children are mentally retarded, with the exception of middle class Americans and Europeans."

The Psychological Corporation has published a revised version of the WISC. The test remains substantially the same. The "women and children in shipwrecks" question has been removed, and other arrangements have been made in various sections. The author now claims that his test can identify reading difficulties and learning disabilities, as well as retardation and brain damage. The standardization group now includes minority children, though the overall averages between the white middle-class group and the minority groups turned out to be as much as fifteen points. Although this revised but still dubious instrument is now available, the old version will undoubtedly continue to be used for a high percentage of evaluations.

Obviously, opinions vary about IQ tests as instruments for measuring anybody's intellectual capacity, just as opinions vary about the need to do so in the first place. This discussion of two sections of the WISC is to demonstrate that even the most respected IQ tests are far from being the reliable measure of inborn ability they are so often assumed to be. Reading through the instruments that are used to obtain these scores can help one understand a great deal that isn't otherwise obvious.

Eleven-year-old Danny Brenner was one of the white Americans Dr. Kagan was talking about, but he wasn't exactly middle-class. He lived up on Bald Mountain, six miles around a lot of curves from Stockdale School. Like many of the mountain kids, Danny hadn't been down to town too much before he went to school. He had very seldom played with anybody besides his relatives.

Danny was only one of hundreds of children in Copper County alone who had been classified retarded by means of the WISC. The story of his progression from mountain farm to retarded class, however, was typical for that area.

When he wasn't in school, Danny's chief regret was that he couldn't be as ornery as he would have liked to be. If somebody could have harnessed his grin, his family would never had had to worry about an energy shortage. He took responsibility for the family garden, and sometimes his big brothers let him have some of their liquor. He was, Maggie heard, a crack shot with a rifle and would take off into the woods with his dog for days at a time. With his sandy brown longish hair, roughened hands, and perpetual squint, he was a right-there kind of kid.

Danny could usually take care of himself — except when he was in school. Anybody who had watched the alert youngster help his dad take apart the Dodge engine up on the mountain might wonder if the silent, slightly bumbly boy down at Stockdale School was the same kid. "Meaner'n hell when you cross him," reported Mr. Dillard. "Otherwise, he behaves himself, but I can't say if he's learning much."

Danny didn't like school worth a damn. He liked his teacher, but couldn't see any reason why he should be at school. Until he hit first grade, he had never ridden in a bus or read a book. He'd never lined up or sat in one place for hours at a time. At home, he knew the reason behind most everything he did. At school, he was constantly required to do things that didn't make sense to him at all.

Maggie wasn't around when Danny entered first grade, but she knew a lot of first-graders like him, so it was easy to imagine that when he came to school, like most children without middle-class experiences, he didn't know what to make of it. Trying to get used to all those other kids, and being confused about things like lining up, keeping quiet, and lunch tickets is bad enough. But it is very likely that Danny also just didn't understand what his teacher was saying. He may not have been familiar with the words and phrases she used.

She'd say, "Put a circle around the duck." He'd see a picture of a duck, but wouldn't understand how to put a circle around it. She'd ask if anybody had any questions. Though Danny may have had questions, he might not have known what the word "questions" meant. To him she might have been saying something like "Does anybody have any crayons?" And, if he *had* understood, he wouldn't have asked in front of all those strange people.

His teacher talked about things he didn't understand, had never seen. She read the class a story about a tugboat in the city. Danny had never even seen a rowboat in the country, and nobody explained. She asked Danny questions about the tugboat, and Danny just stared at her. She asked another child. So it went.

Danny's older brother Billy had gone the same route. Billy had become an EMR when he was in the third grade, a fact that didn't escape Danny's teacher. She watched the silent little desk occupant turn into a scrambling rascal on the playground, and sighed. "Just like his brother. It's a real shame."

From all reports, Danny fell further and further behind. Some of his classmates in the same boat would misbehave and get whopped. Danny just built a wall around himself. If anybody tried to shake him out of his world, he'd get mean. Cuss and sometimes kick. His teachers started talking about emotional problems.

When Danny was in the third grade, his parents got a mimeographed letter from the superintendent of schools. Their name had been ballpointed in, right after "Dear . . ."

DEAR MR. AND MRS. BRENNER,
    We are making every effort to help each student in this school by placing him in classes that will enable him/her to succeed. In order to

do so, we will need to give individualized tests to determine the level of class needed by your child. Children found to be weak in basic subjects will be placed in a special class of approximately 15 students in order to give the teacher time to help each student.

We would like to have your child tested in order to determine his need so that we may properly place him. By so doing, we can be of greater service to each child who needs special help.

Please sign below giving your permission to test your child —— and assign him to a special class that will help him/her to make normal progress.

The superintendent's signature was mimeographed on the bottom.

When Maggie visited Danny's home, Mr. and Mrs. Brenner told her that when they received the letter, they simply didn't know what to do. They didn't want Danny going into "one of those classes," knowing how bad his brother felt about being there. But the paper said Danny needed some special tests. They figured the people down at the school board office knew a lot more about things like that than they did. If Danny was in trouble, they didn't want to stand in the way of help for him. So they signed the tear-off-and-send-back part, which read, "You may test and assign, if needed, my child as requested above."

"They're just going to give Danny some tests," they told one another. "If they try to put him in one of those classes, we won't let them."

But when they signed the test slip, they also gave permission to put Danny in special education. "Come fall," Mr. Brenner told Maggie, "they came and got the boy right out of his classroom and put him in with Billy. And we never had heard one word about what happened on those tests."

"Paul went down and talked to the superintendent about it." Mrs. Brenner nodded, straightening up in her chair. "Mr. Birdwell told me the boy'd scored low on that test," said her husband. "Said he wouldn't get the kind of help he needed if he stayed in fourth grade. Said the law says Danny needs to be in that class." Mr. Brenner folded his arms and studied Maggie's face to see what her reaction would be.

"So we let him stay there," said Mrs. Brenner. "If the superintendent says that's the best place for him, why he's the man who would know, I suppose . . . We certainly want the best for our boys."

Danny was outside working in the garden. Mrs. Brenner called him from the low porch surrounding the clapboard house. "Danny, show Miss Callahan the garden."

The Brenners' place was only about two acres, tiny for a farm, but its situation was spectacular. A whole series of ridges stretched off into the distance on two sides of the house. The mist lay low in the valleys, literally pouring from one to another as evening came on. Maggie walked down to meet Danny.

The garden was beside the woods. Danny pointed out various plants along the way, as well as the rows of vegetables he'd been putting in.

A bird began to sing. "Sounds like the mockingbird," said Danny. "He's around here every day about this time."

"Where?" Maggie swiveled her head around.

"Well, over there, in the mulberry tree . . ."

Maggie didn't know how to spot a mockingbird or a mulberry tree. Danny gave her a slightly incredulous look before diplomatically pointing to the mulberry tree.

Different kinds of learning Maggie reflected. Strange that we value one more highly than the other. To read, a person has to notice the difference between letters. He also has to see that not only are letters different, but some are the same. He has to see that all b's are alike in certain necessary respects and must give them all the name b before he can use them. Reading involves perception both of differences and similarities. But don't thousands of other activities? Danny could read the woods. Maggie was illiterate in comparison. What that meant to Maggie was that Danny shouldn't have had too much trouble learning to read.

"Look at how the trees are leaning around that one big tree," she wondered out loud.

"They're trying to get them a piece of the sky," Danny said perfunctorily. "Big beech is taking up all the sky. They got to lean out to get theirs." Danny smiled as he pulled a briar out of the path.

They walked back toward the house. Maggie noticed that he swung his arms as he walked. At school, he walked as if his arms were wired to his sides.

Inside the house, Mrs. Brenner had some coffee on the stove. "Miss Callahan, we were wondering how long Danny and Billy are going to have to stay in those classes," she said. "Billy was due to go on to the high school last fall, you know."

Mr. Brenner was sharpening a knife. He looked up. "We put a high value on education," he explained, touching his wife on the arm. "Neither of us graduated from high school, but we want at least that for our boys."

They smiled at each other. Maggie didn't know what to say, and Danny didn't say a word. Maggie had seen him that morning, wandering around his classroom while his teacher listened to one student read. The last time she had seen Billy, he had been watching "Sesame Street" with his entire class while his teacher knitted an afghan.

It would be incorrect to imply or assume that, if we could just develop a better test, problems would be solved. Though the tests definitely have their faults, they are also symptomatic of a whole system, and the best of tests depend a great deal on the way they are administered. Along these lines, Maggie thought back to the process by which Danny, Billy, and other kids had been declared retarded. The actual process of taking the IQ test, it seemed, could just about guarantee a poor performance. Test-taking procedures are often arranged for the convenience of the adults involved, and the Stockdale School procedure was a classic example. When children from that school were to be tested, Mr. Dillard got them out of their classrooms, two at a time, and told them they were going to play games with a handsome man. If several children from one classroom were to be tested, Dillard had been known to come in and write their names on the board, to the dismay of those children.

Two at a time, the children were walked three blocks to the Copper County Mental Health Center, where Buzz was waiting for them. The Mental Health office happened to be next to the jail. "I thought I's gonna be put in jail," one wide-eyed little boy told Maggie.

While Buzz tested one child, the other waited approximately forty-five minutes in an outer room. The WISC manual states that children should be tested in comfortable surroundings. When children from distant schools were to be tested, they were brought to the Mental Health Center by car or else Buzz visited the schools. He complained that, when he visited the schools, he was not always given a suitable testing area. At one school, he was placed on the stage while gym classes were going on. At another, he tested kids in a hallway between two classrooms.

The WISC testing manual also says it is highly important that the examiner be a familiar person with whom the child feels comfortable. Although Buzz was a naturally warm person, he barely had time to test, much less make himself familiar to, these stranger-shy children, By the time they got to his office, they were often very nervous, frightened, or apprehensive.

"All I could think of was getting out of there," Danny remembered.

"I even had to miss recess," another child recalled wistfully.

The WISC manual states further that the child should not be pulled out of favorite activities, and that, if nervousness, anxiety, or other feelings prevent her from relating to the experience without noticeable strain, "it is best to discontinue the test and arrange for another appointment." But the psychologist or other testing agent — especially one who works on contract or covers a great many schools — isn't around every day in most school systems. So the child has one shot, and if that shot is missed, that's it. Many of the psychological reports in Copper County reflected such a state of affairs.

Once again, this situation generalizes to many parts of the country. "We take a Stanford-Binet test," writes Oliver Hurley of the University of Georgia, "which has been standardized on basically white middle-class youngsters with a certain style of language and we administer this test to youngsters who differ. They differ in a number of respects. One respect that some of them differ in is their language. There's been a lot of work recently on something called black English. They also differ in another respect, and that is that many of the youngsters are not used to interacting with adults in the way that's demanded on the Stanford-Binet — that is, to say everything you can think of, everything about a subject (if you want to get full credit). So, when these youngsters come into a testing situation, and the tester asks 'What is a bicycle. Tell me all about a bicycle,' this is kind of a crazy question to begin with, from the child's point of view. His response is: 'let me out of here!' His best way to get out of here is to give the person a short answer, as short as possible. So he says, 'Oh, it's something you ride.' O.K., something as short as possible, and he does this continuously.

"There is some research that was carried on some years ago with youngsters who had been labeled mentally retarded, or at least failed the test — 'failed' in quotes. After analysis of the children's responses from a different point of view, the researcher found that these youngsters, once they realized that they were supposed to lay all of their wares out on the table for someone to see, that this is what we want, they then laid them out on the table for the psychologist to see, and their scoring on this instrument, therefore, increased dramatically. In addition, the social setting was modified in one instance that I can remember by the introduction of a second child, and the two children interacted, and the quality of language from those two youngsters increased dramatically.

"There has been research like this. I don't know what a 75 on a Stanford-Binet means when the child can go out and cope with his environment in the middle of Harlem."

In the past, once a child was in an EMR class he would probably wait a long time before an opportunity came to be transferred out. State law for Copper County at that time required that each child be retested after he had been in special education for three years. No program evaluation, but retesting. Danny was a three-year veteran, so he had just been retested when Maggie spoke with him about his session.

A lot of damage can be done within three years, Maggie thought. A child can be badly damaged within one year. He loses self-confidence, maybe receives haphazard instruction, and falls far behind. At the end of those three years, he is retested with the same test, found to be below average, and returned to special ed.

It was a very vicious circle, a conviction without appeal, a kangaroo court, a self-fulfilling prophecy. All in the name of "helping" the children. Maggie asked the regional special education supervisor if any of the seven counties he worked with reevaluated children more often than every three years. "There's only one I know of," he said. "Of course, some counties don't hardly have the money for the initial testing, so it's not likely they'll be retesting every three years."

During a phone conversation with Sam Watkins, Maggie asked what he thought the extent of misclassification in the state was. Sam said he'd always considered misclassification a strange word, for two reasons. "First of all," he told her, "it implies that the problem would be solved if the kid were just taken out of one category and put in another one. But, second, how do you get people to agree on who's misclassified? Now, you've got some kids down there you say are misclassified. Take any one of them, and I'll bet you I could find somebody who'd tell me the kid is right where he belongs, somebody who agrees that he shouldn't be there, and somebody who insists you can only tell by the test scores. It gets worse when you get into more subjective areas like emotional disturbance." He paused and added with a bemused chuckle that somebody had told him that some congressmen were talking about doing a survey which would show exactly how many children in the country were misclassified. "Bet you they come with five pages of figures," he said before hanging up.

13. Interlude

"On June 17th, 1774, the commissioners from Maryland and Virginia negotiated a treaty with the Indians of the Six Nations at Lancaster, Pennsylvania. The Indians were invited to send boys to William and Mary College. The next day, they declined the offer as follows.

" 'We know that you highly esteem the kind of learning taught in those Colleges, and that the Maintenance of our young Men, while with you, would be very expensive to you. We are convinced, that you mean to do us Good by your Proposal; and we thank you heartily. But you, who are wise, must know that different Nations have different Conceptions of things and you will therefore not take it amiss, if our ideas of this kind of Education happen not to be the same as yours. We have had some Experience of it. Several of our young People were formerly brought up at the Colleges of the Northern Provinces; they were instructed in all your Sciences; but, when they came back to us, they were bad Runners, ignorant of every means of living in the woods ... neither fit for Hunters, Warriors, nor Counselors, they were totally good for nothing.

" 'We are, however, not the less oblig'd by your kind Offer, tho' we decline accepting it; and to show our grateful Sense of it, if the Gentlemen of Virginia will send us a Dozen of their Sons, we will take Care of their Education, instruct them in all we know, and make Men of them.' "

— Reprinted from *Touch the Earth: a Self-Portrait of Indian Existence*, compiled by T. C. McLuhan, 1941

IN COPPER COUNTY, March brought its usual battle between winter and spring. The weather kept shifting. Little plants would begin to grow, then snow would cover them up. It wasn't unusual to see snow on the mountaintops when it was too warm to wear a coat down in the town. Clouds on different levels sailed in opposite directions. Children were restless, noses were running, and adults were crabby. It rained hard day after day, and the ridgelines stood out in sharp contrast with the sky. Black and white, shades of brown. Everything and everybody seemed to be pulling inward.

On the first sunny day in March, everybody who could get outside got out there. Across the street from the school, the fourth grade teacher had her kids out in the field, checking their three-foot by three-foot plots of "territory," recording observations about the bugs, vegetation, and so on. "We do it every three weeks," the teachers said. "The kids love it, and it keeps the science book from being so dry, you know. Teaches them to observe in an organized manner, too."

During recess that day, a fight blossomed on the basketball court between Danny Brenner and Pickle. Mr. Dillard had said that Danny Brenner was meaner'n hell if somebody crossed him. Naturally, Pickle crossed him. He tried to assert property rights over the basketball, and Danny whopped him. Mr. Dillard and Anita Maslow finally had to drag the two of them apart, still kicking up gravel and spitting. Danny had a big cut over his eye, and Pickle ended up with a broken tooth. Pickle kept yelling about how he was going to knock out so many of Danny's teeth that "that dumb farm boy'll be eating mashed potatoes and oatmeal for the rest of his life!" Danny wasn't announcing his plans for Pickle.

It was a bad day all around for Danny. Mr. Fairfield, the sixth grade teacher, had bus duty that afternoon. Pickle had gone home early, but Danny had to wait for the bus with Mr. Fairfield. Mr. Fairfield was a teacher who didn't go for any "nonsense" out of kids. His disciplinary policy for children was very simple: "You've got to paddle a child to make sure he's learned his lesson. If he doesn't cry, he hasn't learned his lesson." However, he couldn't stand to see children cry. So he would continue to paddle them until they "straightened up and stopped crying."

Oddly enough, Mr. Fairfield was far from being an ill-tempered person. Much as his policy appalled many of the other teachers, they couldn't dislike him, since he was as generous and thoughtful with adults as he was impatient with and sometimes cruel with children. He obviously felt no inconsistency in his behavior toward people of differing ages. He just seemed to regard children as a separate species and behaved accordingly. When he put his disciplinary policy into effect, he firmly believed that he was acting in the child's best interest.

Mr. Fairfield ended up acting in Danny's "best interest" before the buses arrived. Somebody pulled the fire alarm. Nobody knew who had done it, but somebody had to be punished on the spot. Danny's scuffle with Pickle was evidently fresh in Mr. Fairfield's mind. He collared him, and, without taking an adult witness with him, as school law requires, pushed Danny into a nearby classroom. Within seconds, everybody outside the classroom heard loud whacking noises, interspersed with Danny's yells and resentful denials.

Danny's father paid a visit to Mr. Birdwell the next day, fully expecting the superintendent to administer justice. This put Mr. Birdwell on the spot, since Mr. Fairfield was held in high regard by most of the school board and the superintendent was involved in a tricky struggle with the board over further funding for his vocational school. His position could be significantly weakened by a wrong move in Danny's behalf against a well-liked local citizen.

Maggie went to the school board meeting to watch the inevitable. The Brenners sat in the front row, Mr. Brenner looking ill at ease in his light wool jacket. Mr. Birdwell opened the meeting with a prayer for guidance for "those charged with the responsibility for the boys and girls of Copper County, that we may make decisions which will result in their health, happiness and best interests." The Brenners sat through rat control for Little Creek School, new floodlights for the football field, and other matters. They had been placed last on the agenda. When their turn came, the board called an executive session, closed to the public.

The next morning, Mr. Birdwell told Maggie that during the session he had "advised" the Brenners of his own personal investigation and that their boy had behaved very badly. "We always want to be fair and explain all aspects of the case," he said to Maggie. He avoided looking up from his papers. Maggie couldn't believe he really felt that way. The Brenners made no further noises, so they had evidently been advised rather vigorously.

"Well, you know," Anita said when Maggie relayed Birdwell's comments, "Mark Twain used to call American education 'the organized fight of the grown-ups against youth.' "

Anita was helping two neighborhood fifth graders with their disorganized struggle with long division. Jenny was there too, sitting in the corner of the living room, propped up against a pile of cushions, staring at a book and biting her fingernails. When Maggie went into the kitchen, Jenny got up and followed her.

"How's life?" Maggie asked her. Jenny scuffed at the doorsill with her tennis shoes and wound her hair around her finger. She was wearing lipstick. Finally she said, "How come I don't have homework like the other kids do?"

"You *want* homework?" Maggie teased her.

"Well, what I mean is," she stammered, blushing and grinning, "what I mean is — how come we don't learn dividing like the fifth grade does?"

"Can you do long division?"

"I dunno. I never tried it. I guess I can't." They sat down at the kitchen table with a box of toothpicks and a bag of navy beans, and started with easy division.

Jenny already had a smattering of this process, and, after twenty minutes or so, was able to go on alone, teaching herself while Maggie cooked dinner. They had divided several sheets of paper into squares. Maggie wrote problems on the first sheet, and Jenny illustrated them with toothpicks — starting with a complete pile, and then dividing it into the indicated number of sections.

It wasn't the most entertaining activity in the world, but since Jenny wanted to learn, it suited her. After the first sheet, she made up and worked out her own problems. She started calculating the answers before moving the toothpicks. Maggie was making spaghetti. Every time Jenny missed a problem, she punished herself by eating a piece of onion, which she hated. She was reeking by the time she went home.

Jenny kept coming back to the house the following week for help with division. She made good progress and made up word problems. "There are five hundred and sixty-two leaves on the tree behind my house," she wrote. "I know there are lots more, but the wind makes them move. I can't never count them. The tree has six branches. How many leaves on each branch? That's not right. The bottom branch has more leaves on it than the top one. How can you do dividing on a tree?"

Anita and Maggie made a big deal over Jenny's word problems. Pickle, however, turned up his nose at them. "I could do those kinds of numbers a long time ago," he said, fingering his new snaggle tooth.

"Well, you can't write them down in words," retorted Jenny, safe behind Anita. Flush with her new success, she demanded to know who was smarter, her or Pickle. "He can do numbers, but I can read."

Pickle didn't like the drift of the conversation. He left, after dropping the ultimate put-down. "You don't see *me* down at Gateway, do ya?" It worked. Jenny became very quiet.

A few days later, Maggie took Jenny and Pickle with her up Bald Mountain. They had lived in Davidson almost all their lives, but had never been up the mountain. Maggie had to stop the car at every overlook so they could stare down at the valley and town from a new perspective.

"Look, Jenny! There's the supermarket!"

"Hey! The Dairy Queen!"

"The cars look like bugs!"

"Hey, Pickle! The quarry!"

"Miss Callahan, how come we can't see our house?"

"Your house is too close to the mountain."

A trace of green was beginning to line the hillsides, defying predictions of snow. The ridgelines were softening as the new vegetation appeared. The wind smelled of wet, alive earth, and tiny new plants surrounded them. Burrs clung to the legs of their jeans. At one overlook, Maggie showed Pickle and Jenny some early baby fiddlehead ferns. "If you cook them, they taste great." Pickle ate one raw, while Jenny stared at him, half-envious, half-repulsed.

"Looks like a curled-up worm," she said. "Yuck!"

A ground hog ran across the road. "A rat!" squealed Jenny. They all laughed out loud. Three miles on up, one of Pickle's classmates was riding a pony beside the road. He waved as they went by. Pickle stared at the pony out the back window until he lost sight of it.

The road climbed over 1000 feet in ten miles. "We're on top of the world," Jenny whispered solemnly when it leveled off. The mountain ridges stretched as far as they could see on both sides — purple, blue, gray, traces of green. "The trees look like they're dancing," she added. They did. The branches of the trees in a nearby field swayed in the wind like long, graceful arms.

"Then shall all the trees of the wood rejoice . . ." Maggie said softly.

"Hey, that's from the radio!" said Pickle.

They stopped to see Catherine and Ron Peterson, some friends of Maggie's who lived near the top of the mountain. Pickle got into the pen with their pig and followed it around, scratching its back with a stick. "Sure is a hard pig!" he called. "I thought pigs were fat and punchy!" Jenny was mesmerized by the chickens.

Catherine took them on a little tour of the place, laughing while Pickle chased bugs and inspected the beehives. He was all for disassembling the hives to check out their contents. Jenny was relieved to hear Catherine say that wasn't such a great idea. "It's winter still, Pickle. The bees are all inside and we shouldn't bother them."

They looked in a shed that served as Catherine's silk-screen workshop, and she gave each of the children a poster she had made. Jenny read the words on hers out loud. " 'May the longtime sun shine upon you, all love surround you, and the pure light within you guide your way home.' Do I have a light inside me?" she asked.

"You sure do. You can see it in your face." Jenny made such a weird face that they all laughed. "Not like a lightbulb, lady," Maggie said, mussing her hair. "It's more of a feeling . . ." Jenny nodded, enchanted by the idea.

Pickle wasn't looking at his poster. "Want to read yours, Pickle?" Catherine asked.

"I'll do it later," said Pickle nonchalantly. "Sure is pretty, Ma'am."

They had some hot cider and watched the afternoon shadows creep over the mountains. Then they headed on down. "Wish I lived up here," Jenny said softly. Pickle had two questions. He wanted to know if Danny Brenner lived anywhere around there, and he wanted to know what it said on his poster. Of course, Pickle didn't want to ask Maggie to read his poster. He wanted to read it himself. You usually had to catch Pickle when nobody else was around before he would talk about reading at all. It was a matter of keeping up face. He didn't want many people to know how much it mattered. He didn't want to let *himself* know how much it mattered.

*

Anita had asked Maggie weeks before to give her some ideas for working with Pickle. They both knew that she couldn't just start probing at him as if he were a piece of machinery on the blink. It was very important that he have confidence in her first, that she not threaten him.

"Not threatening" meant showing the right attitude toward his problem when the opportunity arose. He had to see that she recognized the importance of the problem, but at the same time, he had to understand that she didn't see his inability to read as a reflection on his intelligence. That was a delicate, but critical distinction. Many people had already treated Pickle as if he were deficient. He had already asked himself countless times what his reading difficulties really meant. And deep down, he probably wasn't sure. If he sensed that a teacher doubted his capabilities, his chances of working constructively with that person would be pretty slim.

Pickle and Maggie first talked about it one day after school. She was knitting, and he was hanging out. He asked her about her job. She started talking about special ed in general, and, pretty soon, worked her way around to the fact that there were a lot of very bright kids who couldn't read, who had trouble learning in the conventional way. "And lots of times, these kids feel really bad about it when they don't need to. It's too bad that they have that trouble, but it doesn't mean they aren't as good as anybody else. It just means that they learn in a different way than most people do." Maggie was concentrating on her knitting. She could see out of the corner of her eye that Pickle was guardedly interested.

"Mom says we can't afford to have my tooth fixed," he said suddenly. "But it doesn't hurt much." He started tossing a little rubber ball in the air. "I can't read too good," he added after a minute or so.

Maggie kept looking at her knitting, and tried not to change her tone. "Yeah, you probably know exactly what I'm talking about, come to think of it."

Pickle nodded.

"I mean, a lot of kids wouldn't understand why it's hard to have to ask other people to read things for you . . ."

Delicate. Pickle stopped tossing the ball. "Well, it burns me up," he said hotly. There was a lot of energy behind that statement. "It burns me up, because people look at you like you're dumb or something." His face flushed.

"And you *know* you're not . . ." she continued.

"Yeah!" He said it a little too loud for his own taste. "Yeah," he repeated, in a softer tone.

She put the knitting down. "Come to think of it, Pickle, you *are* probably a good example of what I'm talking about. I think you see things in a special way. And, as smart as you are, I'm sure we could find a way to teach you to read so you wouldn't have to ask anybody anymore. We'd just have to do a little detective work."

"Detective work?"

She was watching him closely to make sure she wasn't going too fast or seeming to be too interested. "Uh-huh," she said, untying another skein of wool. "You know. Check around to find out how you see things, how you hear things, stuff like that. It's real interesting. Sort of like gathering clues, and then you go from there." Pickle was starting to fidget. It was time to back off.

"Hey, would you please bring me the scissors off the table in the dining room?" Maggie asked him. Visibly relieved, he jumped up and bolted out of the room. The chance to leave temporarily defused the situation for him. Reading was obviously a very emotional issue. The thought of seriously trying to do something about it probably evoked a strong approach-avoidance reaction. On one hand, he wanted to try. On the other, if he tried and failed, it would be worse than before.

When he came back with the scissors, he wanted to talk about the beehives he had seen on the mountains, but Maggie knew that he would think about the conversation and they would talk about it again soon. So they wound balls of yarn and talked about beehives for the rest of the afternoon.

When Anita came home, Maggie told her about the episode. "He really needs special ed," Anita said hesitantly. "It's ironic."

"It's going to take a while to get him to the point where he's willing to try, you know."

"Can you imagine if he got sent to Gateway?"

"I try not to."

14. Office Lack of Politics

"One of the things we've failed to do is to give the local superintendent and the chief state school officers good publicity on the good things which have happened with handicapped youngsters in their state. If we would do more of that while we point out areas which need improvement, it would tend to reinforce their positive behavior. But what they've mostly been hearing from all sides is criticism and pressures about what *hasn't* been done, what programs aren't there. Now this tends to make a person resentful and somewhat resistant. A good combination of both positive encouragement and criticism might get us a lot further."

— Jack Jones, chief, Aid-to-States Branch,
Bureau of Education for the Handicapped, June 1975

BY MID-MARCH, Blankenship and Coleman aside, many of the special ed teachers were feeling low. A motivated teacher can construct great teaching materials and do beautiful things with very little money, but all the great ideas and training in the world aren't worth birdseed when discouragement sets in. Many of the special ed teachers were feeling their isolation and second-rate status as much as the children were. One teacher even went so far as to express a fear of "getting too good at this job. I want to teach in my field," she told Maggie. "It's O.K. to be the retarded teacher now, but I want to get out of here as much as the kids do, frankly. If Birdwell gets the idea that I like this, he'll keep me down here."

People were just plain discouraged. Maggie spent some time with Miss Adkins and Mrs. Legg to get instruction organized on several different levels. They started talking about expanding beyond the textbooks to paperback books and lyric sheets for country music. Word-construction materials, creative writing projects, and motor exercises for kids like Karen were discussed.

"I'm not trained to do that stuff, and I don't have time to make materials," said Mrs. Legg flatly. "And it's for sure that I can't fork out any money for paperback books."

"You shouldn't. I'll bet we can get some money from the office to buy some."

"Well, I'm not making any plans until I see them right here." She pointed to her desk top, then folded her arms.

Reports of Maggie's promises of funds from the office somehow always got back to Warner, and reports of Warner's displeasure somehow always found their way back to Maggie, usually through Abigail, the reading supervisor.

Maggie called a teachers' meeting at the beginning of March to assess the classroom needs. Abigail told her that "Warner hit the ceiling" when he heard about it. "You shouldn't have done that," Abigail said, shaking her finger at Maggie. "There are at least three reasons not to call meetings around here. One, the teachers don't like them if they aren't on school time. Second, you get much more honest results talking to people individually. They clam up as a group. And third, Warner feels like you're getting onto his turf. Matter of fact, he wants to see you right now."

Maggie's temper was about as long as a mouse hair. She dropped her pencil and marched down to Warner's office. Warner ignored her for several minutes. He was adding up figures on the side of some important-looking papers. Without raising his head, he asked why she had called a teachers' meeting without consulting him. "The special education program is *my* responsibility!" he said briskly. "It is financed almost *entirely* by Title I, so it is *my* responsibility."

Maggie stared at him, open-mouthed. "Warner, what did you want to talk about at the meeting?" she asked finally.

"The Teachers' Burial Fund." he replied testily. Maggie continued to stare at him. After an uneasy pause, he demanded to know why she was still traipsing about the county, leading teachers to believe that there was money available to buy things for special education. As he talked, he gripped the edge of his desk. His elbows were up in the air, as if he might pounce any second.

"Because there *is* money available!" she replied, getting a little red in the face. "You told me about it yourself!" Both of them quickly became red-faced. They began biting off their words. The wind blew around the side of the building, rattling the windows.

"That money is *my* responsibility!" said Warner, jabbing his finger at her. "*I* am the Title I director, and *I* decide how that money is to be spent." He stared at Maggie to let this point sink in.

"There are *other* children in this county besides the special education children," he said finally. "I have *other* things I have to take care of, and special education has *already* had *more* than its share of attention." His mouth tightened into a little ball.

He added that if Maggie really wanted to know, he felt that he had to come to the meeting to make sure she didn't promise the teachers a pie in the sky. "You're wasting everybody's *time!*" he snapped. "It won't do you a *bit* of good to make out lists when there's no *money!*"

Maggie noticed that Abigail had drifted down to the end of the hall and was extending her ear. Impulsively, she asked Warner if the math order had gone out yet. "It has *not!*" Warner huffed furiously. "It wasn't made up with my *permission* and I doubt that it *will* go out!" He began rearranging papers, slapping them here and there.

"I've spent all I'm *going* to spend on special education!" he muttered. Looking directly at Maggie, he concluded, "I don't have *any* more money available for that program, and the sooner *you* understand that, the easier it will be for *all* of us!" He stopped shuffling papers, planted his elbows on top of them, and glared up at Maggie. The windows shook again.

"I've spent all I'm going to . . ." Classrooms and children's faces flashed through Maggie's mind, along with visions of Warner, in the Depression, working for thirty cents a day. He had no way of understanding Maggie's point of view, nor she his. She spun around and marched down the hall to Mr. Birdwell's door. A look of alarm crossed his face when he glanced up from his writing and saw her face. "Come right in, young lady," he said, half rising from his seat.

Questions and descriptions piled out one after another. Individual children, classroom conditions, demoralized teachers, and improper placement. Loss of motivation, humiliation, negative attitudes, and insane evaluation procedures. "There's so much that needs to be done, is crying to be done." Maggie fumed. "And now I'm told that there's not a cent coming for these children! After having been told that a great deal of money was available."

Mr. Birdwell was looking very flustered. He told Maggie he

would certainly attend to these matters and that he hadn't realized things were so bad with those children. "And I'm very glad you're here to keep me informed. That's why we hired you. These children need somebody to be concerned about their welfare . . ." Mr. Birdwell deftly wrapped her in a verbal fire extinguisher. He kept talking until she was doused. "Mr. Jenkins is a hardworking, dedicated man. I'm sure we can all work on this together. In all my years as a superintendent, I've always tried to promote cooperation among my staff members . . ."

He promised that the three of them — Warner Jenkins, himself, and Maggie — would get together first thing in the morning "to get this all straightened out. We have to take care of this right away," he cautioned. "I encourage healthy disagreement among my staff members, but brush fires have a way of becoming forest fires, and that doesn't help anybody."

He hooked his thumb in his belt, smiled his odd, gentle smile and assured Maggie that he would do his best to make sure that every child got what she needed. "That certainly has always been my aim throughout my career in education . . ."

During breakfast the next morning, Maggie made a list of three practical questions: How much money is available for the improvement of the special ed program? How have this year's special ed funds been spent to date? Can we agree on a cut-and-dried purchasing procedure that will eliminate personalities from paperwork?

Anita looked at the questions. "Those questions aren't practical — they're threatening," she said.

"But I don't see why they should be."

"It's just that everyone has his or her own way of doing things, and you're too blunt about the whole thing." Anita shrugged. "But what do I know?"

The previous afternoon's gray skies had turned into sleet, freezing all those new little plants on the hillside. The streets were icy. A gang of Squirrel Hollow kids were walking on the bridge, hugging themselves inside their sweaters, headed for Gateway in the light freezing rain. Maggie made a U-turn. They all piled in. How to make them more real to Warner than those underlined magazines?

By the time she arrived at the office, Warner was already closeted with Mr. Birdwell. "The superintendent said to tell you that he'd call you when he's ready to start the meeting," said the secretary.

A young guy with glasses and a paisley tie kept trying to shake hands with Maggie. "Jack's my name," he said. Jack was representing the regional office of a small educational materials firm. Maggie went to her desk and tried to follow what Jack was saying and read the brochures he spread out before her. Finally Mr. Birdwell opened the door and beckoned. Maggie gathered her wits and list of questions. Warner smiled as she entered the office, and the superintendent said, "Sit down, young lady." The smell of a fait accompli filled the office.

The message of the next few minutes: There are no more federal funds available for special education, and we'll just have to live with it. "Mr. Jenkins has advised me that our funds have been exhausted in that area," intoned Birdwell. He handed Maggie a piece of paper that read "$1000 equipment/$600 materials."

"This paper represents the state funds which are available," he informed her. "That's the way we stand at this time." He folded his hands and glanced at Warner. "Now that we all understand each other, I'm sure we'll be able to work together." He scraped back his chair and said something about getting ready for next month's board meeting. "It'll be a tough one!"

Warner gathered his papers. Maggie hadn't been in the office five minutes. She felt like every pint of blood in her body was trying to crowd into her head. An alarmed expression crossed Birdwell's face. "Do you have any questions?" he asked mildly. She looked at her list for guidance, but all the questions had been invalidated. So her temper took over.

Mr. Blankenship and his cafeteria gang passed through her mind with Jenny, Pickle, and all the others. She banged her notebook on the desk and blurted loudly, "Those classrooms are, for the most part, an outrage and a disgrace! I'm not interested in blaming anyone, but we've got to make things better for those kids and teachers! And that takes money, for beginners!"

Mr. Birdwell jumped. Warner edged his chair away from Maggie. If a piece of furniture had sprung snapping and snarling into action, both might have given it the same incredulous look.

"Somebody has to take responsibility for those children!" BANG BANG "Well over half of those classrooms are substandard, even by county standards!" She banged the desk again, totally beyond good sense or diplomacy. Both Warner and Mr. Birdwell remained speechless, mouths open.

The heating pipes banged loudly, backing her up.

"Most of the teachers are buying basic supplies from their own salaries because they were told last fall that there was no money for special ed!" BANG BANG "It's very hard, knowing that, to see how special ed has had more than its share! The children have been taken away from their normal surroundings and now most of them aren't even getting the basics!" Mr. Birdwell dropped his pencil. Warner's mouth tightened into a hard line.

"And that's not even *touching* the fact that the whole program ought to be restructured, and every kid in those classes should be reevaluated!"

She paused for breath. "And why was the math order approved?" she continued. "I spent almost two days getting it together. If there were no funds, why was I asked to do that?"

"Mr. Jenkins has made me aware of our federal funds situation this morning," responded Mr. Birdwell. "I regret that other commitments have prevented me from examining the county expenditures of federal funds, but these things happen, young lady. We have left that department entirely in the hands of Mr. Jenkins, and he is, of course, the most authoritative source of that information."

Mr. Jenkins huffed audibly. Maggie whirled around to him. "Warner, you told me yourself that sixty thousand dollars was available!"

"None of that money is for special education!" Warner snapped. "I have other children to think about! Special education can't have everything!"

"The law requires at least equal conditions for special ed children!" Maggie snapped back, imagining herself flanked with legions of lawyers. Warner stared back menacingly, as if he would have liked to spank her, at the very least.

Mr. Birdwell, snapping abruptly out of his bewildered detachment, told her that "special education has received, to date, this year, at least seventy-five thousand dollars' worth of attention, and that's more than equal." That comment was mystifying, until Maggie remembered that that was the amount of the perplexing Title I grant.

Warner cut into her thoughts to insist one more time that piles of materials were lurking in closets and desk drawers, if she would only take the time to find them. Warner had regained his balance, slipped back into his standard approach. A heavy fog seemed to have enveloped the conversation, obscuring specific issues. Birdwell took out his pocket watch.

"Warner, may I see the back order forms to get an idea of what materials you're talking about?" she asked.

"No." Warner sniffed, folding his arms. "Special education orders are mixed in with all the other Title I orders. There would be no way for me to separate the two; and you'd be wasting my time and yours." He glanced sideways at Birdwell, who immediately scraped his chair back and said that he had other things to do. He assured Maggie that the county would do its best to give each child what he needed. Back on familiar territory. Unruly outbursts weathered, strangely divorced from the scene of a few minutes before, unreality restored.

Looking at Maggie over his eyeglasses, Mr. Birdwell admonished gently that "you're going to have to start thinking about what is possible if we're all going to work together." Maggie had a lump in her throat and couldn't talk. Mr. Birdwell patted her kindly on the shoulder and said, "I am glad to see that you take your job seriously, Miss Callahan, but we have to deal with realities."

Maggie saw Warner's telephone extension light up the minute she hit her office. Oh boy, she thought. I really blew it. But I'm right in principle, she thought, pulling on her coat. She had decided to take her lunch hour at nine forty-five. But that rightness is probably going to hurt the children more than it helps them. So I must be wrong. At that point, it was hard to understand how she could be so wrong if she was right. So she went home and cried, and ate leftover rice pudding. Brown Eye was very sympathetic.

After less than a half-hour of chewing and calling herself names, she tried to make sense of the morning's events. It turned out to be impossible. She became red-faced angry again and stamped around the kitchen, banging pans and running into furniture.

Around ten-thirty she gave the dog some water and left the house. Mrs. Krebbs was behind her screen door, watching the street. Maggie waved, and she waved back. Jesse, in his gray hood, was picking up trash and broken bottles from under the bridge, dropping them in a burlap bag.

The next few hours were spent driving from school to school, apologetically peering into every cranny. She was at a loss as to what to do next but wanted to eliminate the possibility that some vast deposit of materials had indeed been overlooked before making another move.

"What're you up to?" inquired Mr. McCreedy several hours later. When Maggie explained why she needed to look in his closet, he suggested that Warner might be thinking of the encyclopedias, maps, and globes stored in the music room up at Stockdale. "They were ordered for Title I," he recalled, "only they were too complicated for most people to use, so they ended up catching dust."

The Stockdale music room, sure enough, was piled full of super complicated map/globe kits. And lots of dust. As Maggie stood puzzling over this find, Mr. Higby, the fifth grade teacher, a funny, easygoing fellow, strolled in.

"Oho," he drawled, "you've uncovered one of our buried treasures." He spread his arms expansively. "What you see here before you represents, I hear tell, almost everything that company has to offer." He scratched his head and looked momentarily sour. "I'd like to use some of it with the fifth grade, to tell the truth, but I'm told that it would be illegal to use it with my entire class, since they don't all qualify for ESEA assistance. Apparently, I'd be breaking some sort of federal law.

"These came in the same year we got all those binoculars," he volunteered, offering Maggie half a brownie. "No, I'm not putting you on." He was enjoying Maggie's reaction. "There were several dozen pairs of binoculars." He made his hands into binoculars and scanned the room. "That's so our little slow learners will be able to see the board better. Or if you point them at a book, it enlarges the print and limits the field, you know. Helps with perceptual disorders."

He closed his eyes dramatically for a few seconds, then brightened. "And, of course, no tour would be complete without a visit to the ESEA barometer." He cocked his head. "You *have* seen the ESEA barometer?"

Higby ceremoniously led her down the hall, stopping outside Mr. Dillard's office, where a large, impressive walnut and copper barometer decorated the wall. "This, folks," said Higby in a hushed tone, "is the ESEA Title I German barometer, yes, brought to us by the same folks who brought us the Volkswagen."

Rumble of feet, banging of doors, voices everywhere. "Damn, recess over already?" moaned Higby. "And I haven't eaten my pickle yet."

The herd swarmed by and around them. One of Higby's kids pinched Maggie on the arm and asked her what's purple and lies at the bottom of the ocean. "Moby Grape!" hollered another kid before she could answer.

Left alone as the tide subsided, Maggie felt like Alice in Wonderland. No money for special education?

Abigail was coming in as Maggie went out. "Whew!" She grinned and shook her head as if she had touched something very hot. "I hear you and Warner and the super really got into it this morning." Looking up, Maggie noticed that the hills were white on top. The end of March and snow coming. "They told me about it at the office," Abigail continued. "It sure did tickle me when I heard it, but you're pushing awful hard, lady. Can't say I'd like to be in your shoes."

Maggie looked down at her shoes. They looked pretty shabby. A couple of the special ed kids walked by, last off the playground, shooting her peace signs. Abigail disappeared into the school.

15. Log in Somebody's Eye

"Why do you see the speck that is in your brother's eye, but do not notice the log that is in your own eye?"

— Matthew 7:3

"Psychologists, psychiatrists, social workers, reading specialists, and resource roving teachers are only some of the personnel available to the classroom teacher. One of the major complaints teachers articulate about these specialists is that they define help in terms of what the teacher can do with the child. As one teacher put it, "I do not need someone to tell me what more I should or could do with the child. When I ask for help I am asking someone else *TO DO SOMETHING*." Another teacher put it this way: "The next time someone tells *me* to give Johnny more individual attention, I'll either scream or invite him out." What the teachers have difficulty understanding or accepting is that the number of specialists is pitifully small (both on an absolute and relative basis) to provide the kind of help she desires. In fact, another frequent complaint of the teacher is that special services are available "too infrequently, too late, with too little." If the relationship between the classroom teacher and the special services personnel is not exactly one characteristic of a mutual admiration society, it is in large part due to two factors: both the classroom teacher and the specialist are keenly aware that they cannot give the necessary degree and quality of help, and perhaps more fateful for their relationship, *each tends to be unaware that they are both in the same boat.* It is not unusual, therefore, for the specialist to view many teachers as uncooperative or resistant, and for the teacher to view the specialist as unhelpful and unsympathetic. The loneliness of teachers (and others) has many sources, but heading the list are the feelings that their plight is neither understood nor appreciated and that they have only themselves to fall back on."

— Seymour Sarason, *The Culture of the School and the Problem of Change*, 1971

MAGGIE WENT UP the hill to the Instructional Materials Center, feeling more depressed and confused then she'd felt in a long time. It would have been no surprise to see the Cheshire cat leap out from behind a tree.

The Instructional Materials Center — the IMC — consisted of one room, where many movies, filmstrips, and a few books and kits purchased with Title I funds had been catalogued and shelved, available for check-out to any county teacher. The center was run by an amiable middle-aged fellow named Harry. Harry and his wife had recently bought a small restaurant in a nearby town where they lived. While Maggie poked among the filmstrips and how-to books, he told her how his wife was trying to get together a new menu to exclude harmful food additives.

Maggie collected a pile of items and lugged them up to the check-out desk. Harry put down his Pepsi bottle and whistled. "Boy, now, this is what I call getting on it." He fanned himself. "You make me tired just to look at you. And here I've been working my tail off today." He shot her a big smile.

"Mr. Birdwell called me up all in a twit this morning," he continued, "and told me to get my body right down to Gateway and find out what kind of books those teachers need. Seems like somebody gave him the idea that those teachers don't have what they need. Well, I'm a good boy, so I hurried on down. Just like I hurried on down last fall when those teachers first got in there. It isn't as if nobody's asked them what they want, it's just that they've never gotten around to ordering anything. Bet they didn't tell *you* that." He sighed, took a last swig of Pepsi, cocked his head, and looked at the ceiling. "So I've fulfilled my part of the pecking order."

He swiveled around and sat up straight, looking at her with some curiosity. "Seems Mr. Birdwell had a conversation with you this morning. . ."

"And I'll bet you know all about it. Instant replay."

"Well, I *did* talk to Warner," he admitted, slowly twirling a pencil. "But don't let's talk about that right now. You want a cigarette? I've finished work and feel like running off at the mouth. Why don't you sit down and stop running in circles for a while?" He swiveled back around and got his legs all propped up on the desk. "I like to act like a big shot, even if I am just a lackey."

That friendly tone of voice was just what Maggie needed. It didn't take her ten seconds to drop everything and settle right in. Harry rambled on about his past history and wanted to know about hers. She relaxed and put the morning's events out of her mind. They speculated about the advantages or rambling around to see the world versus settling down in one place. He reminisced about former and fantasy journeys and said that a lot of people seemed to think he was a free spirit beneath his librarian exterior. He told her about the squirrels jumping from branch to branch outside his kitchen window. And he was very interested in hearing her ideas about education.

The building became quiet as other people closed up shop and went on home. The afternoon light was fading. They talked on, about alternatives to self-contained classrooms. Finally, Harry paused for a while "to rest my mouth," then resumed.

"You know, I'm curious about you. You seem like a nice person." He stopped, then added, "That's what I can't understand."

"Huh?" she said.

"Why, I just can't imagine how you could be as insensitive as some people say you are," he drawled. His face was choir-boy innocent.

Maggie started to say that Warner was a little biased, when Harry continued. "You know, the teachers that come through here stop to talk with me and all . . ." He scratched his head. "Nope, I just don't believe it."

Teachers. Teachers? Maggie's heart started pounding. She hadn't expected anything like that.

"What I want to know," continued Harry, "is how come people would be upset about a person who's got such sweet intentions? This puzzles me, yes, this puzzles me. There must be something going on that you aren't aware of."

Suddenly the street noises sounded very loud. Harry didn't let up for a minute. To make sure he was talking to the right person, he related all of these stories. "Now, if I were to believe these stories, you've been making these teachers feel awful insecure, expecting them to do things they don't have the means to do." He sighed. "Why, I hear one of those teachers was so upset that he wouldn't do anything for three days after you visited. And one of the teachers, I won't say who, told me she's going to shoot you dead the next time you set foot in her classroom with those helpful hints of yours . . ."

Harry was making all sorts of puzzlement gestures — scratching his head, shrugging his shoulders, raising his eyebrows. "Why, I know you want things to get better as quickly as possible . . ." In the middle of Maggie's dismay, Harry got a big star for diplomacy. "Now, here's what really puzzles me . . ." He stopped for a moment, deep in thought. "It seems like . . ." He made more confused gestures. "It seems like anybody who knows about teaching children and how you have to go slow with *them* wouldn't be doing what I hear you've been doing with adults. But then we don't always remember that adults and kids are the same species, do we?"

Harry's tone of voice conveyed pure puzzlement, no accusation or condemnation. "Now, I just want to get this straight in my mind. Correct me when I'm wrong, but not too harshly, please. There's one thing that seems important here. And that's the fact that adults react and learn just the way children do. After all, they're people as well, right? Just a different size is all. So the things that make children feel bad probably make their teachers feel bad when they're on the receiving end."

"Am I making any sense?" inquired Harry. He was tracing in the air, drawing a diagram of some kind. Maggie was feeling sort of weak. "Yes, it's kind of a shock to see things from another point of view," Harry sympathized. "Especially when you probably wanted to complain about what Warner Jenkins is doing to you. But anyhow, we're talking about your sins now. Before you or I, or anybody else, can start to condemn these teachers, we've got to give them credit for recognizing their own inadequacies. Most of them *know* they don't know a lot of things they'd like to know. This makes them feel extremely insecure. So it doesn't take anything at all to put them on the defensive . . ." Harry tapped his head.

"Being fairly rural just makes the situation more delicate, because people are very sensitive about outsiders too. Why, I've been working here for five years, and just the other day, somebody asked my opinion on something 'as an outsider.' " He grinned wryly.

"So, here you come. You might be from nearby, but that doesn't matter. You're full of ideas and talk about what could be done. The teachers know you could be a big help to them, but, in another way, you're also a very big threat to their self-esteem. So, before they're going to listen to you, they've got to trust you . . . You know, they have to be sure you're not just mouthing off, or trying to make them feel guilty." He stared at her for a few seconds. "So you have to be extra-careful not to turn them off. They feel insecure, and so they're just looking for an excuse to write you off. And you, see, with every good intention of helping, I'm sure, you've been handing them that excuse."

The noises from the outside had died down. Harry stopped talking and air-writing abruptly. He clasped his hand to his forehead dramatically. "Just listen to me go on," he drawled. "Here I am, working out my own theories on you, practically delivering a sermon, and you haven't said word number one. Now, I'm also known to be a very nosy person. You can slug me if you want to. But first, are you really the helpful terror I hear you are?" He leaned back to listen and almost tipped over in his chair.

Maggie couldn't laugh. She was trying not to cry.

"Oh, shoot," said Harry. "Oh shoot, now you know what, Miss Callahan, or Maggie, or whatever you are . . . This probably muddies your image of yourself, I know, but I didn't want to see you fall flat on your face, and I hate to see you turn the teachers off before you even know what's happening." He grimaced at the threat of tears. "Look, you can cry now, if you want to, but if there's a choice about it, wait until later."

He lit a cigarette and kept talking nonstop until Maggie dried up completely. "Course, there's two sides to every coin," he said. "Tell the truth, now: how do you feel, being new and young when everybody already knows each other?"

Maggie blew her nose. "Scared a lot," she said. "It's pretty hard to go in somebody else's classroom anyhow."

"Now, I'll bet you none of the teachers realized that you were feeling scared. Well, you'd probably be better off just coming out and admitting it. Now I'll give you a compliment. I haven't seen too many supervisors who were willing to even try to be helpful in the classrooms. Most of them I've seen either camp out in the administration building where they're safe, or else, when they do come in classrooms, they just watch and leave. I used to have one I called the snoopervisor. You've got the right idea but the wrong approach. So, see, you could use build-up, just like the teachers." He looked at his Pepsi bottle seriously. "Now that I've given you a compliment, you should stop that crying."

Maggie asked him where he got his diplomatic training, and he said his grandmother had beat it into him. "No, seriously," he drawled, "I've learned from experience that if you want to get things across, then you've just got to build people up before you say anything that might be interpreted as critical. You don't have to lie. Even a varmint like me has some good things about him. I think.

"For instance, I really do think you're a nice person, and I really like to talk with you. And, if I'd passed on all those stories without telling you how nice I think you are, you might've busted me one with all those notebooks. Now, isn't that true? You'd feel awful and would never want to speak to me again. Am I right?"

Maggie sighed. "Well, I don't understand why you bothered to tell me all this, but I'm glad you did."

Harry look disgusted. "I get a lot of pleasure out of watching the show go by," he said, "and every now and again, I stick my fingers in it. While I'm busy being a busybody, I ought to tell you that you've got Warner, poor man, running in circles." When Maggie started to object and fill him in on the situation, he held up his hand. "Nope," he said, "I'm not jumping in anybody's quarrels. I only have one point to make: Dealing with Warner Jenkins professionally might be like trying to speak Yiddish with an Arab. However, once he gets outside that job, he's a very warm-hearted man." He lit another cigarette. "O.K., I can see that he rates alongside Jack the Ripper in your book, but I'm just trying to give you a little perspective."

Maggie lifted the lid of a geology kit beside the chair and looked over some plastic cross-sections inside. "Those older kids at Gateway would really dig this," she said.

"Stop trying to avoid talking about Warner," Harry replied. "I can tell you about a lot of really thoughtful things that man has done." He crossed his heart and Boy-Scout-honored. "Food, clothes, and other things to families that need it . . . he's a real Good Samaritan at times."

Maggie put down the lid to the geology kit and shot him a puzzled look.

"Oh, I know," he said, "It's a lot easier to look at him in black-and-white, good-and-bad terms. Who is it, Ralph Nader, who refuses to ever meet or see car company executives. He doesn't want to see them as human beings. He wants to maintain that pure rage. And he's got a good point, for his business. But you've got to deal with the whole person. Nader's work doesn't depend on getting along with anybody, but yours does.

"All I'm saying is that Warner's got an awful lot of good in him. And he also has other priorities besides special education. And, if you won't buy peace on that basis, maybe you'll buy this: Warner controls all the federal funds in this county, as you may have noticed. There's a lot to be said for willingness to stand up for what you believe in, but it's not going to get you anywhere if you do it the wrong way. It sure isn't going to do those kids any good after the shock effect wears off. If you get Warner dead-set against you, he's going to cut off every penny for special ed. You may have noticed that too."

Harry didn't give her time to reply. "Besides that, Warner has a lot of influence in hiring and firing, and the teachers know it. They won't go against him. He can ruin anything you want to do with just a few phone calls, and don't think he can't. This place is a lot different from the city maybe. Maybe not. Scotch tape, pencils, and paper can be used for politicking. What you say down at the drugstore might have a big effect on how much cooperation you get for your next project. The drugstore clerk might run into Warner at the church social."

His voice grew quiet. "You know, some of us try to explain why things happen as they do by theories. And, in more specific instances, we write proposals and outline plans and actually expect them to come out as we said they would. But, over the years, I've come to believe that things happen as they do largely because of what I call 'the random personal element.' The random element as often as not doesn't have much to do with the actual *issue* at hand.

"The example that comes immediately to mind is the Murphy Clock Factory. The city council went through all kinds of gyrations to get that clock factory in Davidson. Well, it's located fifty miles from here, and I have it on good authority that they went there, not because the advantages to the plant were greater, but because the president's wife's best friend is married to a lawyer over there. That's the random element. It happens all the time. An important meeting doesn't go well because so-and-so had a stomachache and couldn't come. We can't put so-and-so in this teaching position because a board member's aunt wants it. This person has a lot of influence because he's having an affair with that person. A lawyer I know claims that the county court operates on the 'What did the judge have for breakfast?' system of justice. It's people, not theory. And the point I want to make, my girl, is that it's happening in your program. You have all your theories about what ought to be happening with children, but what's really controlling events, in great part, is the fact that you aren't getting along with Warner. The issues are secondary. If you want to make sure they get considered, you have to take care of important things — the random element — first."

Maggie frowned. "Well now, Maggie," Harry continued, "I've heard you hold forth on the subject of politics, but you must have that straight by now. Don't think about it as being dishonest in any way. Think about it as making people feel good, adding a ray of sunshine to the world's store of sweetness and light." Harry grinned. "Then you'll be at peace with yourself, because, honest, there's nothing wrong with building up Warner either. He responds to that, just like a child does, like we all do."

Suddenly, Maggie realized that it was getting dark. Harry had to drive fifteen miles over the mountain to get home. Maggie gathered up her things, apologizing madly for keeping him, thanking him too many times. Harry looked disgusted again and said he enjoyed telling other people what was wrong with them. "And spreading oil on troubled waters gives me a tremendous sense of accomplishment that seems to be lacking from my daily errands."

His smile faded. "Besides that," he said, getting up to put on his coat, "what do I know? At least you've got enthusiasm. When I first came here, I was going to do great things too. But they wear you down, and pretty soon you don't care. Pretty soon you're content to be a delivery boy and glad that they don't bother you too much."

He looked out the window, down the hill, through the town, toward the river and the railroad tracks. "All I care about now is getting my restaurant going. It's invigorating to fight a big war, but a thousand daily insanities and frustrations will always wear you down."

The town lights were coming on as Maggie picked her way down the hill, trying not to bust her tail on the ice. Snow was moving down from the mountaintops into the valleys. Those ferns had come out too soon. She sat in her car and thought about the importance of people and right attitudes. A woman struggled up the hill, leaning at an extreme angle into the wind.

Well, what do I know? she wondered, starting the car. What do any of us know?

As she drove past the Yellow Castle, Warner was just locking up. He peered at her suspiciously as she got out of her car. But, when she apologized to him for having lost her temper, he seemed to be genuinely touched. That kindly grandfather she had met when she first came showed himself again. She told him it was hard to maintain an objective, impersonal attitude when the kids and teachers needed so much help, and he said they'd all work together.

Somebody told her later that Warner had decided then that Maggie was a sweet girl after all. If Maggie was honest about it, part of her was being a sweet girl, but part of her still hoped to loosen up those federal funds.

16. Hindsight, New Attitudes, and Rewards

"The Senators are good men, but the Senate is a wild beast."
— Roman proverb

A FEW DAYS after she and Harry had talked in the Instructional Materials Center, Maggie found a note from him in her box at the Yellow Castle. It contained a quotation from Longfellow: "If we could read the secret history of our enemies, we should find in each man's life, sorrow and suffering enough to disarm all hostilities." "I can't resist corny notes and preaching," Harry had written underneath. "That word 'enemies' isn't exactly right. I left it in to preserve Longfellow's integrity. What I really meant in this situation is 'people who irritate the hell out of us.' "

Maggie looked at the note in her hand for a moment, then pulled another paper out of the box. It was an ad for a consulting firm that would come in and explain how to set up a program for emotionally disturbed students. The two papers together struck her funny, and gave rise to assorted thoughts. It can seem very easy, she thought, to look at an educational program from the outside and pick out problems and prescribe repairs. Car needs new plugs, change plugs, car runs. Only that approach doesn't work in school systems, since people are coming from so many different life situations, attitudes, points of view, etc. And there's also politics.

She thought about the idea of the six-hour retarded child and the objections that had been raised to looking at the child only in the school context. Isn't it true too, she began to think, that when we work with other adults, we often see them only as nine-to-three people and forget about the other hours that make up their lives? The six-hour crabby bitch? How clear or fair is that?

The more Maggie thought about the outside factors affecting the lives of the special ed teachers, the more uncomfortable and insensitive she felt. Low pay, poor treatment from the school system, small children at home, liver trouble and gallstones, serious marital problems . . . and two teachers had to hold down part-time evening jobs to make ends meet. Not that they shouldn't be expected to do the best they could in their jobs, but Maggie began to see that a much more sympathetic approach on her part would help them to do so, much more than pressure and implied disapproval.

When she first came, Mr. Birdwell had advised her to lay low for the first month or so and let people get used to her, but that hadn't seemed to be a top priority. She had noticed that the teachers seemed to expect supervisors to ride around in their cars a lot and issue mimeographed nonsense. It had seemed more to the point to offer to help one teacher set up a behavior modification schedule for the destructive behavior of two children, to demonstrate concrete math activities, to advise on organization of reading groups, to tell a teacher how to make maximum use of her aide.

In hindsight, she saw that her ideas, like many other good ones, had been largely canceled out, not because they weren't needed, but because she hadn't paid sufficient attention to the feelings of the people who would be receiving all this advice and help.

She also remembered an incident Miss Adkins had described to her. The previous year, one of the civic organizations in town had collected a lot of clothes for children who needed them. They had come to Gateway School and arranged for the teachers to distribute the clothes. The children had seemed to be pleased in general and had taken the clothes home. "But do you know," said Miss Adkins, "that most of those kids have never worn a single one of those items to school, even on cold days when they show up with nothing but a thin sweater? Shirley told me her pa wouldn't let her wear hers, because he said it was charity." Winding one of her ponytails around her finger, Miss Adkins had added, "It's not enough to know what's needed or have good intentions. You can't force things on people. I guess you've got to find some way for the need and what's needed to connect."

Maggie began to see that she would have accomplished a lot more by being pleasant and noncommittal for the first month or so while producing concrete objects like tape, glue, library books, and puzzles where possible. She also saw that it wouldn't have been so much *what* was being done as when and how it was done. It would have been better just to have spent a lot of time in the classrooms getting to know the teachers and the children, keeping any critical vibrations to a minimum.

The talk with Harry had given Maggie much to think about over the weekend. A sentence she had read somewhere kept running through her mind: "If you expect people to learn, you can't take them to the drinking fountain and turn on the fire hose." The longer Maggie thought, the more situations that sentence seemed to apply to — until "turning on the fire hose" amounted to a national means of operation. The federal government, turning the fire hose on the states, demanding the creation of *programs now* . . . the states, doing the same thing to the locals . . . herself, down on the local level, doing it to the teachers and Warner . . . teachers, drowning children with expectations. All of them saying, "Here. I insist that you perform this complicated operation sensitively, accurately, and constructively — *even though, I'm not going to give you adequate time, guidance, or resources*. (However, I will punish you if you don't do it.)"

Many others have had those same thoughts. "On a national level, the U.S. Congress is presently doing what so many of us would be naturally wanting to do in a local situation," remarked Ed Martin, director of the Bureau of Education for the Handicapped in the summer of 1975. "They're saying that things should be the way they're supposed to be, right now or within a very short period of time. And it's hard to argue against it, and I'm really not arguing against it, in principle. I'm just saying that some of the proposed requirements concern me, because I'm afraid that we may get backlashed if we impose, all at once, much more stringent requirements than school systems are able to fulfill at this time. The requirements should be there, but the timing is very important."

In some ways, maybe the fire hose whacks down hardest on adults, Maggie speculated, experiencing a fresh whack of guilt herself. Adults are so rarely viewed as still learning. If a grown-up makes mistakes, it usually isn't seen as part of a learning process. It's likely to be seen as a defect in the person's character.

*

Despite those reasonable thoughts, Maggie was feeling pretty defective herself. On the Monday following her talk with Harry, she went to school with spirits dragging on the pavement, feeling that she'd managed to alienate the very people whose cooperation she needed most. But an odd thing happened. Her apology to Warner the preceding Friday had demonstrated a new attitude, something that was to be encouraged in Warner's book. So he called her into his office early in the morning and told her he had "found" $7433 hidden away in Part B of the previous year's Title I funds. He asked her to spend the money for special education and mentioned several other possible avenues for funds.

The windfall knocked Maggie back a few paces. Beyond the fact that the funds were offered, she was dismayed to find herself feeling grateful in a personal way. It didn't feel as if Warner were releasing funds because the children needed them. It felt as if he were giving her a present as a reward for her change in attitude. No mention was made of Friday's meeting. What had been said on that occasion no longer applied. But it was crystal clear that no money would have been directed to special education without the apology — or maybe even without the hassle preceding it. Personalities were the deciding factor.

Warner explained that it would be necessary to rewrite a section of the federal proposal to define the new usage of the $7433. He presented Maggie with an official Part C proposal-writing guide, along with a short list of words to use and words not to use. "You have to know which words catch their eye this year and which words will turn them off or you won't get *anywhere*," he explained in an earnest fashion. "That's one of the most *important* things to know when you're trying to get money from the federal government. He circled "words to use" to emphasize his point. He himself, he said, was kept up to date on the latest words to use by the state Title I director.

"Go *to* it!" he encouraged Maggie. As she exited with the Part C guide, Mrs. Pearl had replaced her in the chair beside Warner's desk and was showing him some catalogues.

*

In response to Maggie's new attitude, Warner did his best to patch up relations. At lunch a few days later, he drank a cup of coffee with her at the diner. He told her he was feeling very tired. "But it always makes me feel a little better to get these big orders out of the way." He showed her a spoon he was carving, then said he had just mailed out a check for $25,000 "to cover Alpha I and Dimension 99 kits." Maggie almost choked.

This was the first time in a while that they had discussed work informally. Warner explained that the state Title I director was coming the following week, and the Part C proposal should be finished by then. Maggie told him that putting it together was tough. "So many different kinds of information to get together to do it right. Warner, how do you ever handle as many programs and write as many proposals as you do?"

Warner hesitated, studying her over his coffee cup. "I don't," he shrugged finally, pushing a few strands of gray hair behind his ear. "I don't do a good job on any of them. I couldn't possibly, since I'm only one person and rarely get out of the office. We can't do it the way it's supposed to be done, so what I do is just jump in there and do what I can. If I didn't do it, it just *wouldn't* get done." A curious toughness shaded his voice.

Warner was right. It wouldn't get done if he didn't do it. While he put on his coat, Maggie was admiring his willingness to jump right into that mass of paperwork. However, after he left, she had second thoughts. Not about his willingness to work, but about the assumption behind all this jumping right in, about the idea that "something is better than nothing."

If the government told Copper County to build an Apollo rocket, Warner would probably start ordering parts, she thought irritably.

Between Monday and Thursday, the Part C proposal sucked up approximately fifteen hours of writing time. Maggie used the right words, talked to teachers, dug through catalogues, consulted other supervisors, tried to run down salesmen, estimated prices, and tried to make everything add up to approximately $7433. No luck.

By Thursday, it was obvious that it would be impossible to prepare an accurate and realistic proposal in just one week. Sure, a slick piece could be shipped off to pass muster, but it wouldn't reflect the needs of the program as it should. Thursday afternoon, she visited Warner.

"What do you do when you can't get together adequate information in the amount of time you have?" she fussed. "Suppose I put down 4000 dollars for language arts materials, then find out later that it would be better to spend that money for something else?"

Warner seemed to be somewhat taken aback and slightly amused by the question. "Oh, no." He shook his head vigorously. "You don't *understand*. That's not the way it *works*. It doesn't matter if the figures are *accurate*. The main thing is to get the proposal *approved*. You just write it any way you want. Fake what you don't know. After you get the money, you can spend it however you *want*." He seemed pleased to be consulted.

"But what happens if they come and check up on you?" Maggie persisted.

Warner shrugged. "In that case, you just tell them you changed your mind. It's as simple as that. The federal people are used to it. They understand how hard it is to get these proposals exactly the way you want them when you've got other duties too." He paused, then added, "But they almost *never* come."

These remarks took a while to digest, but Warner didn't seem to notice Maggie's silence, perhaps because he didn't consider the subject a matter of opinion. He wasn't telling her how to pull the wool over the government, he was merely explaining procedure.

"Don't use round figures when you estimate prices," he continued. "The federal people are suspicious of round figures. It looks as though you didn't do your homework. I always write in $1523, for example, instead of $1500. That's more likely to pass.

"And if your proposal involves training workshops for teachers — in-service workshops — you're supposed to fill in the names of people who will conduct your in-service, day by day. That's another thing that doesn't have to be accurate. You can just put down anybody." Maggie fantasized telling Title I that Zsa Zsa Gabor, Bob

Dylan, and Sigmund Freud were coming to Copper County. "Once, I even put down the name of the Title I man who approves the proposals," Warner chuckled. Then he sighed. "Lots of times, I end up doing the workshops myself."

After working a while on the proposal, Maggie realized that the Title I money couldn't be used for basic supplies, so she asked Craig Bailey, the business administrator, if he could do anything in that department. "Well, don't they have that stuff?" he said slowly, squinting at her in a businesslike way. After hearing that some of the teachers were spending their own money, he looked up at the ceiling. "Listen," he said in very measured tones. "You make up a list of what's needed, and we'll get it. If there isn't money in the special education accounts, we'll just take it from somewhere else." His face showed a trace of anger.

"Nobody's come to me about this before," he added, "so I assumed the classrooms were getting what they needed." He paused. "My job isn't to investigate these things, you know. I assume I'll be informed." He looked at Maggie, then leaned back in his chair. "Now, you're wondering how I can take such a passive attitude." They both smiled. "Look," he continued, "there's no shortage of things around here I don't like. But I can't afford to initiate too many crusades. I have my own personal changes I'd like to see made, like fair pay for the office help. I'd also like to be elected to the town council, because there are many things I think I could get done from there. If I go sounding off about everything I don't like, I'd cancel out every little bit of influence I've got.

"So you can see why I wouldn't be anxious to initiate a complaint about other things. But now that *you've* told me, that's different. I can do something about it, since you started the ball rolling, and that's your department." Maggie went away wondering why she and the teachers hadn't understood that Craig could help.

Outside the Yellow Castle, she ran into the music teacher. Mrs. Pearl's usual bright smile was gone, and she looked pooped. Her greeting contained a trace of anxiety, so Maggie avoided shoptalk and carried on instead about a couple of beautiful farms between Davidson and Goshen. Mrs. Pearl's smile came back, and soon they were talking about local musicians. She enthused about the church choirs and talked about a couple of people who shared her love of classical music.

Maggie asked her if she knew any good banjo players or guitars pickers. Mrs. Pearl mentioned one man in particular but seemed to have something else on her mind. Maggie brought up the fact that the special ed kids were crazy about bluegrass and gospel music, hoping she'd pick up the ball.

The afternoon sun slanted low, and the castle cut jagged chunks from its rays. Mrs. Pearl left the ball where it was, squinted into the sun, and pressed her lips together, hanging on the edge of speech. The constable and his buddies were arguing with a man in a checkered shirt in front of the J.P.'s office. One of them kept pointing to a battered green pickup labeled "farm use" in white paint.

"You know," said Mrs. Pearl, startling Maggie out of the little drama across the street, "I really didn't think I wanted to take this job. I mean, after six months, I still don't know how to work with special ed kids." She pushed back a small strand of her hair with a jerky motion and said she didn't know if Maggie would be that interested in her problems. That comment knocked the green truck completely out of Maggie's head.

Maggie said she had plenty of time if Mrs. Pearl did. Rechecking the strand of hair, Mrs. Pearl gathered her thoughts. "Well," she began, still not sure if Maggie was interested, "I told you before that I have a music background, but I just don't know very much about working with retarded children, to tell the truth."

When Maggie asked how she had become interested in special education, Mrs. Pearl spoke warmly of her neighbor's child in the town where she used to live, who apparently had great difficulty performing basic functions. Her experience with this child's needs had persuaded her, she said, to tackle the job. "After I signed my contract, the more I thought about it, the more inadequate I felt, but I at least wanted to try."

Remembering her earlier unkind thoughts, Maggie felt a sudden rush of sympathetic warmth for Mrs. Pearl's efforts.

"I didn't know where to start," Mrs. Pearl continued, words rushing out. "I mean, I did read a book on teaching music to retarded kids. It said to use a lot of rhythm exercises, said they needed that. I'll show it to you" — Every sentence was punctuated by a questioning look — "but, the thing is, I just don't know what else you can *do* with special education children . . ."

Oh, Mrs. Pearl, Maggie thought, with these particular kids, the same things you do with any kids. They're just children, as far as music is concerned, not a different species. Special education. Forget what you've been told and what you've read, and just look at them. Look at Jenny Krebbs and see Jenny Krebbs. Don't see your neighbor's child. Don't see a big sign that says "retarded" or "special ed."

Maggie didn't say any of this, not right then. Mrs. Pearl was twisting her hands together, obviously upset. "I do try," she said, "but I just don't have the training necessary to work with special ed children. I do all I can. I even walk around among them while they're marching, to help them march, you know."

She was so obviously sincere, obviously making a real effort, and certainly deserved a great deal of personal support. "I touch them on the left shoulder when I want them to lift their left foot." She laughed nervously. "I don't know if it does any good, touching them, but I use whatever I can think of . . ."

Mrs. Pearl stopped to think, and the familiar inner debate began inside Maggie: "This person is saying, 'I care, I'm putting myself out.' Her effort is genuine."

"Yeah, but her approach affects the children, and you could tell her how to do things that would make everything better all around. Those things she's doing are probably very good for a few of the children, but counterproductive for most."

"It's too soon. Wait until she trusts you. Adults are sensitive, just like children. Remember what Harry said."

"Yeah, but as a professional, she should be able to take professional criticism. Especially in the interest of the children . . ."

"Should be able to doesn't have anything to do with reality and can get you in hot water besides. If a child came to you and told you he felt inadequate, would you start telling him what he *should* be able to do?"

"Of course not. That would be the worst thing I could do. It would convince him that there was no hope for him."

"Then don't do it to this lady. Find another way. Feelings and learning aren't confined to children. Mrs. Pearl can and will obviously learn if you don't fire-hose her."

Mrs. Pearl was watching Maggie anxiously. Maggie told her she wished everybody cared as much as she obviously did. And that was the truth. "Maybe I'll be able to help you out if you'd like me to . . ."

Mrs. Pearl relaxed considerably. "By now," Maggie ventured, "you must have noticed how bright and quick many of these children are . . ."

It was almost too much. Mrs. Pearl gave her a strange look, then murmured, "I have to admit that I haven't been too successful in communicating with these children. I guess I don't know how to." Her face fell a little. Maggie remembered the wooden faces of the children as they marched. "They seem to be so unreachable, to me anyhow," continued Mrs. Pearl. "They don't seem to be able to carry on a conversation . . . and it's so hard for them to memorize the songs . . ." She looked up, pushed back that same strand of hair and brushed some lint off her plaid coat.

"It takes a while . . ." Maggie began, but Mrs. Pearl interrupted rather urgently.

"Can *you* talk to them, Miss Callahan? I mean, will they talk with you? Carry on a conversation?"

She was showing such a willingness to take another look. It would have been too easy to say something sarcastic or condescending. "Well," Maggie began delicately, hoping she had learned something from Harry, "they wouldn't talk to me at first, me being a stranger. But I always come in informally, so it's sort of different with me. I mean, you're pretty well tied down by your schedule and have to rush off to the next class, so I guess that doesn't give you much informal time with the children . . ."

"That's true . . ." Mrs. Pearl looked sideways, apparently examining the parking meter. "I really don't have the kind of informal time I'd like, to let the children get used to me . . . but Miss Callahan," she hesitated — "can they really talk with you intelligently?"

She met Maggie's eyes again. "Yes, they can," Maggie said softly. "Most of them can, just like any child."

17. Teaching Teachers in School

"I've spent a lot of time visiting programs while we were putting the federal special education legislation together, and the one thing I found absolutely frustrating, as we looked at program after program, is that it seems that everything comes from quality of personnel, and yet the quality of personnel varies without any apparent correlation with amount of training. We simply don't know what to do about that in a legislative way.

"You go from one program to another, looking for the critical variables, asking 'What makes this one productive and this one destructive?' and nobody's sure what those variables are. Some say program structure, others say personnel, some say both. If it's personnel, I'm not sure how much training has to do with it. The very good people we saw were either not trained at all or were exceptionally well-trained. And the very bad were either exceptionally well-trained or not trained at all. Training seems to be important somehow, yet some sort of personal characteristic seems to make the critical difference.

"The law can require that children be mainstreamed in regular education wherever possible, and we can require that teachers be certified and that parents be given the right to a hearing. But Congress can't require teachers to have a caring attitude. We can't make it illegal for teachers to call kids dummies or communicate low expectations in other ways. And yet, these intangibles are necessary to the spirit of the things we *can* write into the law."

— Lisa Walker, legislative aide,
U.S. Senate, July 1975

IN 1968, Robert Rosenthal and Lenore Jacobson published *Pygmalion in the Classroom: Teacher Expectation and Pupil's Intellectual Development*, an often-cited research study of the effect of teachers' expectations on their students. Rosenthal and his colleagues worked with eighteen elementary teachers of grades one through six. At the beginning of the school year, they gave each teacher a list of children who were supposedly rapid learners with hidden potential. Teachers were told that, regardless of previous performance, those children would show unusual gains in interest and academic progress during the year.

All children were tested before the experiment began and afterward. The children on both lists were chosen *at random*. At the end of the year, those pupils who supposedly had hidden potential had made significantly greater gains as a group than those other pupils of whom nothing special was expected. The difference between the two groups was especially large in the first and second grades. Many other studies have supported the same idea: children tend to do better or worse, depending on what their teachers expect them to do.

Rosenthal called *Pygmalion* a study of the "self-fulfilling prophecy," meaning that what one person expects another person to be can actually influence or determine the second person's behavior. *Pygmalion in the Classroom* focuses on the positive results of expecting that children have positive potential. Communicated expectations are equally powerful in a negative way, when poor performance is expected. If you tell a person he is clumsy often enough, for instance, he will probably start stumbling and dropping things when you're around — especially if he sees you as influential or important. If a boss treats employees as if they're incompetent, if a father sees his children as all thumbs, those expectations will get across somehow, either verbally or nonverbally, and there's a good chance that the people involved will feel less like working, will accept the "all thumbs" judgment, and shy away from trying.

After her encounter with Harry, Maggie understood that she had been communicating the wrong expectations to most of the teachers. Her first chance to clean up her act came with Danny Brenner's teacher. Danny was a boy who had been heavily influenced by the expectations of the adults around him. He moved stiffly at school and talked through his teeth. "But if you think he talks through his teeth now, you should've seen him at the start of the year," reported the teacher's aide assigned to his class. "His whole body acted as if it had lockjaw."

"Mr. Bigelow's made a big difference," she continued. "He treats Danny decently, as though he likes him, as though he thinks he's worth something. Danny relaxes around him."

When Maggie first came to Copper County, she equated Danny's teacher in her mind with Harry Blankenship, who taught in the cafeteria over at Goshen School. Like Harry, Jerry Bigelow expected that the children were interesting, reasonable people and that there were no limits on their capacity to learn, given interesting opportunities.

"Why'd you want to be a teacher, Mr. Bigelow?" Danny asked him one afternoon, rasping through his teeth.

"So I could push around big guys like you," replied Bigelow. Grinning broadly himself, Danny feigned a punch before slipping outdoors to recess.

"He needs to know that he can poke at me," Bigelow said, unconsciously echoing Blankenship.

"Why *did* you become a teacher?" Maggie asked.

"To save my immortal soul," he replied instantly. "I was lying awake too many nights in the Marines, praying that God wouldn't punish me too badly for participating in a killing machine." He swung his feet up on his desk and ran his hand across his army-style haircut. "I used to be in charge of hundreds of men. Now I'm in charge of the kids they put out behind the school."

Jerry Bigelow had grown up in Copper County and had gone to Stockdale School as a kid. "He was on the basketball team," breathed one of the girls, "and he used to date *my* mother!" In his late thirties, he was involved in community affairs, spending a lot of time with his family, working a part-time job after school to make ends meet.

Jerry had been put in charge of sixteen children, ranging in age from eight to twelve. His class enrollment also ranged considerably, from week to week, mainly because Mr. Dillard had taken to punishing troublemakers from the regular classrooms by assigning them to Bigelow's class for a "cooling-off period" — "And, if you don't straighten out, I'll *leave* you there."

When these extra kids appeared in Bigelow's class, they sabotaged his academic program. Even after Maggie convinced Mr. Dillard to hold back on deposits, Bigelow didn't make any bones about needing help. "Maybe my kids are feeling better about themselves, and that's fantastic," he said. "But I know what's going to happen to them in a few years if they don't learn the basics too. I've seen it too many times. As far as this system's concerned, feeling good about yourself is worth less than nothing if you can't read decently. That just makes you a happy retardate.

"Now, I'm supposed to be curing their academic problems," he continued, "but I'm still teaching with a how-to book in one hand." He pulled at the collar of his sweater. "I'm taking as many courses as I can handle, commuting to school, and I took a bunch last summer. But somehow, they never seem to get down to the nuts and bolts."

Jerry never doubted that progress was possible for the children, and he had confidence in his own ability to bring it about. A few visits to his classroom showed that he had a natural instinct for teaching. In academic terms, he was denying his own instincts in favor of the safer ground of teaching the way he himself had been taught; but so many little things showed that he was cued into the kids' ways of learning. One day, for instance, when Maggie came by, the children were all worked up over the Empire State Building. "It said in one of those reading stories that the Empire State Building's one thousand four hundred and seventy-two feet high, with its radio tower," explained Jerry. "I asked those guys how far one thousand four hundred and seventy-two feet is, and one of them said, 'To the end of the playground' and then the rest agreed. They had no feeling for that kind of distance. So it seemed like a good idea to get our coats on and go step it off."

"If the Umpire State Building was laying on its side, Miss Callahan, it'd reach down over the bridge!" interrupted one girl.

"Wish we had one of those in this town," said another. "I'd skinny right up it."

Since Mr. Bigelow already had positive attitudes and natural ability, a little bit of practical training made a big difference in his classroom from the start. As it happened, he and Maggie started with reading. Bigelow's children had all been in school for at least three years, so any bad feelings about reading had had plenty of time to ferment. Only one of them, a constant talker named Arthur, read "at grade level." All the others were at least one year behind.

Arthur was the class spokesman. He would interview strangers and generally act as master of ceremonies. Sitting behind Arthur was a boy from Bald Mountain named Chet, who apparently couldn't read three words in a row. However, Chet *could* look at a page and tell you the sense of its contents in loose, general terms. "I dunno how I know what it says, I just know," he would say. A mop-haired, apple-cheeked, and cheerful little fellow, Chet was popular with his classmates and wasn't one for a conscious put-on. He really seemed to believe he couldn't read.

And then there was Willy, an equally cheerful ten-year-old with a very bad speech problem. Understandably, Willy didn't like to read out loud, so he avoided any activities likely to put him in that position.

With great sympathy, Bigelow told Maggie about Sheila, who took care of her four younger brothers and sisters and was seldom awake enough to take full advantage of anything that was going on. A tall thin girl with limp, light brown hair, Sheila obviously had trouble keeping her attention on classroom activities. She wore thin cotton dresses in the middle of winter. Bigelow frowned. "When I think about her getting those kids up, fixing breakfast for the family, and then coming down on the bus to be in a retarded class . . ."

Charlie, whose middle-class parents gave him pills every day to slow him down, told Maggie, "If I don't take my pill, I go at three thousand r.p.m.s. Like this!" He let out a good imitation of 3000 r.p.m.s. Sheila bolted straight up in her chair, then sagged down again. Bigelow cringed and asked Charlie to shift gears. Charlie obliged by letting out a roar that sounded more like 1500 r.p.m.s.

And there were eleven other kids in that class, all below grade level, mostly indistinguishable in conversation and action from average nine- or ten-year-olds. They giggled a lot when Maggie first started coming around and groaned when they found out she was going to be working on reading.

"How come we didn't all learn to read good already?" demanded Arthur. The other kids were too shy to ask questions like that, but everybody's ears were extended.

"I don't know. Different people learn different ways." They talked about reading being like a puzzle that different people put together in different ways, and then a few kids told war stories about reading groups. The whole group relaxed.

"How come Bigelow don't do this by himself?" persisted Arthur.

"Because I'm learning too," the teacher cut in. "And she knows how to do some things I don't know how to do yet."

"But when she gets finished, you'll know. You'll pick her brains."

"You got the idea, buddy." Bigelow winked. He sounded relaxed and matter-of-fact. Knowing that the teacher was learning too was a great piece of information for the kids.

A couple of mornings' work turned up the fact that, with the exception of Arthur and Sheila, none of the children had an adequate grasp on which sounds were associated with which letters. Most knew a certain number of words by sight but had no tools with which to attack unfamiliar words. It wasn't that they had forgotten those letter sounds; most, apparently, never had learned phonics in the first place.

Phonics is the study of individual letter sounds and of the sounds letters make in combination with other letters. For some children, trying to read without phonics is like trying to build a brick house without bricks. With the exception of Willy, all of Jerry's kids responded very positively to phonics instruction. Even Chet.

Jerry began to worry that the kids would see phonics instruction as baby stuff. He had gone next door to ask Mrs. Cales what phonics materials she had that he might borrow, and she had showed him a bunch of duplicating masters with pictures of little ducks and doll babies. He was feeling frustrated. "It's just that I don't know where to start," he said, rubbing the back of his neck, adding that he was getting mostly theory in his teacher-training courses.

Jerry wanted "nuts and bolts" help on the job, with real children, and the nuts and bolts activities to make sense in terms of a total program so that he could go on to develop teaching devices of his own. He didn't want to have to look in the teacher's manual to find out what to do next.

Jerry expressed those needs to Maggie one afternoon as the children were lining up for the buses to go home. Maggie was delighted to have the opportunity to try again. They were sitting at a couple of student desks. Somebody was blowing a whistle outside. "Line up! Line up!" Bigelow was tracing the initials and cuss words carved in the desk with his finger. "I'll do my best to talk about the teaching framework," Maggie said.

"I'm listening," replied Bigelow.

"O.K," Maggie began. "We've got a particular situation here in which some teaching guidelines come in very handy. We want to teach something that's basically abstract and has possible overtones of baby stuff to a bunch of kids who ain't babies." Bigelow nodded. "Well, I'll come up with some specific ideas for tomorrow. The nuts and bolts. Maybe they'll work, and maybe they won't. In any case, it's probably useful for you to know about the general guidelines I happen to use in deciding how to approach any teaching problem. All these ideas have come to me from other people, so I'll pass them on to you."

Bigelow pulled out a piece of paper to take notes. Maggie smiled. "First thing is making sure the kids understand what's going on or what's going to happen — right now and in a bigger sense as well. How does what's going on right now relate to what happened yesterday and what's going to happen tomorrow. What are we doing this for?

"Another one is something nobody has to tell you, Jerry: relate to every child as if he or she is likable, normal, and interesting. Communicate the best of expectations to him. If anger or disappointment is called for, make sure he understands that you may not like what he's doing, but you still like him.

"A third guideline is more down to nuts and bolts. Involve as many senses as possible in the learning process. Try not to go at a particular lesson in only one way. For math, let the children see, hear, and touch the quantities. Involve their motor functions. Let them jump off the numbers, or step them off. Write it, say it, hear it, jump it, and so on, but use more than one approach. Make it fun, and let the kids move.

"That's also something else you already know, Jerry," she added, remembering the Empire State Building.

He looked up and smiled. "Cut the diplomacy and get on with it."

"Well, O.K., here comes another one. If the kid doesn't understand what you're doing, the lesson content's probably too abstract for him. Make the lesson more concrete and simple. Bring it closer to something the kid can relate to in a physical way. A number like 'five,' for instance, is an abstract symbol. A picture of five apples is more concrete. Five actual apples are concrete. If he eats them, they are even more concrete to him. He gets a stomachache probably. Find the level of concreteness that suits the child. To do that, you've got to know where you want to end up. In this case, you want the kid to be able to use the abstract symbol five effectively."

"Give me another example," said Bigelow.

"Well, when you plan a lesson, it's a good idea to start whenever possible with actual objects, then progressively become more abstract at a rate that suits the children involved. If you were trying to teach young children about maps, you could start with a map of a simple area they know, the school and its yard, for instance. They'd all walk around it first. Very concrete. They they'd make a 3–D model of the building out of paper and put it on a flat surface representing the yard. Then maybe they'd replace the building with a flat piece of paper the shape of the roof. Next, maybe they could make a map of their neighborhood at that point. Or map a room in their house. Pirate maps. Treasure hunts. Aerial photos with map overlays. And so on until you get to road maps."

Bigelow had been writing all this down. "I've never thought about it specifically that way," he said, "but concrete understanding's really important for kids around here." He tapped the pencil's eraser on the desk. "Even a city is abstract for a lot of them. If you've never seen one, it's abstract."

"Yeah. So you've got to use their *own* concepts to lead them toward understanding of things they haven't seen. That reminds me of something else. It's closely related to concrete-to-abstract. One of my teachers used to call it 'giving the child a handle to grab onto.' If you can relate whatever you're trying to teach to the child's own experience, you give him a handle to grab it by. The learning has to start *inside* him, not be imposed from outside. He's got to have a handle, if he's going to learn, not memorize. So if you're talking about the Amazon River, first say a few words about the river running through Copper County, or better yet, go down there and talk about rivers. Compare the two. Tack the Amazon onto the river the kids know.

"You'll end up with your own guidelines," she concluded. "This is just to give you an idea. There are so many — making sure the child understands the meaning of the words you're using, and the importance of letting the kids do work for themselves, or of ending a lesson with something they can do. Anyhow, you'll find your own."

"Gotcha," said Bigelow, folding his notes and sticking them in his pocket.

Phonics, the nuts and bolts in this case, turned out to be a roaring success in Bigelow's class. The kids talked some more about "sounds" being one way of "unlocking" words. Arthur got up and spontaneously acted this concept out, twisting an imaginary giant key, spitting out sounds. Jerry involved the kids' ears, eyes, and bodies to make the sounds come across in as many ways as possible. The kids ran relays, had quiz shows, raced with word puzzles, made up and acted out stories about "word families," and made up lists of alliterative insults. Jerry and Maggie introduced the children to a cartoon character called The Runaway Word to help them relate to words that don't follow phonetic rules. Each week he'd be running up different parts of the wall with new words like *would* on his back.

Best of all, Jerry took what he saw and expanded it in his own program, making good use of the concrete and of the kids' own experience. He laid heavy emphasis on building up the children's vocabulary and expanding the concepts within their grasp so they would understand what they read as they read it.

The most exciting moment during Mr. Bigelow's program that spring occurred in April on one of those days when the weather couldn't make up its mind. Dark patches were coming and going across the playground. Same thing, down on the river. Maggie was heading for her car when Jerry whooped at her from his doorway.

"Come in here!" he yelled. "It's Chet! He's reading!" Chet, it turned out, had picked up a third grade book that day and simply started reading. Just like that. All the kids were clustered about him, and, with a very pink face, he was reading for all of them. He held the book as if he thought it might disappear.

"I never thought I could do it. I didn't think I could do it," Chet kept repeating in an awe-struck tone, running his hand nervously through his sandy mop. "I just never thought I could do it."

"I can't believe I ate the *whole thing*," said Arthur. Everyone laughed, including Chet.

Bigelow and Maggie suspected that Chet had had the ability to read for a long time, but that some psychological block had prevented him from using it. He may have doubted his own ability so much that his brain wouldn't accept the messages his eyes sent him up from the page. Perhaps the message leaked through at some level, which accounted for his mysterious knowledge of the subject matter that he literally "couldn't read." All speculation.

Phonics seemed to have given Chet the means of double-checking the messages his eyes had been sending him. The casual accepting classroom atmosphere gave him the courage to try. As he read aloud, he made heavy use of phonics. When he was shown words printed on a card, he would mouth the word silently in some cases before sounding it out. Only after he had double-checked would he say the word aloud.

"What made you think you couldn't read?" Maggie asked him.

"Aw, you know . . . people said so . . ."

"What people?"

"Teachers and all. An' I guess I told myself too." He went back to his book.

Oddly enough, Maggie felt angry as she left Bigelow's room. Chet's success was wonderful, but he was a child whose school experiences evidently had caused him to think so little of his own abilities that he wouldn't even believe the evidence of his own eyes. Jerry's "new" strategies were just good teaching procedures, not magic tricks that could only occur in special education.

Beyond that, it didn't seem fair to Jerry that he was paying for teacher-training courses that didn't give him what he needed to deal with the actual problems he ran into in the classroom. This is a common problem in all parts of the country. "Out of the research and data gathering over the past few years," remarked a Virginia learning resource specialist in 1975, "we're finding that the greatest percentage of potentially capable people are already with us out in the schools. But they have many training needs, and this means that either the separation between the teacher-training institutions and the schools will have to be broken down, or else we have to by-pass the teacher-training institutions altogether."

"No doubt about it," agreed Dr. Tom Behrens of the Bureau of Education for the Handicapped. "There has been greatly increased dissatisfaction with the ivory tower approach to teacher-training. Many public school people have been saying in effect that if the teacher-training institutions were private industry, many might have to close after their first year of operation. And just a few years ago, that was universally pretty true, because no university that I know of was doing a thorough job of investigating the actual needs of the public schools around them. But changes are beginning to happen, mainly because the teacher-trainers themselves are concerned about the gap. I hear them saying, 'We've got to get more cooperation programs going with the schools.'" Speaking in the summer of 1976, Dr. Behrens pointed with satisfaction to a series of meetings in the Northwest, in which three colleges in a 300-mile radius had gotten together with public school personnel in the same area to compare needs and offerings and to air gripes.

The Bureau of Education for the Handicapped is also trying to narrow the gap between teacher-training and the public schools. In the mid-sixties, they required all teacher-training institutions receiving funds in any given state to offer courses in line with the needs reported by that state division of special education. The bureau is also encouraging teacher-training institutions to take their courses out into all parts of the state instead of requiring working teachers to make the trek in to a central campus. The Office of Education also encourages practical media presentations that can be used to help train student teachers on campus or teachers already teaching in the schools.* Many school systems

---

*A good example is California's video-cassette program, involving hundreds of short videotapes of actual children of varying ages. Each tape zeroes in on a specific problem or behavior and is accompanied by a practical discussion and information.

and some state divisions are putting together their own training programs, either in cooperation with or independent of the teacher-training institutions.

In fairness to teacher-trainers, getting cooperative arrangements going with the schools isn't always easy. "The state division of special ed has put together some terrific training opportunities," remarked a Vermont Head Start official, "but some systems won't take advantage of it. They'll tell you it's because they don't want the state messing with their school system."

Whatever the circumstances, the same messages do keep coming from the schools. First of all, there is too big a separation between what teachers need in the schools and average offerings on college campuses. An increasing percentage of training should occur in the schools where the children and real problems are. Second — especially as mainstreaming becomes more common — the schools are increasingly dissatisfied with teacher-training institutions which do not prepare *all* teachers to deal with individual differences. As mainstreaming forces schools to backtrack and supply additional training, pressure is increasing on teacher-training institutions to give teachers-in-training more practical preparation for dealing with individual differences. As teacher-training improves, children in general will benefit, and it's possible that many of the difficulties of children like those in Jerry Bigelow's class will be prevented.

Maryland's videotape series "Teaching Children with Special Needs," set up to be used in conjunction with a training program for early elementary teachers in the public schools, is another.

18. Mainstreaming

". . . Basically it [mainstreaming] *is* a thrust toward integrating handicapped children into regular schools and classrooms, with many opportunities not only to join in the usual activities of a normal school day, but also to be accepted members of their own society of non-handicapped peers, to be 'counted in.' On the other side, one thing it is *not* intended to be is a wholesale elimination of specialized services, programs or classes designed for children with exceptional needs.

"In simple terms, the mainstreaming philosophy maintains that as many physically, mentally, and emotionally handicapped children as possible should be included in regular classes — with as much extra support from professional specialists as each requires. Extra professional support covers a wide gamut, including intervention by teachers who are skilled in helping youngsters deal with emotional difficulties, tutoring by math and reading specialists trained to work with learning disabled children, mobility training for the blind — to give only a few examples. Even when disability is severe, and the child needs to spend a greater amount of time away from the regular classroom to get the kind of teaching and help he requires, he can still be encouraged to take part in all the activities which have always been open to other children — such as art and music, shop and P.E.

". . . But it is important to point out that all the program reforms, new techniques, and special resources which are now being debated, developed, and tested must stem from a basic change in attitude. When we talk of the 'supports' that have to be provided to the handicapped child in the mainstream, our starting point *has* to be our genuine conviction that every child is worthy of the best we can give . . . We have to really mean it when we say that to be different from the 'norm' is not just okay — it's what being human is all about."

— winter report, Closer Look, National Information
Center for the Handicapped, 1974

ONE AFTERNOON after the kids left, Jerry Bigelow, Maggie, and Mr. Dillard stood on the playground, talking about the idea of trying to take some of the special education children out of the segregated situations. The sun reflected on the river below the school, and Jerry shaded his eyes as he spoke. "A few of them would make it with no trouble," Jerry speculated, "but I think most of them would need some extra help for a while anyhow, maybe a half-hour, an hour a day. Of course, a lot of that would depend on which regular classroom teacher they got placed with . . ."

"And how disruptive they are," added Dillard with a half smile and a sharp eye on Maggie's face. "I'll bet Miss Callahan here's getting ready to tell us that you can't keep a child in a class for the retarded because he's too noisy or wreaks havoc. Weren't you?" He looked very serious, and Maggie turned a little red.

"Now Miss Callahan," Dillard concluded, a twinkle in his eye. "You know I'm beginning to see some sense in this mainstreaming idea, but I want you to tell me how I'm going to convince our Mr. Fairfield, who already has twenty-six kids and a renowned short temper, that he ought to take in a few of these children who have been short-changed, as it were, by their school experience. Mr. Fairfield, as you may know, isn't the most flexible good soul in this school as far as classroom approach goes."

Before Maggie could open her mouth, Dillard added, "And don't tell me that the basic problem is that he has twenty-six kids to begin with. That's true enough, but what do I do about it *now*?"

Jerry and Maggie described different possible ways to set up a mainstreaming program for kids like those in Jerry's class. Then they talked about ways of getting Fairfield involved gradually and diplomatically, and then they conceded that he still might not want to do it.

"Sure," Maggie said, "mainstreaming isn't any magic trick to guarantee that every kid will get better if he's just put back in a regular classroom. There are some teachers who just won't want to see it happen, so they can damn well make sure the children have a poor experience with it. I guess you've got to start with basic willingness to give it a try, to make it worth going through some initial hassle."

"And are you going to tell me how I can get Mr. Fairfield to view it that way?" Dillard wanted to know. "Now look here, Maggie and Jerry, imagine two teachers in the process of changing their classroom plans for mainstreaming. If I'd ask one of them, 'What are you doing?' he'd say, 'I have to do all this blankety-blank work because they're putting those retarded kids into our rooms.' The second one might well come out with something to the effect that she's helping build a society in which people aren't rejected because they're different or have problems. Now, that's a pretty wide spread in perspective on the same activity. How do I get teacher number one to see things the way teacher number two does?"

"I don't know for sure, but better think about that when you hire teacher number three," answered Jerry.

"Not immediately helpful, Bigelow," said Dillard. "See, basically, to make this thing work, we'd need to give some regular class teachers a lot of support," Dillard concluded, getting up to go home. "I'm not willing to just dump kids back in, and the Lord knows, I don't want teachers fighting among themselves because everybody's short of resources. So you have to figure out some way to do it with the particular people we have without any feathers flying." He winked at Maggie. "We want to keep that federal money too, remember."

This kind of conversation could be heard in many school systems over the past few years. Mainstreaming has sometimes been described as a movement teetering in the balance. On one side, tremendous potential for improvement of entire systems and, on the other, the fear that many children will be as ignored or humiliated in the regular classrooms as they often had been in self-contained. There's no getting away from the fact that the mainstreaming movement aims at fundamental change or that much of its success depends on the extent to which people believe in it. And, to a greater extent, the degree to which adults are willing to work together.

Mainstreaming has met great success in some schools and has run into difficulty in others. Those programs that are running most smoothly inevitably seem to have an administrative staff that takes the needs and differences of the teachers into account. The common difficulties that do arise between a special education resource teacher and a regular classroom teacher are much like those Maggie had been encountering with the Copper County teachers as supervisor. All the people involved in a situation can have very good intentions, but the reality of one professional coming in to "help" another creates delicate diplomatic and ego problems. Like Maggie, many resource teachers have been unpleasantly surprised to receive lukewarm or cold receptions to their helpful efforts, until trust is built up.

A good resource teacher needs to think through all those problems in advance. In 1976, Whyla Beman, an experienced resource teacher at Belt Junior High School in Wheaton, Maryland, passed on some good advice about the communication process between teachers in a mainstreaming situation. "When mainstreaming programs are set up as an alternative to self-contained special classes," she said, "they're often set up with the assumption that teachers are automatically going to be willing to work together. That's very seldom true. We're people, and so a lot of time and effort often have to be expended getting to the point where we can work together productively. A resource teacher ought to be prepared for that, because it's the first big part of the job.

"The first year's usually the hardest. Teachers naturally feel threatened when somebody comes in who's supposed to 'help' them. After all, they don't know who that person is, and lots of teachers have never thought of special ed in any sense other than sending kids out. I've been here for five years. There are teachers I tried to approach during the first year or so — or who tried to approach me — and we didn't get very far, because it took a while for us to understand where the other was coming from to be able to talk about what was happening with the child without threatening each other. Saying, 'We'll work together to change the child's program where necessary' is a whole lot different than 'I'll take the child off your hands for so many hours a day.' And saying 'I need help' can be very different from 'I'm willing to sit down and really look at this child's program.' Or even more difficult, 'I'm willing to look at what I'm doing in relation to this child.' We both feel vulnerable and have to get past that barrier. Both resource teacher and classroom teacher need to be able to talk about what isn't working too well for them without embarrassment. You need to know the other person isn't going to put you down.

"A lot of resource teachers are young, and that adds another delicacy to effective working relations with older teachers who've been around a long time. One thing that makes it hard is the implication that the resource teacher is there as some kind of expert who necessarily knows better. So what I say is 'I have something I'm good at, and you have something you're good at. So let's get together, because I can't do it by myself, and you've asked for help, so obviously you feel you can't do it by yourself.' It takes a while to really get that working, because teachers are so used to people coming into their class as experts, you know, sitting there, not saying anything, taking notes and leaving. Maybe they're looking down their nose or even going to go report to the principal or something. By the way, that's something I *don't* do, take notes in someone's classroom.

"I want things to be on an equal basis. I have something to offer, but I sure need that teacher's help and commitment, and I understand that the teacher needs to know I can be trusted and that working with me will be productive. The principal's help and commitment is essential too.

"Now, in my fifth year at the school, relationships have been established so I can go in and out of classrooms more easily, and we can work with the total staff. But building up trust and keeping personal relationships good are still an essential part of this job. We learn a lot by the process, and that's never going to change, although, in time, it'll be a lot easier if all teachers come out of teacher-training expecting this kind of working relationship."

Although Copper County hadn't started mainstreaming that year, Maggie had been working with Jerry Bigelow in pretty much the same way a special ed resource teacher might work with a regular classroom teacher. She worked with Pickle Krebbs in a similar way. (If she had been a resource teacher at Stockdale, Pickle would have come to the "resource room" periodically to work with her. As it was, they worked at home. The situation with Maggie, Anita, his teacher, and Pickle was simple compared with the situations many real resource teachers face every day, because there was no need to deal with such problems as school schedules and interruptions. Furthermore, Maggie and Anita already trusted each other, so there was no professional jealousy or adult communication problem. This situation provides a good example of how a child, a resource teacher, and a regular classroom teacher might work together.)

The working arrangement really began the day Maggie took Pickle and Jenny up Bald Mountain. A week or so later, Pickle asked Maggie, "You know that detective stuff you were talking about? What happens when you do that?"

"Well, I try to find out how a person sees and hears things, for one thing," she told him. "For instance, I try to find the reasons why it's hard for him to learn to read. You know — maybe he doesn't see the same thing other kids see when he looks at a word."

"Whaddya mean?" Pickle was fidgeting a lot, shifting from one foot to another. He had a homemade slingshot and kept twanging the rubber band.

"Well, some people see words backwards, for instance. They look at c-a-t and see t-a-c. Or may they start reading at the wrong end of a line of print." She got a book and showed him what she meant. Pickle raised his eyebrows, as if he had made a connection. "And lots of people get mixed up if there are too many words on a page. They have trouble keeping their place because their eyes keep seeing all those other words at the same time . . . so if something like that turns up, you can do certain things to train the kid's eyes to see in a way that will let him read."

There was a long silence while she took the dishes out of the drainer and put them away. "You interested in seeing how it can be done?" she asked finally.

"Might be," he said, aiming the slingshot at the door. And that was it. In a disinterested way, Maggie told Pickle that she'd be willing to show him how the investigation worked if he'd come back after dinner. It was good, she felt, for him to take the next step, to actually decide to transport his body there.

He came back. Although both of them knew that his reading problems were the reason he had come, they still kept pretending that Maggie was just showing him how she worked with other kids. After the first few sessions, this pretense could be dropped without comment, but to get himself involved with minimum discomfort,

Pickle had to feel that he could back out without losing face. After the first few sessions, he began to see them as just taking advantage of a chance to do something about a problem. "Like going to the doctor, right?"

"Right." But they still didn't work when the other kids were around.

That habit of saying "right?" at the end of a sentence meant something, Maggie thought. The only time she heard him do it was when he was doing something that involved reading. Otherwise, he didn't seem to question his own statements much.

During the first session, Pickle didn't have to deal with any written words. They worked with pictures and objects and played games that seemingly had nothing to do with reading. Throughout their working time in the upcoming months, whenever words made Pickle uptight, Maggie would change the subject.

Working with the material Anita had given her — "I *know* he's familiar with these words" — Maggie found that Pickle had two major areas of difficulty. First, he had a lot of trouble with figure-ground discrimination. This meant it was hard for him to see one detail among many. He could read the sentence, "The boy likes to play ball" with no difficulty when it was written by itself on a piece of paper but when it was included in the context of a printed page, he had trouble with it. He kept skipping words or even skipping from one line of print to another. Maggie discovered this after noticing that he had trouble picking small objects from pictures that included many objects. He also slid his finger along the page as he read, moving from word to word, stabbing each with his finger as if it might move if he didn't keep it pinned down.

It turned out that Pickle also had a lot of trouble with visual discrimination. In that respect, he was no different from a large number of children in the school system, special ed and regular. Shown a picture of a triangular-shaped tree, he had trouble matching it with an identical tree, pictured with trees of other shapes. He said that a picture of a round-faced woman with long dark hair was identical to a picture of a woman with long dark hair and a long thin face. He said that Φ was identical to ϕ. To a much lesser degree, he had some difficulty in choosing the longest stick from a pile of varying lengths. But he had no trouble whatsoever with volume or depth perception. No spilling while pouring, no trouble stopping his finger a fraction of an inch before touching a pane of glass. About average motor coordination.

His auditory receivers were well tuned. He had no trouble hearing what Maggie was saying, even when she turned the radio up loud, scraped a chair, and banged a spoon while talking. He was used to that. This was the auditory counterpart of figure-ground discrimination, where he had so much trouble. His ears could do what his eyes couldn't.

When Maggie left spoken sentences unfinished or left out words, he still knew what she meant. This was not true when words were left out of sentences on the printed page. He often had to read them aloud to catch the sense. If Maggie showed him a list of five numbers, he couldn't repeat them back unless he said them out loud while he was looking at them. Though he floundered with visual problems, he shone with their auditory counterparts.

It wasn't surprising to find that Pickle read out loud to himself when he was asked to read silently. "He doesn't even know he's doing it half the time," Anita told Maggie. "If I try to make him stop, he just starts up again in a few minutes."

Anita was adjusting Pickle's classroom program in accordance with Maggie's findings and suggestions. The adults worked in two directions: building up Pickle's weak visual areas and taking advantage of his strong points. He sat down with them every week for a conference, sometimes came up with good ideas himself, and enjoyed being involved in the whys, wherefores, and adjustments in his own program.

He began waiting for Maggie after school, bouncing a ball off the side of the house. The program was set up so that he could keep track of his own progress, repeating certain exercises at regular intervals. He thought of it as "racing myself," since he could see the evidence of his progress, which seemed to add a lot to his continued motivation.

He usually worked with Maggie for about a half-hour. At first, they made all kinds of concrete helpers. Sandpaper symbols, for instance: triangles, squares, lines. Pickle would feel them and match them by touch, then pick them out of a bag, only taking out those he could identify. Then he would do it by sight. This was a build-up to working with letters.

They also played a game called Monkey See. Maggie would take a sandpaper line, for instance, and place it on the right side of a sandpaper circle. Pickle, sitting beside her, would do the same. Maggie would put the line under the circle, and Pickle would duplicate this with his own line and circle. If Maggie could "fool" him, she'd get a point. After she got three points, they'd switch, and she would duplicate his constructions. She deliberately made mistakes, and he knew it. His job was to catch them. To make the game harder, they'd speed up, allowing less and less time for duplication, but always keeping the constructions within his grasp. The next step was to discard the sandpaper and begin drawing the symbols. Moving toward the abstract, she'd draw a symbol and he'd copy. Finally, they'd move on to the letters of the alphabet.

What Pickle *could* do was at least as important, academically and psychologically, as what he couldn't do. Taking advantage of his well-developed coordination, for instance, they got some masking tape and made big symbols and letters on the floor. Pickle would walk over them with his eyes open, then try to see if he could do it barefoot and blindfolded. If he was walking on a "B," he had to remember which side the "circle" was on. They traced letters on each other's palms with pencil erasers and guessed what they were — anything to make Pickle more aware of the distinctions between different shapes and letters. "You've got to get it into the muscles," one of Maggie's favorite teachers had liked to say. That's what they were trying to do.

They made cardboard letters and developed a game in which she would set out all the letters but flip ten of them over backwards. Pickle's job was to right all the backwards letters as quickly as he could. He was trying to break the Pickle World Record for Letter Flipping. They made playing cards with letters and words on them, and played Fish and Old Maid. Every now and then, they'd change the letters and words on the cards.

As identification of letters became easier for Pickle, he began to respond to phonics. A puppet named Lovejoy suddenly turned out to be very useful. Pickle liked to play with Lovejoy as much as he did any of the kids. Some days, when Pickle was feeling insecure, Lovejoy could often do what Pickle could not. What was threatening for Pickle was entirely possible for Lovejoy. If Lovejoy made a mistake, it was Lovejoy's mistake, not Pickle's. Lovejoy wasn't afraid to be wrong.

One afternoon, Pickle came up with a very unusual idea. "Want to hear what a B sounds like?" he asked. He made a noise that sounded as if something were falling rapidly, followed by a noise like a circle. The noise was an obvious B. "Now, do ya wanta hear what a D sounds like?" He reversed the process, making the circle sound first, then dropping the line. Maggie burst out laughing. It was the first time Pickle had shown solid awareness of the difference between those two letters. Anita came in to admire his invention. "It just came into my mind this morning!" He beamed.

Pickle developed noises for letters that dropped below the line, letters and lines that went off at an angle, letters that curved. His noises became a secret code, and the game was a natural for him. At the height of the noisemaking, very weird sounds were coming out of the kitchen. Pickle got into spells when he refused to communicate in any other way.

"Now, you're starting to bug me!" Anita told him. "I'm not as good at this sound business as you are." Afterward, she wondered if he felt equally lost when he couldn't read the sentences she'd written on the blackboard. He wasn't as good at that visual business as she was.

It was firmly understood between Pickle and Maggie that if he didn't feel like having a session, he didn't come. And if he became very anxious during a session, that was the end. She'd switch to an entirely different subject, like beehives, to end the session positively.

Rule number one while working with a child like Pickle was Don't Overload. Don't take him to the water fountain and turn on the fire hose. Especially in the beginning stages. As they got used to working together, when Pickle began to fidget, Maggie would have to make a delicate decision. Did he need encouragement or was he truly frustrated? Once again, Pickle simplified matters. She told him frankly that it would be very helpful if he'd just look inside and let her know how he was feeling. They talked about frustration and recalled times when they both had felt frustrated.

Pickle took to peering down the neck of his T-shirt when she asked if he was feeling frustrated. "I just looked, and there's frustration in there," he would say. Other times, he would tell her matter-of-factly, "I need a push." Then they got to the point where she could ask him, "Do you need a push from me, or can you give it to yourself?"

It wasn't easy, by any means. Like so many children with similar problems, Pickle found his new success somewhat unsettling at times. A particularly good day or series of days could be followed by a particularly disruptive or disinterested day. There would be days when he would seem to have totally forgotten everything and days when he would flip over every letter on the table and throw the cards on the floor.

He had a habit at those times of attributing his frustration and uneasiness to the nearest adult. His blue eyes would go flat, and he was temporarily convinced that all adults were simply trying to push him around for some evil purpose.

Without the adjustments that Anita was making in Pickle's classroom work, the activities Maggie and Pickle did in the kitchen would have had a much more limited effect. Many of the changes Anita was making centered around figure-ground discrimination. A child with Pickle's kind of visual problem might be thrown for a loss when asked to copy from the board, for instance. The more material on the page or board, the more confused he gets. *Rows* of math problems are also likely to be frustrating, even if the math itself is no problem. When copying from a book, the child may copy part of one problem, then switch to another.

"I used to think Pickle was just being careless or smart-alecky when he'd do that," Anita said, batting herself on the head. "He'd even write numbers on top of each other, and we've been making him copy those papers over all year." She wondered if the appearance of his papers reflected the way he was seeing the printed matter he had been copying.

As Pickle's teacher, Anita began saying directions out loud, as well as writing them on the board. She had her aide make a point of checking Pickle's understanding of written directions. She also shortened his copying assignments and made some use of a tape recorder. The point, she decided, was that he grasp the concept, not that he produce a lot of written work.

Since Pickle's frustration point was considerably lower than many of his classmates', Anita encouraged him to keep several projects in his desk, including some of those he had worked on with Maggie. "If you start to get really frustrated," she told him, "work on something else, then come back to it." After some dickering with the principal, she got permission for Pickle to run around the playground when he felt that he was about to blow his stack.

She made adjustments to help him build up eye-hand coordination. Since Pickle's words also frequently ended up on top of each other, Anita got him to write in "telegrams." (A friend had sent her a telegram a month or so earlier, and he had been fascinated by it.) Pickle's telegrams were mimeographed sheets filled with word-sized boxes in rows, like this:

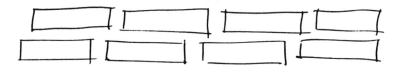

They were designed to help him isolate each word, to develop the habit of seeing each word in relation to the other words in the sentence.

Anita made sure that Pickle always had an adequate supply of telegrams. The first week after he began using them, she came home elated. "It isn't just the improvement in his work," she said. "We also don't have to go through so many of those song and dance routines he used to put on when he had to write something down."

Other children in Anita's class began to request the telegram sheets. "And it's helping some of them," she said thoughtfully.

"You know, since we've been working with Pickle, I've noticed similar problems in other kids in the class, and I feel better able to deal with them. So all this work isn't helping just Pickle."

It's worth repeating that Pickle's situation was very easy compared to what might have happened among three strangers in a school situation, or among three people who didn't trust each other so well. Many of the usual roadblocks never appeared.

In 1975, the New York State Education Department published an "occasional paper" from the commissioner of education called "Mainstreaming: Idea and Reality." The paper emphasized that there is no one right way to mainstream, and that mainstreaming means different things for different children. It does *not* mean that all handicapped children should be placed in a regular classroom. For very severely handicapped children, for instance, mainstreaming might amount to field trips or eating with nonhandicapped children. A less severely handicapped child might be able to participate in special school programs or art and music classes. As the handicaps become less severe, the possibilities for different mainstreaming arrangements expand, depending on the child. The goal is to help children become involved in normal society, to the maximum extent possible and appropriate for each individual child.

The paper summarized the case for mainstreaming as follows: ". . . educators are showing an increased interest in programs that encourage the education of handicapped and nonhandicapped children together. There are a number of reasons for this preference. First, studies done of the effectiveness of special class vs. regular class placement have failed to reveal any conclusive results. Secondly, many educators are concerned about civil rights issues in school districts with high enrollments of handicapped children in separate facilities. Also, the benefits to the handicapped children of contact with nonhandicapped children are increasingly evident. Studies show dramatic improvements in coping and in interpersonal relationships for children in mainstreamed settings. Finally, many educators are convinced that the nonhandicapped child makes important gains in understanding and values by having the opportunity to grow up with handicapped children. Each of these reasons for mainstreaming underlies the value and importance of this trend in education."*

Many authorities also believe that segregation of handicapped children from nonhandicapped children has had a negative effect on the whole society, since children form values and impressions in school about life that often remain with them all their lives. In this respect, special education mainstreaming is especially important to physically handicapped people of all ages. Since most people, until recently, have grown up with little contact with blind, deaf, or orthopedically handicapped people, many physically handicapped people have found that the inappropriate reactions of nonhandicapped people make it difficult for them to achieve natural and maximum participation in the adult society. Such reactions are often due to lack of familiarity with handicapped people in general.

Four adult handicapped people discussed this problem for *The Exceptional Parent* magazine in 1973. Evelyn, who was born with cerebral palsy, mentioned the frequent assumption that a physically handicapped person is also mentally handicapped. "Just coming here," she commented, "I was with someone getting on the airplane at the airport. And the man who was going to help me on the plane asked the person I was with, 'Can she walk?' Behind my back, he went like this, making walking motions with his fingers. He thought I didn't see what was going on or that I was too stupid to know what was really happening."

During the same interview, Dennis, a blind college student, provided another everyday example: "In a restaurant, eye contact has to be established between the waitress and the customer before the waitress will say something. So a lot of times, I'll go in, especially with another person, we will sit down, and the waitress will come up and say, 'What does *he* want?' And I'll say, 'I'd like a hamburger.' And then she'll look over at the guy again and say, 'What does *he* want to drink?' And I'll say, 'I'll take a Coke.' And she'll look back at the other guy and say, 'Does *he* want any dessert?' I just can't believe

*See pp. 341–42 for additional material from this paper.

it, but that happens pretty often. I don't think it's any real cruelty on the part of the waitress. I don't think she knows how to approach it all."

Strong as the case is for mainstreaming, it would be a mistake to present advantages without talking about the problems. Though it is now widely agreed that each child should be going to school in as near-to-normal a situation as is appropriate, people still frequently disagree on important practical questions like "How do you do it?" "What's appropriate for this child?" and "How should responsibility be divided between the special and regular teachers?"

Many people have also expressed fears that mainstreaming will be abused in some places, unless efforts are made to make the general system more flexible. These are still the children who have traditionally come last in the school system pecking order. Special needs children could simply be returned to regular classrooms with no attempt to provide adequate support services. In that case, mainstreaming could become another means of denying children the specialized attention that many of them do need. Particularly good teachers should be placed in the resource "support" positions in the regular schools, for instance, to assist regular classroom teachers with any problems.

The Bureau of Education for the Handicapped conducted a widescale research project on mainstreaming entitled Project PRIME (Programmed Re-Entry into Mainstream Education). Headed by Martin Kaufman and researched in the early seventies, PRIME involved approximately 2000 students, 20 researchers, and 520 observers. "The results of the project make it very clear that the problems of implementation of mainstreaming are much more complex than most people originally anticipated," Kaufman observed. "Where children are not getting the kind of programs they need, we have often found that school people have been defining mainstreaming in terms of time blocks — 'Sally is 60% mainstreamed' — rather than what goes on during those time blocks. We also found that lack of communication and cooperation between special ed teacher and regular classroom teacher cut down on the effectiveness of the child's program, since under such circumstances, it often isn't clear who is responsible for the child's total program.

"Among other things, PRIME makes it clear that effective mainstreaming can't be accomplished simply by placing a child in a regular classroom for part of the day and in a resource room for the rest. What's going on while he's in both places is what counts."

Similar reports from many parts of the country support Kaufman's statement. A Massachusetts high school teacher tells about the severely retarded boy who was assigned to a "buddy" who shepherded him from class to class, apparently under the mistaken belief that mainstreaming means every child should be in the regular classroom. On the other extreme, a Kentucky special ed teacher reports with frustration that she has eight or nine children who could easily spend most of the day in a regular classroom, "but the principal won't let us arrange it, because he says it would mess up the schedules. He lets them eat lunch and have music with the other kids and reports it as mainstreaming." An Indiana teacher tells of the well-equipped special school in her district that was largely disbanded after the state urged a "policy" of mainstreaming. "It would have been great if they'd planned it all out, but they just put the kids in regular classrooms without making any effort to pick teachers who were sympathetic to the idea, or to help the teachers carry over the children's program, and, of course, a lot of children really got confused and were suffering from it. When this sort of thing happens, people are likely to blame the idea of mainstreaming, rather than the way it was carried out."*

For one of his courses, Jerry Bigelow was reading accounts of successful mainstreaming projects. "So I know it's being done well in a lot of places," he told Maggie. "I read about what people are doing, and my head's filled with ideas." Jerry had daydreams about how it could be some day for kids like those in his class. "I see myself as a resource teacher in the main building, and each of those kids might come to me for an hour a day, or every other day, or whatever they needed. We'd zero in on their specific problem, and

*See pp. 343–46 for descriptions of a variety of approaches to mainstreaming.

then I'd work with the regular classroom teacher. There'd be lots of materials available, of course, and I'd be able to share them with the regular teachers. And the school systems would arrange workshops on individualizing instruction for all of us." He swung his feet off his desk and leaned forward on his elbows. "You know, after a few years of adjustment, I'm sure mainstreaming would get easier and easier. Teachers would be feeling a lot more comfortable with the whole thing by then. You know — as people learned new ways to individualize instruction, there'd be better programs all through the school, and you'd eventually have less and less kids ending up with the kind of heartache mine have had to go through."

Jerry sat quietly for a few seconds, looking out the window. "And God knows, we wouldn't have this thing of stigmatizing and seg-regating most of the low-income kids anymore . . . Sheila, Chet, anyone who talks or walks funny . . ." He smiled wryly. "My own boy is going into first grade next year, and I don't want him coming home and telling me in effect that people who are different or poor ought to be sent somewhere else. That's not the way I want him to grow up seeing life."

Maggie didn't say anything. "Guess I'm getting into a little pie in the sky, huh?" Jerry asked. "I know that the number of kids in the regular classrooms is high already and that there are teachers who would want convincing before they'd give it a try. I don't expect that it would come out as beautiful as I was painting it, but even if it didn't, it could still be better than what we're doing now. At least we'd be trying to do something about the whole system, instead of putting the kids somewhere else and saying it was their fault. Damn, there's so much at stake."

Bigelow talked about some of the mainstreaming methods he had read about. "But I also think it's just as important, when you start thinking about mainstreaming in your own school, to take into account how Mrs. Jones enjoys having kids move around the classroom, and Mrs. Brown doesn't. Personal preferences. Seems you'd have to start where people were at, wouldn't you?"

Maggie told him Harry's theory about "the random element" and why things happen as they do. "Those are really important to pick up on," she agreed. "Otherwise, you could have a kid like Chet getting left in the dust because Mrs. Hershaw and Mrs. Davis had a falling out at church last year and don't like to work on the same kid's program together. Or maybe Mrs. Garvin feels she needs some math materials, but didn't get any."

"Well," Jerry concluded, "it seems that, if a good percentage of the teachers in a school got to the point where they were determined to give it a try, we'd be halfway there. All those other factors would be a lot easier to work out."

"How would you get most people to see it that way, in this school for instance?"

Bigelow looked as though he had too many words in his mouth, but all he said was "Well, I've come to feel that way by getting to know these kids, as people. Maybe the same thing would work for others. But I think there's probably more to it than that."

19. Severely Handicapped Children and Comprehensive Planning

> "The special educator has traditionally placed the majority of services in the middle of the continuum, or range, of handicapping conditions. The responsibility for educating the severely handicapped has been left to others or to no one . . ."
>
> — *Mainstream Special Education: Issues and Perspectives in Urban Centers*,
> edited by Philip H. Mann, 1974

THE INCLUSION of programs for severely handicapped children in the public schools is another different aspect of "mainstreaming" or "least restrictive alternative." The overall focus of special education is shifting toward these children. As years go by, increasing attention and resources within special education will be paid to severely and multiply handicapped children, while, at the same time, general systems will hopefully be increasing capacity to help children with "minimal" problems in the general education programs, through mainstreaming. So, in large part for economic reasons, the entry of severely handicapped children into the schools will most likely accelerate the mainstreaming movement for children labeled "minimally handicapped."

Most special educators agree that this is as it should be. In the early seventies, the Council for Exceptional Children estimated that at least one million handicapped children were legally excluded from a public education on the allegation that they were "ineducable." Since special education was originally created for children with severe handicaps, and since the children's parents have been forced to make do as best they can, correcting this situation has been regarded by the courts and the federal government as a number-one priority.

The first major test of the exclusion laws occurred in Pennsylvania in 1971. The Pennsylvania Association for Retarded Children sued the state on behalf of fourteen severely retarded children who had been turned down by the schools. The children's lawyers established the following: all mentally retarded children can learn through appropriate education programs, and there is no such thing as "ineducable." For some children, learning to feed themselves is as much education as learning algebra is for others. It just means shifting one's ideas about what constitutes education. Furthermore, testimony established the fact that the sooner in life the children can get help, the greater their chances will be of correcting serious disabilities or learning new skills.

The need for cooperation among agencies is greater than ever. Some agencies have much more experience with the severely handicapped than the public schools do. A whole range of agencies deal with handicapped children or children who are having problems. There are departments of mental health, child welfare departments, social work agencies, developmental disabilities, Head Start, vocational education, vocational rehabilitation, agencies like Crippled Children's Hospitals and Easter Seals, the advocacy groups for the different handicapping conditions, institutions, private schools, family counseling services, the Office for Child Development, public health services, agencies dealing with minors in legal trouble, drug abuse programs, and many other local variations. Each one has at its disposal certain resources and expertise, which — put together — could give an education system a real chance to work effectively with many degrees of handicapping conditions.

The main problem now is getting agencies to work together and with the schools. "People in agencies inevitably get into a turfsmanship kind of mind-set," says Wayne Largent of the Bureau of Education for the Handicapped, "where 'you're not going to get over on my area' and 'you stay within the confines of your responsibility and don't get over in mine.'"

"You can't always just go knock on the door of some agency and say, 'Hey, we've got to cooperate,'" remarked another BEH official. "There has to be either some outside mechanism or a working relationship that gets the ball rolling. Often this can be most effectively accomplished when so-and-so from Agency A knows and gets along with so-and-so from Agency B. There's already a personal relationship going. So very often, the whole program can make or break on that one factor. Without the good working relationship, bureaucracy can take over."

Yet, the benefits of coordinated efforts are becoming increasingly obvious. In an eight-state region in the southeastern United States, for instance, Head Start, special education, developmental disabilities, and the universities have all been pulled together by the Outreach early childhood project from Chapel Hill, North Carolina. They have pooled resources to produce one of the best early childhood efforts in the country. "This kind of thing is so rare at this point," commented Jane DeWeerd of the Bureau of Education for the Handicapped in 1975. "The good feeling and growth that have come out of it have been just tremendous, and it looks like we'll be seeing much more of this sort of thing in the future."

Ms. DeWeerd's prediction is a pretty safe bet, since some aspects of the new laws are promoting this kind of cooperation. As a requirement for receiving federal funds for special education beginning in 1975, each state had to begin pulling together all the agencies it felt could contribute to a total range of services for handicapped children. This process is called comprehensive planning.

HEW also told those agencies receiving federal funds that they wouldn't get their money unless they cooperated with comprehensive planning. Despite much initial apprehension, some states that plunged in wholeheartedly have reported happy results. Kentucky officials, for instance, report that the whole sit-down-together has turned out to be a real plus for everybody involved. "They really are pleased with it," said Wayne Largent of BEH. "They say they're finally really getting to know each other. It's the kind of situation where people suddenly say, 'Oh! So *that's* what you're doing! Well, here's what we've got over here, and look, if we'd put them together, we could . . .' "

Comprehensive planning has unlimited possibilities. It's already generally known that certain agencies work with children with special needs. But, beyond that, the "comprehensive planning" structure also gives the schools a chance to draw on other resources that can help with important needs in a child's life which the schools don't ordinarily reach. For instance, nutrition — what a child is eating — can make an incredible difference in the way a child learns and deals with school. If serious financial and nutritional problems are interfering with the child's ability to concentrate or enjoy, for instance, the best academic program isn't going to touch the root of the problem. In this case, under comprehensive planning, a public health worker might naturally connect the family with as seemingly unconnected a program as the Women, Infants and Children (WIC) food program run by the Department of Agriculture. A system of comprehensive planning should make it much more likely that such connections will be made.

"The benefits to the schools and the children of this kind of cooperation don't have much limit," continued Largent. "But local people don't have to wait for the state people to get their ducks in a row. They can go ahead and do their own comprehensive planning on the local level, to pull everything available together. The sooner it happens, the better."

In Copper County, while all these changes were being planned on state and federal levels, approximately thirty county students were on "homebound instruction" or were kept at the Day Care Center. Not all these students were severely handicapped, but informal reports of cases throughout the county indicated that a fair number of handicapped children were kept at home. If the special ed kids in school were the rejects of the regular system, the children out of school were the rejects of special education.

The Day Care Center in Copper County was administered by the Mental Health Department, which was not under the jurisdiction of the school board or Mr. Birdwell. On Maggie's first visit, some of the dozen or so children were taking naps on canvas cots in an otherwise bare room. One of them, a very pale boy with a burr haircut, lifted his head to look at her.

"Awful bad home conditions, some of these children have," commented the director, a warm, elderly lady named Mrs. Scarrola. "They don't get adequate nourishment at home, and it affects the way they are when they're here. That one tells me more often than you'd like to think that he had Rice Krispies, nothing else, for dinner."

The program had very limited resources: no blocks, physical

exercise equipment, very few toys. As Mrs. Scarrola showed Maggie around, a heavyset boy with a lagging tongue followed them. He didn't say anything, but he did show Maggie a couple of big marbles he had in his pocket.

"He can talk a little," commented the director, "but he hardly ever does."

A couple of other boys were playing with blocks on the linoleum floor. "You ain't agonna pull that 'un out without all of 'em falling down," said one boy, slurring his words badly. The other didn't say anything. He just pulled the block out and the others didn't fall.

Most of the children looked to be at least eight years old. "Why don't these children go to school?" Maggie asked curiously.

"Most of them, their cases are too bad," the director said, shaking her head.

By the time Maggie left, the little boy who ate Rice Krispies for dinner was up and walking around. Maggie was on her way to the Davidson Diner for lunch to eat some liver.

Often when Maggie felt frazzled, she'd go down to the diner and eat liver and onions. With its high nutritional value, that meal seemed to help her rally and keep going. After visiting the Day Care Center, Maggie couldn't help but have thoughts like, "If I get out of sorts and lose effectiveness when I don't eat right, how much more are these children's whole lives affected when they rarely get the nutrition they need?" And, "If that child keeps eating on the order of Rice Krispies for dinner, it's not likely that he'll be prepared to deal well with something like school. And if he can't cope because he's malnourished, how appropriate will it be to label him retarded and try and solve his difficulties by concentrating on spelling, reading, and math?"

Maggie had gone to visit the Day Care Center that day because there had been talk of putting Malcolm Jordan there. Malcolm was a child who could be greatly assisted by the new law, as one of the few severely handicapped children enrolled in school. At age nine, he had not yet developed coherent speech and had very poor muscular control. In his more alert periods, he recognized the function of common objects like keys but had a lot of difficulty putting a key in a lock. He couldn't handle number concepts greater than two. In his most confused periods, he wouldn't respond to his own name. One reason Mrs. Quigley wanted to send Malcolm to the Day Care Center was his temper tantrums. When he sat on the floor yelling in frustration, she was at a loss.

Malcolm couldn't adjust to Mrs. Quigley's classroom activities. Everything was too hard for him. He didn't know how to copy from the board, do math, or read. He didn't color neatly and wouldn't stay in his seat. Malcolm was frustrated. He failed at everything. Mrs. Quigley's class just wasn't an appropriate program for him.

There was so much Malcolm could have been learning. Maggie had seen him after school, sorting objects into piles at the junkyard. If he could do that, he could learn other skills. Education for Malcolm could mean improving his muscular and emotional control through a well-structured program of physical activities of gradually increased difficulty. Strengthening his memory would be education for him, as would learning to handle simple tools to discriminate more accurately among differing quantities, distances, and thicknesses. Malcolm could learn to finish projects, to organize his belongings, to get around town with reasonable efficiency, and much more that would be invaluable to him later and would undoubtedly make him a better citizen of his community.

Education for Malcolm couldn't be books, paper, and pencil, certainly not at the beginning. His progress would be very slow, and there would be many setbacks and emotional scenes. The greatness of his achievements couldn't be measured against that of other children. The new laws, if properly funded, will eventually make it easy for schools to provide special education programs for children like Malcolm who have formerly had makeshift arrangements at best.

Annie Jones was another Copper County child who would benefit by such laws. Annie was in a different type of situation: she had been placed on homebound instruction, an arrangement whereby the child stays at home and a teacher on wheels comes to her house two or three times a week. The teacher, who usually stays about an hour, can be an invaluable service to students who are laid up and literally unable to come to school. However, homebound instruction can also be a means of excluding other children from school.

Each of the twenty-some students on homebound instruction in Copper County had a doctor's recommendation specifying a medical problem. There was a psychological report from the Veteran's Hospital in Annie's folder that said she was mongoloid, incapable of speech and in need of lifelong assistance to perform basic functions. Annie's mother, continued the report, was prone to irrationality and would not accept plain evidence of her daughter's condition. Maggie read the report after Miss Foster, Annie's homebound teacher, asked her to come along to Annie's house. "We need some fresh ideas," Miss Foster said.

They stopped to see a couple of other kids before they got to Annie's. The first was a ten-year-old boy on an isolated farm near Goshen. This child had only a small percentage of his vision. Miss Foster appeared two times a week, sometimes carrying books with giant-size print, which he read. That was school for him. He wasn't actually allowed to go to school because "he would have trouble making his way around." It was unclear how the homebound arrangement was going to help him make his way around in later life.

Next they went to see a young girl named Darla, who had broken both her legs when she fell over a sawhorse. Homebound was the best possible solution for her. Miss Foster picked up Darla's lessons from her teacher, and they went over them together.

Annie Jones lived way up on Bald Mountain. As they drove to her house, Miss Foster explained that Annie's optometrist had recently discovered that Annie had very bad eyesight. "Her little face has always been squinched up," she said heatedly, "and she didn't seem to be able to relate to her surroundings. That's why she was always bumping into things. She's been wearing increasingly stronger glasses for three months to build up her eye muscles, and she's stopped squinting enough to let some beautiful brown eyes peep through."

Annie's house was balanced on the top of a steep hill. As they parked down below, a very loud voice yelled: "M'Fosta!" A small figure standing on the porch above banged a stick on the railing and waved vigorously. "C'mon e'bo'y! M'Fosta here!"

"This kid is incapable of speech?"

"You just wait," promised Miss Foster. "You ain't seen nothing, lady. This is one spunky kid!"

They didn't have to wait long. Within ten minutes after they came in the door, Annie, waving a battered old ukulele, had organized them all — her sister, her mother, Miss Foster, and Maggie — into what she called "Th' Jo'y Cass So." After a few rounds of Johnny Cash, Miss Foster, who had sung as Merle Haggard, asked Annie to go to her room and bring out her blocks, pattern cards, and blue truck. She brought all three without hesitation. Miss Foster showed Annie some alphabet cards, all of which she identified readily.

"Annie learned all those letters in the last month." Miss Foster beamed. "Soon as she was able to see them clearly, she learned them!"

They spent the next hour happily fishing around for ways to hook into Annie's fascination with music. She shied away from verbal counting, for instance, but was very willing to hold up two blocks when they sang "Annie has two blocks," with the ukulele.

When they got up to leave, Annie organized them into a parade to march out onto the front porch. She bundled up in her coat and told Miss Foster that she had something to show her. Before anybody knew what was happening, Annie jumped on a big plastic go-cart and roared down the forty-degree hill, pulling up in a sharp curve just before she would have smashed into Miss Foster's jeep. If she had seen a kid with normal vision do that Maggie's heart would still have been in her throat. By the time they got their own coats on, Annie was inside the jeep, trying to find out why the horn wouldn't blow.

"Scares us to death sometimes, but she's the light of our life," said Annie's mother. She and Annie's older sister had shown great sensitivity as they worked with the little girl, making up additional activities as soon as one was suggested. Annie was exceptionally lucky where her family was concerned.

She hadn't been too lucky at Goshen School. Annie was a bona fide special ed reject. She had been enrolled in one of the classes for the first two months of school. Her teacher had earned a reputation for hard work, but Annie's problems had evidently been too complex. "I'd find her lots of times out sitting on the steps in front of the classroom," said her sister bitterly. "Just sitting there."

Finally Annie's teacher had decided that she couldn't make it in school, that her problems were too bad. So she had been sent home.

As Maggie and Miss Foster walked down the hill, Annie's mother followed them, asking questions as fast as she could. "I've had to bear a lot of insults to prove that my girl can learn," she said through the jeep window. "People wouldn't pay any attention to us because we haven't got the education. But the girl can learn."

"Anybody who says that child can't learn is full of baloney," said Miss Foster. "We all know it."

"Do you know," Miss Foster said in an angry tone, as they drove away, "that they are trying to take that child off homebound and send her to the Day Care Center? Somebody got hold of the hospital report, and now Warner is telling me that we can't justify spending the money on her anymore." She scowled. "He won't believe me when I tell him how fast Annie is learning. I was hoping you'd go tell him too."

Maggie promised to do that, if Miss Foster would get Annie's doctor to write a letter contradicting the Veteran's Hospital report to be put in Annie's folder. Maggie wrote one herself when she got back to the office. Then she sat staring at it. Of course, a lot of dust would be raised in having Annie transferred immediately to school. To what school? Mrs. Coleman's class was over twenty miles from Annie's house, and it was hard to picture Annie in Goshen's cafeteria class, in spite of Harry Blankenship's good will.

Although, under the right conditions, Annie could have been learning a lot more in the right program at school, she was learning and growing at home too. More importantly, she was being treated well. Until her eyes grew stronger, it almost seemed as if she needed protection *from* school. Finding the right answer wasn't as cut and dried as it might seem in theory.

Homebound can have such a valuable function for a child who's laid up, but what does lack of alternatives within the total system do to children like Annie? And to their parents? "It's very likely," observed Ed Martin, director of the Bureau of Education for the Handicapped, "that, if special education is making some differences, it may be in ways that are relatively unmeasurable. For example, if you're the mother of a significantly handicapped child, and you have no special education program, versus if you have a special education program, what's the impact on you? I'll bet you that one of the major societal benefits of special education programs — when they are productive — is the impact on the families themselves, on the ability, on the mental health, on the basic quality of life. We are just now getting a widespread societal response on behalf of severely handicapped children, which helps the parents share the anxiety."

As people try in all states to set up effective public school programs for significantly handicapped children, objections have often been raised as to cost. In 1976, Ronald Conley, author of *The Economics of Mental Retardation*, explains that the expense of a public school program, when it is inappropriate for a given child, is actually much lower than that of institutionalization, which is the only other legal alternative: "The cost of a public school program for a severely retarded child, per year, is probably about three times the normal cost per child. But it is also about three times less than the expense of institutionalization, per year. Taxpayers don't usually see that, since the public institution is usually supported through state taxes and therefore one step further removed from their immediate view than the county-supported school systems are. And taxpayers have become very sensitive to anything that increases costs. So, even though the cost of public schooling is actually much less, the taxpayer sees that cost much more clearly. The cost of the public school program looms deceptively larger than the actually much larger cost of an institution.

"Beyond that, you have to think of the savings to society in terms of the later life of the severely retarded child who develops at least rudimentary skills through an effective program. Taking a long-run social point of view, it is certain that, through a special education-type program, the majority of severely retarded persons are going to be able to produce more and enjoy life more. Studies clearly show that many who have received public school programs do work and pay taxes in later life. And, with additional help, in my opinion, it is at least probable that anyone whose IQ measures above forty, who has no serious physical abnormalities, is going to be employable. A child in a similar position who does not get a good training program (many children in institutions don't) would not be employable. This person may well end up being cared for at public expense in an institution, unless he finds a guardian angel somewhere. You have to also consider the tendency to keep people in institutions once they are placed there.

"There are two cautions I would like to mention in relation to my comments here, however. The term 'institution' is very misleading. What you're really talking about is out-of-home care. The general image is of a big ugly impersonal institution without any developmental services. That's not necessarily so, as there are those small homes and schools where the child who cannot profitably live at home undoubtedly receives good care. Only five to ten percent of the so-called retarded would need such care, but, when they do, they should not be placed in the public schools to satisfy somebody's notion of mainstreaming. The success of the severely retarded in later life, of course, is dependent on their ability, at least in a minimal way, to get along with people in the society they may hope to return to, and this is another argument for educating them as close to that society as possible. But public schools aren't going to be the best place for all children.

"The second caution has to do with cost estimates. The cost of institutionalization, like the cost of special education, varies a great deal, from place to place, from person to person. But, assuming the institution and special education program are providing the treatment the child needs, I do think the three times estimate will hold, on the average."

As part of comprehensive planning, Childfind efforts to find severely handicapped children and get programs for them are now under way in every state. Childfind means that local communities under the direction of the state division of special education organize volunteers to go out and find children who have been left at home with no educational program. People do this by house-to-house canvassing, radio and TV ads, leaflets stuffed in grocery bags and bank notices. One state reports that posters in gas station bathrooms led to information about many children.

Some states such as New Jersey have been in the financial position to do this kind of search very effectively for several years. Other states haven't been in as financially secure a position. A BEH official reports, for instance, that the governor of one state told the state special ed director in 1975 *not* to find any children, because there weren't yet any funds to establish programs for them.

Despite funding problems, many systems are finding inexpensive methods of paving the way for the severely handicapped children's entry into school systems after they have been located and enrolled. Some schools are making special efforts to develop a receptive attitude in the "regular" children. As children with all types and degrees of handicaps come into schools, some in regular and some in self-contained classrooms, many thoughtful regular classroom teachers across the country are making a special effort to give other children some background on what handicaps are all about and to help them look beyond the handicap to see the individual. (Where the diagnosis of handicaps have been more based on opinion than say, physical handicaps, many teachers are doing the reverse, making no mention or fuss about the fact that the child in question had been considered mentally retarded or emotionally disturbed.) Handicapped adults have also been visiting classrooms to talk about handicaps and to show that a person with a handicap is just another person.

It's important to promote general community preparation and awareness of what the whole mainstreaming movement, in its biggest sense, is about. "I contend that we've got four basic messages that we've got to get out to the public," says Fred Weintraub of the Council for Exceptional Children. "One is: handicapped kids are kids. They smile, they laugh, the most severely handicapped kid likes ice cream as much as any other kid likes ice cream . . . they're kids. They go through all the turmoils that other kids go through. We've got to get people thinking of them as human children.

"The second message is: handicapped kids can learn. That's a very important message because it not only has to be conveyed to the general public, it has to be conveyed to special educators — because many of them *don't* believe it. Our present communication to general audiences is really not learning-oriented. We, as special educators, talk about these kids in terms of the problems they have. We make centerpieces for banquets. Handicapped kids make good centerpieces, handicapped kids can draw good, give concerts . . . they put on shows and things like that. But the message is — they ain't good learners.

"What I've been doing to try to combat this, as I go around to different parts of the country, is to suggest to people, 'The next time you're asked to do centerpieces, instead of the usual thing you do, put out reports on the tables with facts about learning . . . the number of children you've taught who are now employed . . . a picture-story of a child who couldn't walk, but now can . . . the kids who learned to talk . . . the kids who learned to read despite their handicaps . . . that's what the public needs to hear. We've got to get away from this idea that handicapped kids are kids who can't learn, that they're those poor kids that the Kiwanis Club takes on a picnic every year.' The way in which the public and the teachers themselves view the children can make all the difference in the children's program and progress.

"The third message is: handicapped children are not getting what they need. Thousands of children are still sitting at home. I don't think the public understands the magnitude of the issue. A necessary corollary of that message, perhaps, on the other extreme, is that not every child who has a handicap needs special education. Some do well educationally in regular programs. The main point is to give each child an *appropriate* education program in the least restrictive environment possible.

"The fourth message is: I think we can do it, especially if all agencies can learn to work together. This is my kind of continual optimism. Every handicapped child, no matter how severe the handicap, can have an effective program."

Before the American courts began to order the schools to provide programs for severely handicapped children, very sharp comparisons were often drawn between excellent services some European countries (notably the Scandinavian countries) provide for severely handicapped kids and the near-total lack of public services in the United States. It was often said that the difference in services reflected the difference in the attitudes of the two societies toward those who are less fortunate. A representative of the National Society for Mentally Handicapped Children in England took another view of the whole subject. Asked if the good programs and general social acceptance of severely retarded people in England and Scandinavia meant that Europeans are more tolerant than Americans, she said, "It's quite the other way 'round. Attitudes [in England] have changed *because* there are good programs. For example, doctors do not any longer necessarily recommend that a retarded child be placed in an institution, because it is recognized that there are now alternatives in the community." Her comments support those people who contend that, difficult as it may be, the process of establishing public programs for all children, no matter how severely handicapped, will, in the end, make our country a more humane and tolerant place.

"Depending on the attitudes people are able to take, programs for severely handicapped children could turn out to be one of the most broadening things that ever happened to the schools," commented a teacher of severely handicapped children at the Brookmont School in Brookmont, Maryland. "But you can't expect that positive attitudes are just going to happen. You have to work for it, help people to change their way of looking at these children."

"These kids are love, they're life, they bring me much joy," added another Brookmont teacher. "They make you laugh, they make you cry, they make you think deeply about the blessings we take for granted and the meaning of life itself.

"You know, there's an old saying about how a society can be

judged by the treatment it gives its least fortunate members," he added. "I hope that people all over the United States will be as good to the children coming into the mainstream, so to speak, as people here have been to ours."

20. Buying

"Materials and media must be considered as an integral part of the environment that must be modified accordingly for the learning disabled child. Success or failure for many learners is determined not only by the expectations, intentions, and skills the teacher brings to the task, but also by the interpretation and organization of the myriad of commercial materials that are available. The dilemma isn't so much where to obtain materials any more as it is the evaluation of available materials for their functionality and appropriateness."

— Philip H. Mann and Rose Marie McClung,
Mainstream Special Education, 1974

TEACHERS OF severely and multiply handicapped children, teachers who work with specific disabilities, and regular classroom teachers who want assistance with children mainstreamed into their classrooms — all share the need for something beyond regulations and theory: practical programs and materials that suit each child's needs, programs and materials that can give a teacher a structure within which to build a meaningful program. At this point, the quality of many programs is much dependent on the type of program materials available to the teacher.

In 1976, more than two billion dollars per year was tied up in special education on a national scale. A good percentage of that money went for educational materials and equipment, and the educational materials manufacturers haven't missed that fact. In 1971, to illustrate, there were 159 materials exhibits at the Council for Exceptional Children convention. In 1976, there were 297.

Finding the right programs and materials for specific children can turn into an incredibly time-consuming and frustrating task. School employees are amazed by the number of truly fine programs and materials that have come on the market since 1972 and also frustrated by the amount of expensively packaged junk that is passed off as special education material.

In Copper County, the educational materials boom was represented by the constant stream of sales representatives who went in and out of Warner Jenkins' office. Many of these people represented companies that gear at least part of their products toward the special education market.

Some had good luck with Warner, others didn't. The SVE educational materials representative was a familiar face around the Yellow Castle. He said that Warner had bought almost everything in his catalogue. "One of the best customers around," he boasted. Warner added that the SVE salesman was a fine young man, respectful, and always interested in sitting down to explain the latest developments.

Because Warner rarely had time to get out of his office to visit classrooms and determine specific needs, he leaned toward packaged programs, expensive boxes of materials whose producers often promised that educational miracles would be forthcoming in a short time. The year before Maggie came, Warner bought dozens of reading kits and cassette-tape programs designed to diagnose reading problems at a cost that averaged out to hundreds of dollars per kit. Stockdale School alone had six cassette kits.

Abigail Robin was pulling her hair out over the cassette kits. "Those damn things might have been worthwhile if we'd been able to put together the teacher-training to go along with them." Abigail was firmly against Warner's policy of imposing materials on teachers who had not chosen them. Beyond that, the inflexibility of the number of days school had to be in session didn't allow for workshop time to help the teachers make the best use of the programs they did get. "Seems as if people have the idea that these machines are going to do the job by themselves," Abigail complained.

Warner obviously did put great faith in programs and machines. One day, soon after Maggie began to work on the Part C proposal, she found a note on her desk to see Warner. As soon as she walked into the office, he told her enthusiastically, "The *nicest* young salesman came by to see me this afternoon, and he told me about the most marvelous machine. I wanted to order several when I heard about it. It's just the *perfect* thing for special ed . . ."

"What is it?" Maggie asked. Warner's secretary stopped typing and swiveled around to listen.

"Well, I don't exactly know yet," he said. "But he said it was absolutely guaranteed to teach any nonreader to read in just eighteen lessons!" He paused. "The whole program is only four hundred dollars. And he *did* say, though, that it might be harmful to a child who could already read a little, and it should be for a child who has the capacity to read . . ."

He stopped and eyed Maggie with something that looked like apprehension. "He asked what *kind* of special education we have here, and I told him the children are retarded. He said his machine was probably just the thing we need, and I'm *sure* he's had lots of experience with these kind of things."

Maggie hugged her notebooks. "Could he bring it in for us to look at?" she ventured. "It certainly sounds like a wonderful machine."

"Well, that's what I wanted to talk to *you* about. He's willing to come *demonstrate*, but he'll need a child to demonstrate *on*. So I want you to get one of the nonreaders out of special education."

He began organizing his papers with an "everything's settled" air. Maggie told him she'd get together with the reading supervisor to see if they could find an absolute nonreader. "We don't have any absolute nonreaders to fit his definition in special ed," she explained. Warner's mouth dropped, then tightened into a line. "Well," he said doubtfully, "we'll have to do the best we can . . ."

"What about Billy Stewart?" Warner's secretary suggested. "He can't read."

Warner threw up his hands. "Mercy sakes, *no!*" He shook his white hair vigorously. "His father's a *prominent* doctor in town, and he just throws a *fit* if anyone ever suggests that something's wrong with the boy."

He kept shaking his head. That child was definitely out. "Lawd, you should've *heard* him when one of Billy's teachers said Billy ought to be in *special ed!*" He put his hands over his ears, as if he could still hear the doctor.

Maggie checked with Abigail. "Sounds like that machine must float on water," Abigail said. She didn't know any nonreaders who fit the requirements either and said she didn't like the idea of that kind of demonstration in front of so many people.

"So that pretty well cancels the machine, right?" Maggie asked her. "No demonstration?"

"Wrong." Abigail smiled. "You ought to know that by now."

They decided to ask Sally, an outgoing, ten-year-old reading on first grade level, if she'd like to do it. "If it's such a great program, she'll have fun with it," said Abigail.

At exactly ten o'clock a few days later, seven school officials were scheduled to gather at Gateway School. Maggie went early and found the company representative, who turned out to be a very likable fellow indeed. He was very anxious to know if the child involved was a genuine nonreader, and was unhappy to hear Maggie's "not quite."

"But the program was designed for *true* nonreaders," he murmured, adjusting and readjusting his thin gray tie. "Mr. Jenkins told me there were many such children in special education." Maggie apologized and the salesman decided to carry on anyway.

Abigail and the reading aide from Goshen arrived early to look over the apparatus, which turned out to be a plastic record player with a color-coded armrest. They decided that it would survive approximately two weeks of childlike manipulation.

The others showed up, milled about, shook a few hands, and settled behind a long table and stared at the salesman. Maggie went outside to wait with Sally until they were called.

They were leaning against the wire fence behind the school, watching the creek. "Been swimming yet?" Maggie asked her.

"Nope, still too cold for me. I been fishing."

"In a boat?"

"Nope." The river was pretty high. "I'd like to go in a boat." The school disappeared, for them, when they turned their backs on it.

"Been in one?"

"Coupla times."

Sally rocked on the loose fence post, and Maggie told her about the rubber-raft trips that went down the river a couple of counties away. "One of those rafts holds sixteen people." Sally liked that and wanted to know how come they didn't sink.

"They're full of air, like a tire."

"Oh. I had a tire one time." She frowned and stuck out her lip, then smiled. "I wish I was in that tire right now," she said. "Just float on down that river as far as I could go . . ."

Some of the Gateway kids came bursting out onto the playground, and Sally turned to stare at them curiously. Although she was special ed too, due to the bus schedule she had been placed in a classroom at Stockdale School, a regular school. That made a big difference in status. The Stockdale special ed kids got teased by the regular kids at Stockdale, but in turn they themselves would tease the Gateway kids.

When Maggie and Sally were called in, the salesman showed Sally how to pick the first color-coded card out of a box. With the card before her, she placed a record on the machine and rested the color-coded needle arm in the corresponding slot. "The dog" read the card. "The dog" said the record. "The dog" said Sally. The salesman told her to move on to the next card as soon as she felt ready to do so. While she operated the machine, he fielded questions from the audience.

The questioning turned up the following facts: The program might be harmful to a child who was just beginning to read, if that child did not respond well to repetitive tasks. The program would deaden the interest of a child who already knew simple words by sight. No hard data was available on the program's success.

In a quick postdemo survey, everybody rated the machine thumbs down, except Mr. Morris, the truant officer and director of transportation, who said it might be all right, and Mr. Dillard, who had left in middemonstration, despite his earlier declaration that he would do anything to get away from Stockdale School.

Marvin Sizemore, the regional special ed supervisor, had slipped into the building sometime during the demonstration. He caught up with Maggie as she left. "Had lunch?" he wanted to know. They decided to eat and confer at the Burger King.

Mr. Sizemore was a retired superintendent. His job was to oversee the programs in seven counties and to provide assistance when necessary. "What'd you think?" Maggie asked him, watching

Warner Jenkins gesturing to Mr. Morris, who nodded genially and smoked his pipe.

Mr. Sizemore jingled the coins in his pocket. "Knew it was a piece of junk as soon as I saw it," he said. "But I didn't feel it was my place to say anything, seeing as how I just wandered in on this meeting, not invited, you understand . . ." The little dining room at the Burger King projected out over the river. Maggie watched the water slide by while Mr. Sizemore reminisced about the time Warner had ordered all those maps and globes. "Lord, the post-man dumped them all at one schoolhouse," he recalled, tsk-tsking. "You realize that you've got to handle him with kid gloves," he said, lowering his tone and looking over his glasses' rims. "He's very powerful around here." Maggie suddenly felt very tired. I wish I was in that tire right now. Just float on down that river as far as I could go, she recalled.

"Well, I get tired of politicking around just so these kids can get what they should've had a long time ago," she blurted pettishly, instantly regretting the outburst, as Mr. Sizemore began to sympathize and tell her that after she'd been in the business as long as he had, she'd just accept the facts of life. "Don't take the job so much to heart," he advised.

As they rode back across the bridge and drove past the railroad cars and the junkyard, he continued in the same vein. "I know how you feel . . . but you're beating your head against things you probably can't change. I used to do that myself, but not anymore."

Something in his tone of voice made Maggie pay particular attention. For some reason, Mr. Sizemore seemed to have dropped his usual evasive manner. She studied his face as he pulled over to the curb in front of Gateway. He looked somewhat bitter. They lingered to finish their conversation on the sidewalk.

"So what do you do, if you don't do that?" she asked with real curiosity.

"Well," he said, "I cover seven counties, and after a while, it gets pretty simple. Sometimes I go into a classroom and see that nothing's going on in that class. Well, the county hired that teacher, and I can't teach her class for her, as much as I might like to. Even if I didn't have all this territory to cover. So what are you going to do with a situation like that, and with all the other ones similar to it?"

he asked. "You can either go home and not sleep, thinking about those children. Or else you can go home, think about the nice things, and sleep. I sleep. That's what I do. You just have to realize that there are some things you can't change."

Mr. Sizemore had told Maggie that the neighboring county was much better supplied with materials than Copper County. So a few days later, she took a trip there to borrow some books for the older kids at Gateway from their middle school. Copper County had none of the high-interest, low-reading-level books designed to appeal to teen-age students whose interests far outran their reading abilities.

The principal of the school, Mr. Baumgartner, was ready for her. "We've got lots," he'd said on the phone, and he had a big pile of workbooks waiting on his desk. He told Maggie to select a few.

They stood together outside the school and watched the children pile into the school buses. Then he showed her the new Astroturf covering the front steps. "They had to spend a big hunk of federal money before the government took it back," he explained. "We need that money for next year, you know, and if we didn't get it spent this year, we'd get less next year. Turned up with some unspent money at the last minute, so they got this Astroturf."

Maggie scuffed her foot on the Astroturf. "Too bad there's not some place you can call that could give you some ideas about how to use extra money the best way . . ."

"Yeah." He nodded absently, gazing after the departing school buses.

Later that same afternoon, Maggie was digging through catalogues when she heard Mr. Birdwell in the hallway of the Yellow Castle, asking Warner Jenkins for his impression of the reading machine.

"Well, I wasn't as impressed as I had been," Warner began. "As a matter of fact, I'm not at all convinced that this system could work. It would take a long time before we could be sure if it was any good at all."

Well, lucky that's out of the picture, Maggie thought.

"So since we don't know," continued Warner, "I think we'll have to buy one. Otherwise, we'll never know. If we could teach even one child to read this way, it will be worth four hundred dollars."

"That's certainly true," said Mr. Birdwell hesitantly. Maggie strolled out into the hall, available for questioning. Mr. Birdwell smiled as she appeared. "Mr. Jenkins was just saying that it would be worth four hundred dollars to teach just one child to read."

"I agree." Maggie smiled back. "And for even less than that amount of money, we could buy a wonderful perceptual development program I've just been looking at in one of the catalogues here. It could help dozens of kids learn to read better. While we're considering programs, I think we should look at this one."

Maggie produced the catalogue, and Mr. Birdwell advised Warner that it looked like an excellent purchase. "Should I have them send it on approval so we can look it over too?" Maggie asked. Warner looked the other way, Maggie turned a little red, and Mr. Birdwell made a quick exit.

When Maggie got home, she asked Anita what she made of the exchange. "I don't know." Anita shrugged. "Maybe Warner didn't want that nice salesman to go to all that trouble without buying anything from him."

"But you know that money could be much better used, even for basic supplies. We need it for so many things."

Anita shrugged again. "You aren't sure that perceptual program is the best use of the money either."

It's not entirely unusual to find that the materials which are available determine the type of program the children will have. And materials manufacturers have often been criticized for promoting the use of a label like EMR for their own economic reasons (as have been the pharmaceutical companies which manufacture drugs for children labeled "hyperactive"). The whole process of trying to decide which educational programs and materials are worthwhile is a real problem for many people associated with education. Much time and benefit to children can be lost through trial and error.

Robert Audette, presently director of special education in Massachusetts, published a written protest against a rising flood of expensive junk in the July/August 1973 issue of *The Exceptional Parent*. The "bright package with 'psycho-linguistic' this and 'perceptual-motor' that proved to be, at close inspection, essentially hula hoops and frisbees at the sale price of $45. Five pages of instruction was apparently the justification for the price. As with so many expensively redesigned and repackaged products — such as walking beams, pegboards, and ball games — the only distinguishing feature was the jargon and the claims of 'research.' Even these claims of research have little to justify them.

"Recently, I visited fifty-one commercial booths at a convention in order to inquire about products on display." Audette continued:

- Only one company was able to provide a booklet citing specific studies that had been done with their materials. Naturally, they 'discovered' that the product was an effective one. However, the anonymity of the authors of these studies cast a substantial doubt on their value.
- Eighteen companies said that their job was to develop materials, not to collect data. But they said they had much personal testimony from educators.
- Six companies said they did not know about data-gathering.
- Six companies said that their materials were supplemental to regular curricula and thus data were not necessary.
- Four companies indicated that they had no data but were interested in soliciting teacher feedback.
- Seven companies said that data gathering was the responsibility of the educator, not theirs.
- Nine companies replied that the data could be obtained by writing to the company. So I wrote; few responded. The only evidence they submitted were case studies, flimsy support for their advertising claims. . .

"The result of this advertising mumbo-jumbo is an atmosphere of confusion for parents and professionals who are trying to evaluate programs and materials from some objective standpoint . . . Advertisers can confuse and mislead parents and professionals with unfounded claims and expensively dressed materials. There are certainly situations where new materials are necessary and should be obtained. But, if a frisbee will suffice, call it a frisbee, not a 'motor control device.' "

Special education personnel know that good, useful materials do exist in good quantity, but as Barbara Aeillo, who edits *The Exceptional Teacher* for the Council for Exceptional Children, cautions, "Some of the best materials on the market for special ed kids don't come under the 'special ed' label, so don't limit your looking to materials designated 'special education.' "

Some of the best programs on the market are also designed to individualize instruction for all children. There are now comprehensive school programs like Individually Guided Education (IGE), a "multiunit school organization" that involves the planning and operation of entire school curricula. (IGE is designed for a range of achievement levels and allows a school to accommodate the great majority of children with varying needs and learning styles, without making actual differentiations between regular and special.)

Materials manufacturers are also beginning to gear their products toward mainstreaming. Ms. Aeillo commented favorably on the number of nonspecial-ed-labeled materials that are including components for children who have physical problems. "When I see this, I see materials development paralleling the good things that are beginning to happen in our society — the opening of doors between groups of people who have previously been isolated from each other.

"The main thing which still bothers me about materials is exorbitant advertising claims. Even with good materials, nothing replaces a good teacher. I would like to see materials advertisements say that 'there's a good chance this will make learning easier for the child' or 'try this and expand on it to meet your children's needs,' rather than claim that 'this is it! This is the cure!' It would also be good to get away from materials demonstrations in which a salesman says, 'This is such a wonderful material' to demonstrations featuring good teachers who can say, 'Here is an array of good materials,' which allows teachers to make some choices."

The Bureau of Education for the Handicapped has been responsive to these kinds of concerns. In 1973, HEW set up a network of information and service centers designed to give state and local school systems access to informed evaluation and information about everything on the market, from a plastic record player to complex commercial programs for multiply handicapped children. Under this system, Warner and Maggie would have a reliable place to get an informed opinion on whether XYZ product is expensive packaged junk or a solid, usable material.

Since the process from local system to national system is complicated and often involves considerable waiting time, many states are developing or have developed similar resource centers within the state to suit their own needs. Some local school systems are doing the same. As the whole network begins to build up, the national centers will be able to work more as places to get advice, which may turn out to be their most important function.*

So far, the system has been used primarily for special education, but officials working with the program say there's no reason general education shouldn't be able to use it too. "As a matter of fact, it could be very helpful with mainstream programs in particular."

---

*The Regional Resource Center Network, as planned, would provide a whole variety of services. See pp. 347–49 for further description.

21. State Level Headaches

> "I think you've got to consider everybody involved in a change process when you want to institute new programs. This is an extremely complex business these days, and we have to find human-oriented ways of going about things. If we start shooting at each other, we aren't going to get anywhere."
>
> — Landis Stetler, director of Special Education,
> Florida State Department of Education, March 1975

SAM WATKINS, Maggie's favorite person from the state division of special ed, stopped by the Yellow Castle one afternoon. He and Maggie went out to get a cup of coffee. "I'll tell you," Sam said. "Things are getting complicated. The responsibilities are getting mind-blowing. I'm glad to see the laws, but the problem is — the legislature just loves to pass these sweeping bills for educational or social reform, and then, when it comes time to deal out the money, they don't give us half the funds or personnel we need to carry them out. So we've got a mandate for severely handicapped coming up, and then required preschool programs in 1978. Mainstreaming's going to be pushed, nondiscriminatory testing, Childfind . . . it's all coming." Sam crossed his eyes and flopped against the back of the booth. "And it'd all be much less overwhelming," he said, perking up, "if they'd just give us the cash to do the job."

Maggie fanned him with the Title I papers. "I know." He smiled. "You probably think it isn't such a bad thing that there isn't more money for EMR classes. But on the other hand, I know you must agree with me about severely, preschool, and" — he sighed — "more positions at the state level." Maggie nodded soberly, and they both laughed.

It was true. There just weren't enough people at the state level to cover the state needs — present and upcoming — with any effectiveness, or to maintain responsible control over what was already going on. Sam was one of less than a dozen people employed to work in the state central office. Over 15,000 children were enrolled in state special education programs that year, and if the amount of time Sam spent on the road was any indication, he more or less ran himself ragged trying to fill in where help was needed, all over the state.

The state special education mandate would soon be legally effective and lawsuits might be coming out of counties that were not maintaining the required programs. People like Sam Watkins would be personally named in these suits. Such lawsuits, particularly those involving severely handicapped children, are often initiated, put together, and carried out by organized advocacy groups representing the interests of handicapped children.

Alan Abeson of the Council for Exceptional Children is a man who has played a leading role in the use of courts of law to force the establishment of special education programs for children who had been excluded entirely from school or programs. He sums up the more militant advocacy point of view: "If we're talking about Right of Education for the Handicapped . . . O.K., let's take a state that has a new mandate. I would give them a reasonable number of months, say six, past the date the law goes into effect to demonstrate that they're really trying to do the job. That's what a court would say. If, after X months' time, a plaintiff can demonstrate that the defendants really aren't doing diddly, then they should walk right into court and sue them. And I think that's about as much time as they need.

"I have two pet theories that relate the change. One is called 'the maintenence of threat.' That suggests, very simply, that 'I want you, public official, to know that we are watching. We'll work like hell with you, but we're watching. If the time comes that it's determined by us, or by anybody else, to our satisfaction, that you're not doing the job, we're going to do whatever we need to do to get the job done. And that may include going to court.' Now there's a new weapon. Maintenance of threat is a relatively new concept in special education.

"The second theory is 'the baseball bat theory of change.' You can apply it to group homes for retarded citizens, for instance. There are two ways of opening up group homes. One — you come into the community and you open it. You don't tell the neighborhood officially that you're coming. And then you have all kinds of chaos. Or two, you tell the neighbors that you're coming and try to help them see how successful and meaningful these homes have been in other areas. And then you have all kinds of chaos.

"Now, I believe you deal with it directly and say to a neighborhood, 'Here we are! Now, adjust.' Either way, you face the same problem of prejudice. Reeducation is nice in theory. But you're going to have to do that anyhow, so why waste all the time, when the thing that convinces people most is contact with the actual people who live in the group home?

"I'm convinced that you have to deal with resistance directly, on the head. The same thing goes for public school officials."

Recognizing that public school officials are themselves frequently frustrated by bureaucracy and lack of resources, Dr. Abeson points out in his *Legal Change for the Handicapped through Litigation* that "changes sought through litigation may be very similar to directions the party named as 'defendant' has tried to produce, but whose ability to achieve those objectives has been frustrated because of barriers such as inadequate agency commitment or financial support. In this sense, litigation (or the threat of litigation) may be used as a level to bring about the action desired by both the potential defendant and plaintiff . . .

". . . Litigation is not necessarily a personal attack upon parties named as defendants," Dr. Abeson emphasizes. "Frequently, complaining parties are aware that the party named as defendant has tried to produce desired changes. It is also known that in some of the cases . . . named defendants have spent days preparing defenses for the suit, and nights assisting the plaintiffs prepare their arguments. It is in the best interest of the handicapped to prevent litigation from becoming personal, because, regardless of the decision, it is likely that the named defendants will retain a major role in implementing the desired change."

Dr. Abeson was referring to people like Sam Watkins. In spite of the personnel limitations of the state division, Sam was an exceptionally sensitive and effective officer who felt frustration as keenly as anybody on the local level could. He also understood that one of his most important responsibilities was to maintain and encourage a positive attitude in the individual school system personnel. Give them a shoulder to cry on, make them feel appreciated, then turn them around and send them back to keep on plugging.

Part of Sam's job also involved keeping up formal communications among the local supervisors in each region. Three or four times a year, he set up a series of regional meetings for the special ed supervisors. Maggie's early spring meeting was to be held in the next county. The mountains surrounding Davidson seem to rise very high in the wintertime, almost penning in the town, stark and inescapable. The spring thaw comes as a relief from that frozen black-brownness. Winding up the mountain toward the meeting, Maggie's car plowed through slush, slid on the ice, and rolled through water washing across the road. She finally arrived, her mind full of questions about local problems.

The main purpose of the meeting was the demonstration of instructional materials from a central materials center in the next state. Several supervisors, however, like Maggie, seemed to be waiting for the opportunity to get together and compare notes. During lunch, Maggie sat with the supervisors from Hadley and Sloan counties, Carolyn Smith and Harriet Caldwell. Carolyn was about Maggie's age. Mrs. Caldwell, an easygoing sort, looked to be in her early fifties.

"What're you doing about the entry forms for the special Olympics?" Carolyn asked Mrs. Caldwell.

"Same thing I always do with them," said Mrs. Caldwell, busy with her steak. "File them in the nearest garbage can. And, as long as they call those games 'Olympics for the Mentally Retarded,' that's exactly where they'll be filed."

She stopped eating and turned to Maggie. "You see," she explained, "those games can be the most wonderful thing in the world for severely retarded children, but most of the children in our program are what people like to call mildly retarded.

"Now, we get some very negative reactions to that word in our part of the country. It's not the way it should be, God knows, but that's fact. I've spent six years supervising in Sloan County, marching up and down hollows, trying to eradicate the words 'mentally retarded' from the parents' minds and everybody else's vocabulary. As soon as I'd send a busload of kids up there, some parent'd turn on the television, and there would be a reporter talking about how nice it is that all those retarded children can participate in sports."

Maggie was immediately in love with Mrs. Caldwell.

"Now, I'd love to see our kids included in a tournament with all kids," Mrs. Caldwell told Carolyn. "We've got over five hundred children, and a lot of them could whip the pants off any kid around. The fact that they're having trouble in school doesn't make them any less physically able."

They ate silently for a while, then started talking about evaluation procedure, trading test names and organizational difficulties.

"We use a battery of four tests, plus the required IQ test," said Mrs. Caldwell. "I'd walk over the mountain backwards before I'd place a child by one test."

"My regular teachers have referred over one hundred and fifty children for only fifteen slots," Carolyn said. "There's no way we could give all those children a full battery of tests and a medical exam, so I'm screening them myself. Eliminating down to the kids who *will* be formally tested. And I'm wondering if I'm going to have fifteen kids left. Those teachers refer kids at the drop of a hat." She scowled. "They keep sending me a lot of kids with IQs way up in the hundreds who're having trouble with reading. I write PLEASE TEACH THIS CHILD TO READ in big letters across the referral sheet and send the child right back where he belongs."

Carolyn was right, it seemed, but Maggie felt a sudden twinge of sympathy for the regular teacher who received this note — and for the child who might take the brunt of the teacher's frustration.

Maggie asked Carolyn if her county had any way of giving regular teachers resource help.

"No, ma'am," Carolyn replied in a businesslike manner. "We have our hands full . . ." Her faintly hostile expression broke, and she smiled and shrugged. "Well, it's like this. You work with what you can, hope to do more in the future, and you've got to be a tough broad to take the criticism." She looked Maggie over, maybe to see if she was tough. "I even get threatening phone calls at times . . ."

"Why?" Maggie asked, wondering if she would ever get one. "Because I'm there, I suppose."

In the car on the way back from lunch Mrs. Caldwell started talking about psychologists. "I'm always suspicious of any psychologist who tells me he has 'evaluated' more than four children in one day." Mrs. Caldwell's sarcastic quotation marks surrounding the word 'evaluated' were quite audible.

"When I first came to Sloan County," she told them, "I checked the evaluation records and found out they'd been bringing in some hot-dog psychologist from Andrews County who'd been averaging fifteen or sixteen kids a day. Didn't know up from applesauce about what he was doing."

She turned around and looked at Maggie in the back seat. "You pay attention to all this. Anyhow, this yo-yo was a licensed psychologist. You can bet we fixed his wagon, one-two-three. Now, we have a man who comes in on a staff basis and gives us the best services I've ever seen, including teacher counseling, workshops, and program design."

"What happened to that psychologist from Andrews County?" Maggie asked. "Did he get in any trouble?"

"Shoot," said Mrs. Caldwell, running her hand through her gray hair. "We reported him to the state psychological board, and they smacked him with a wet noodle." She looked truly disgusted, and they all laughed. "He's still doing the same thing down in Andrews County is the sad part. But at least he's not doing it in Sloan County."

"How do you manage to pay your new staff psychologist?" Maggie asked.

Mrs. Caldwell turned around and looked at her with some surprise. "Why, you just write him into your federal proposal," she said. Maggie didn't think that Copper County had ever asked for such a thing.

Maggie spoke to Sam before he left for the next day's workshop, two hundred miles away. He was feeling typically frustrated by the shortage of everything and had some unkind things to say about the legislature's lack of concern. "They get the publicity for passing

the law," he grumbled. "Then they seem to expect the laws to behave like magic wands." He wondered if it was possible for state
employees to sue the legislature for not providing adequate funding.

In the parking lot, Mrs. Caldwell invited Maggie to come visit in
Sloan County. "I'll just take you under my wing," she said. "We're
all in this together." Maggie told her what Sam had said about the
legislature. "Well, now, I'll second that," Mrs. Caldwell agreed. "I
get sick and tired of hearing people pick at Sam for not doing this
and not doing that, when, if you looked at the man with half an
eyeball, you'd see that he's doing all he can with the responsibilities
he's got. So, yes, I'd take it back to the legislature — or even back to
the people who influence the legislature, I guess that's you and me,
among others."

Having heard two respected people cast aspersions on the legislature, Maggie was interested to see that the following week the Public Broadcasting System was airing a show on the problems of state
legislatures. She and Anita watched the show. When they tuned in,
the narrator was saying, "The President says that the best government for our two hundred and ten million Americans is not in
Washington, but here at the state local level where it is closest to the
people. The President's plan rests, in large part, on the ability of
the fifty states to govern themselves with wisdom and with a degree
of orderliness as they're given new responsibilities for major programs that the big daddy federal government has been handling."

The PBS staff had picked a state legislature they felt was typical
in terms of the problems all the state legislatures were facing. A discussion with a group of legislators, lobbyists, newspapermen, and
assorted citizens began with the fact that, during the sixty-day session just concluded, the legislators had introduced 1417 bills. Of
this number, approximately 110 were passed. Maggie imagined a
special ed bill floating somewhere among all those others.

"I wonder at you and your fourteen hundred bills," a citizen
commented. "How do you find time to read them, much less do
anything about them? It's worse than the want ads. The want ads,
at least, are classified."

The following half-hour was filled with comments on organizational difficulties and the impossibility of making wise decisions under the time and input circumstances: "Many of the bills weren't introduced, oh, until halfway through the session." "We don't have any staff experts who can give this input on an earlier basis." "A number of what were regarded as important pieces of legislation kind of got lost in the shuffle at the very end." "We don't have a place where we can work alone to study something out." Special interests . . . lobbyists . . . lack of time to assimilate the volume of material . . .

Toward the end of the program, the narrator introduced Charlie Davis, Executive Director of the National Conference of State Legislative Leaders, who explained, "The problems that these people have articulated here are problems that are occurring everywhere in the country." Mr. Davis concluded that the discussion "only demonstrates to me that the problems across the country are very much the same, everywhere we go. We're faced with the same kinds of problems, social and human problems that have never faced us before."

22. Parents and Early Intervention

"One who recognizes all men as members of his own body is
a sound man to guard them."

— Chinese proverb

PEOPLE WHO KNOW how to cope with all the complexities and still
come up with good individual programs are especially valuable at
the local level. Sam Watkins told Maggie that he appreciated just
knowing that Harriet Caldwell, the Sloan County supervisor, actually existed. "She's always in the classrooms or out in the homes," he
said. "When she tells you what's happening with a child, you know
it's not hearsay, and you know she's not just reading off a report."

Soon after the regional supervisors' meeting, Maggie accepted
Mrs. Caldwell's invitation to come over to Sloan County and learn
something. Sloan County was a steel mill community, where black
smoke touched everything within five miles of the county seat. An
unusual feeling of energy pervaded the county — wildflowers,
waterfalls amid freight trains, forthright people. Maggie also found
that the Sloan County schools had something going for them that
made their problems seem much less defeating than those of Copper County. She had never seen a whole group of school administrators who were so child-oriented.

Mrs. Caldwell had suggested that Maggie come with her on her
day's rounds throughout the county. "You already know I don't
supervise from my office," she told her. "To tell the truth, I get to
feeling antsy if I stay around the office too long. I get out of touch."

Sloan County's special education program included over 500
children, most of whom were placed in self-contained classrooms,
sometimes in totally separate buildings perched on steep hillsides.
A high percentage came from the county's isolated hollows and

mountain areas. Most of the others came from the crowded low-income areas of the valley towns. On the surface, the Sloan County program sounded as if it might be a larger version of the Copper County program. In some unavoidable respects, it was, yet the program was in transition. Mrs. Caldwell didn't claim she had all the right answers. She saw that the self-contained structure was having unexpected negative effects on the children. So, without any qualms about changing her tune, she was slowly converting to resource programs for most of the kids. In important respects, even the self-contained program wasn't a duplicate of the Copper County program, primarily because Mrs. Caldwell had been there for six years. "I'm the watchdog," she joked.

It was an education just to follow Mrs. Caldwell around and watch her operate. From the reception she received, her visits were obviously frequent and welcome. She practiced very conscious low-key diplomacy: a motherly, supportive attitude with a young, insecure teacher; prodding humor with an experienced "but slightly lazy" teacher; impersonal, but friendly "Can I help you?" for an ambivalent principal; unfailing warmth for the children. She knew how to use her own behavior to produce positive results for others.

She also seemed to know almost all of the children and their individual problems. They greeted her affectionately and joked around with her. "How's Minda getting along with fractions?" she asked a teacher, or "Did you finish patching that quilt, Ginny?" "Dougie, have you and Fred made up after your fight?"

While Mrs. Caldwell discussed particular problems with the teachers, Maggie wandered around, copying names of the materials that filled each classroom. Well-planned educational programming seemed to be the strong point throughout the day. They visited fifteen classrooms, and Maggie saw only one that wasn't well equipped. And most of the teachers displayed good practical understanding of the potential uses of the items she asked about.

"We in-service teachers to death until they develop a working familiarity with these kinds of things," explained Mrs. Caldwell. "We don't have the kind of in-service where somebody gets up and preaches. We have the kind where you wear your slacks and get down and learn to make something useful. And then, I in-service almost every day, whenever I come around."

Over the years, through in-servicing, constant friendly contact, and teacher involvement, Mrs. Caldwell had brought most of her teaching staff up to a fairly sophisticated level. They had all collaborated on a set of behavioral objectives for each developmental level and had contributed to the program's curriculum guides for each major subject area. "We don't make teachers that way so much as they come with inborn ability and interest," Mrs. Caldwell claimed.

The teachers, in general, gave Mrs. Caldwell great credit for their success. One man, a retired military officer, reported that he never would have made it without Mrs. Caldwell's guidance and thoughtfulness. "When I was first beginning," he remembered, "she let me start with only four children, then kept adding more each time I'd get my feet under me. At the end of two months, I could handle sixteen kids comfortably. If I had begun with the full classroom, I wouldn't be able to do what I can do today and would still be trying to get out from under my own confusion."

Special education in Sloan County was not a dead end. "We're sending fifty-three children back to the regular classroom this year," Mrs. Caldwell told Maggie. "We watch them closely, and also check their progress through achievement tests at least once a year. This baloney about coming back and checking a child three years later just doesn't work. We give each child a full reevaluation every two years, at the very least, and sometimes twice yearly if the child is progressing rapidly. After we move a greater percentage of the program into resource, evaluation should be even more frequent and flexible."

Mrs. Caldwell was moving toward mainstreaming many of her pupils with resource support, but she moved with caution. The very existence of the large self-contained program had made the establishment of resource programs more difficult than it would have been if the teachers and principals had not been accustomed to the idea that troublesome children are removed. Mrs. Caldwell wanted to lay the groundwork well. "I don't want those kids ignored when they go back, so I'm working to make the teachers as receptive as possible."

"Now, you're always going to have a few self-contained classrooms," she said, "because there will always be children who need that kind of structure. But we have tried in the past few years to move as many children as possible back into their home schools, particularly the older ones. Our problems, oddly enough, have not been with the teaching staffs as much as with the principals. The children add an administrative chore, since, if they aren't scheduled to the greatest advantage, your program isn't likely to be as effective as you hope. We cut down the principals' resistance by offering to help with the scheduling. The kids are our responsibility now, as much as ever, even though we're sharing duties."

"If we can just get more individualized instruction going in the general system," mused the county superintendent, "we'll be able to do a much better job with severe handicaps and preschool when the time comes. Mainstreaming will be much easier."

The Sloan County program did have many trimmings the surrounding counties lacked: The county system employed a psychologist three days a week. Many high-school-age special education pupils participated half of each day in an outstanding vocational program and spent the other half of the day with academic subjects. The Head Start program was recognized as one of the best in the region. Mrs. Caldwell had an assistant supervisor. The school system maintained a diagnostic team for academic difficulties.

Sloan County had been able to develop such a full program primarily because the superintendent, Mrs. Caldwell, and several other people in the county administration were crack proposal-writers. Apparently, they knew how to get every available nickel of federal and state money. They had a formidable edge over programs without supervisors, and those counties that didn't employ personnel who understood the ins and outs of the money game. (Present federal legislation which stipulates that a percentage of the federal money go directly to local systems without passing through the state division cuts this advantage somewhat.)

Sloan County's program might have been enough to make a person decide that a lot of money can create good programs — until that person remembered that, if Mrs. Caldwell, her superintendent, and others like them weren't there, the county might be using money to cover steps with Astroturf.

The Sloan County staff was anticipating a shift in special education priorities. Mrs. Caldwell herself believed that the greatest hope for the child commonly called "disadvantaged" or "developmentally delayed" lay in early intervention. "If the day ever comes when our services are no longer needed in this county," she said, "it will be the greatest day of my life. And, if we ever want that day to come, we've got to get these children while they're very young.

"Here in this part of the country," she explained, "we have what I call a façade of retardation. Ten years ago, when this program was starting, we picked up young children in wholesale lots, because they were not ready for books and other standard school devices. They needed to learn about a lot of other things first. The psychologist who was testing the children, for instance, told me that many children were stymied when they were asked to lay a pencil on the book, in the book, and so forth — that's one of the items on the Stanford-Binet. Those children didn't pick up the pencil or the crayon, not because they lacked intelligence, but because they didn't know what he was talking about. So we picked up many children back then who were lacking experiences we take for granted.

"Kindergarten and Head Start have done much to counterbalance all that. In this county, at least, those two programs go heavy on concepts as well as motor skills. This means that the kinds of problems which used to be so common have begun to disappear by the first grade. As a matter of fact, I'm delighted to say that special education in this county is almost out of the catch-up business, as far as the young children are concerned. I might add that we now have dozens of older children who would never have been in special ed if we had begun to develop these kinds of programs when they were four or five years old or even sooner.

"If you'll allow me to generalize," she continued, "the greatest single schooling needs which children who fail in school have had are vocabulary and basic concepts. Individual children's needs differ greatly of course, but almost all of ours have shared those two.

That's why it makes great sense for the special education people in the public schools to have some input into the Head Start and kindergarten curriculums, and vice-versa. Not to label the children, but to make sure they get the kind of experiences all along that will keep them from being defeated before they even begin. We feel that, if we all work together, even though Head Start isn't under the same management, the kids will have a much better chance. Each program can build on what the last one already did. Too often, that doesn't happen, and then you get criticisms of Head Start for not having a lasting effect. Well, of course, if children get an enriched program in Head Start and maybe kindergarten, and then go into an elementary program which either repeats or else has nothing to do with what they've already done . . ."

"We try to avoid that here, even if it does mean a few extra pow-wows here and there, or a few program changes on the part of the schools. I feel strongly that we should be into prevention at least as much as we're into remediation."

The Sloan County superintendent of schools agreed with Mrs. Caldwell. "But, if I had my way, I'd go even further back," he said. "You see, like most places, we have a high percentage of parents who get married in their teens, who are in no way prepared for the twenty-four-hours-a-day reality of a child, much less a handicapped child. I think we're missing a great opportunity to get at the source of many of the children's problems before they happen. I've been agitating for two years now to get mandatory parenting courses put into the schools at the junior high and secondary levels, and I wouldn't mind seeing them in the elementary schools either. Teach students about children's nutritional needs, about basic developmental stages children go through, about research which would let them know how good it is, say, to talk to your baby, to play with the baby, to hug the child . . . To my mind, that would be real prevention. We have trouble getting funding for that at this point, but I do believe it could make inroads on nutritional problems and some of our child abuse problems besides."

He studied Maggie thoughtfully. "Now, don't you get the idea that I'm saying we have a bunch of bad parents," he said. "In cases of nutritional deficits or even child abuse, lots of times the parents just need personal support and information. Educating for parenting could go a long way in cases like these, cases where we have to backtrack now, mostly after a lot of ground has been lost for the child." A few years later, the superintendent could have conceivably fit his ideas into the "Comprehensive Planning" frame work.

Like Sam Watkins, the Sloan County superintendent couldn't think of anybody better at working with parents than Mrs. Caldwell. "If we have to rely completely on after-the-fact assistance," he said, "I'm glad we've got her." After talking with the superintendent, Maggie told Mrs. Caldwell about some of the parents she had already met in Copper County. "So far, we haven't found any effective way to get good relations going with most parents who don't live right in town." she said. "The system holds Parents' Night twice yearly, but most of them don't come. The ones I've met really seem to care, so I guess Parents' Night isn't the right way to reach them . . ."

Mrs. Caldwell shook her head. "I know exactly what you mean. Parents' Night won't do it by itself. One of the greatest strengths we've had," she said pointedly, "has been getting the parents on our side — and that has been really hard in Sloan County. It has entailed a lot of hiking, walking up hollows and mountains, and not being afraid of being rejected. I don't think we've missed a valley or hollow in this county, and we haven't missed very many of the mountains." She looked out her office window at one of the hillsides.

"Our parents are proud people in general, and they want to know *why*. But once you go in and explain what you're doing to their satisfaction, we've had unbelievable cooperation. But it takes a lot of time, personnel, and persistence. You've got to plan for it and allocate money for it. You've got to have administrators who feel that three thousand dollars' worth of good visiting time can be worth far more to the children than three thousand dollars' worth of something you can point at, like overhead projectors.

"Like anything else, it has to be done right. You don't just march into a home, say who you are, and start talking school business immediately, as if you aren't interested in the people personally. Not around here anyway. You have to win parents' trust, in my experience, so when you make a home visit, you sit down, and you *visit*, without turning up your nose at this or that circumstance you might not like in the home."

She chuckled. "I know I insulted a young man in a class one night not too long ago. He said that he didn't want to do this, that, and the other . . . and the parents wouldn't do this, that, and the other, and told some story about a home in which whiskey bottles had been out on the table. Well, I'm real bad about speaking before I put my brain in gear, so I told him that if he would stop looking down his middle-class nose and go in with some empathy, he'd find parents a lot more receptive to his efforts."

She frowned. "It's true that there are certain things people ought to know if they go visit in some parts of the county. For instance, if you start up a rural hollow — and I hear this happens in the inner cities as well as in this part of the country — if you stop at the first house to ask directions, be sure and tell who you are and what your mission is. Otherwise, everybody up that hollow may know you're in the hollow before you get where you're going, and if they think you might be from the welfare department and if you have a paper or a pencil in your hand, you may well not get into that house.

"But this is understandable. I get particularly tired of hearing people talk about how low-income parents won't participate. These are people who are trying desperately to make a living, many of them. And I know that some of them do a much better job on what little bit of money they have than I could ever do. A lot of people are quick to say that parents don't care when they don't show up at these meetings and conferences we hold down in town. But they are very concerned indeed. They don't come to our meetings, it's true. But there are reasons for that.

"Quite often, their problems have to do with having a way to get to the meetings. In having clothes to wear to the meetings. Many of our parents are in circumstances which, but for the grace of God, all of us could be in, and they don't want to look different from the other people. They need somebody to give them enough — I guess it would be courage — to go out and be in another situation.

They're afraid, as everybody is always afraid of the unknown. And they often have to be thinking about things like where next week's food is coming from. It's a struggle to maintain any sort of peace of mind under those circumstances, and the last thing they need is to go someplace where they might be embarrassed or where somebody is going to lay another load of worry on them.

"We rely on home visits, but we do have meetings occasionally. And one thing we try to do is make these meetings as attractive as possible. We always provide a little entertainment, something like a fashion show, where the children show off the things they've made in school or an open house, featuring the children's accomplishments, something positive.

"To solve the transportation problem, we've tried sending out school buses to pick up parents, and we've made arrangements for car pooling, and this kind of thing. We've had to work like crazy to get car pools set up when we've needed them. But car pools tend to fall apart if you try to use them on a regular basis.

"So we've had limited success with PTA-type groups and conferences in town. Our best way of reaching the parents is still legwork. Home visits, where they see that you've made the effort to come see them." She laughed and looked down. "I guess that's how we keep our figures.

"It always pays off. The more parents can understand about what you're trying to do, and the more they see you putting yourself out, the more they're able and willing to help." She gave Maggie a significant look. "And the children whose parents get involved usually show the most progress."

Mrs. Caldwell often ended up teaching parents as well as children. "Some parents will follow through automatically with their children at home, once they understand what you're trying to do. But, very often, we need to teach the parents to follow through. We can't expect them to do something they haven't learned how to do, any more than we can expect it of their children."

She frowned and added, "Of course, then you have those parents who will give you lip service, and then not do anything after you get out the door. Those things, if you would let them bother you, could really get to you, but I try to maintain a positive attitude and just keep on plugging. We fail with a few children, but we've been able to make it pretty well with most of them, particularly when the parents are participating.

"Parents, of course, don't cooperate to the same degree or with the same willingness, though most do try to help. With parents, as with any other group, what makes the difference in the amount of help the child gets is the degree to which the individual parent cares for other human beings."

The school psychologist, Tim Higgins, worked with the parents, as well as with children and teachers. "He's one of those presents the Lord sent us," Mrs. Caldwell told Maggie. "And Title I had a little to do with it too." The psychologist and the superintendent sometimes acted like a one-two combination when the interests of a child were threatened unjustly.

"I'll give you a current example," Mrs. Caldwell said. "We have several severe behavior problems, all of them resulting from unusual home conditions. These children's teachers don't seem to want to take the problems into account at times. So we're having a session with some teachers tomorrow over a little boy whose father lives in Pennsylvania and comes home periodically to make worthless promises to the boy. He gets him all upset and then leaves again. The boy's teachers don't understand this, so they get all upset when he periodically goes crazy in school. They would like to see him put in special education.

"Now there are two ways of dealing with situations like this. Sometimes, they can be handled simply by the psychologist, principal, and teachers. Under these circumstances, Tim Higgins, the psychologist, can say, 'These are some of the approaches that will help you deal with this child in a manner which is constructive on both sides.' Other times, when the school personnel aren't willing to work with the psychologist and the child, problems have to be handled through an administrative order, which has to come through the superintendent.

"Of course, I'm hoping that when we get more resource programs built up, we'll have the capability to handle problem situations as they arise, to give the classroom teacher assistance on a temporary basis when children have temporary problems. And we'll be able to do it, you can bet, because the superintendent is backing us, and the board's backing him."

Child support seemed to come naturally to the Sloan County superintendent of schools. "I get tired of these teachers discriminating against children because of IQ scores," he told Maggie, a twinkle in his eye. "I've been considering giving all the teachers IQ tests and posting their scores on the classroom doors."

"We'd never be able to do as much as we do without his kind of support," Mrs. Caldwell told Maggie. "We've gotten to the point where we can go anywhere in this county and be welcomed, and you don't do that without a reputation for supporting the interest of the child. And you can't follow through with that support if the superintendent or the other administrators are working at cross purposes."

On the way home, Maggie sat in her car at a railroad intersection, waiting for a train to go by and trying to recall the details of some "early intervention" projects she had read about. All the research projects she could remember had shown what common sense would suggest — that adequate nutrition, medical care, verbal stimulation, and affectionate contact with others are extremely important to a child's healthy, "normal" development, especially during the first two years of life. She vaguely recalled studies suggesting that a high percentage of children who ended up in EMR classes did not receive some of these benefits in early childhood.

As Mrs. Caldwell's words echoed around her head, they were joined by something her neighbor Lucy had said: "Even if you think you've found yourself a right answer, you've got to find a right way of putting it into effect, or it could turn out wrong." Maggie wondered how early intervention could turn out wrong. Almost as soon as the question crossed her mind, she remembered Dr. Hutschnecker's plan.

Dr Hutschnecker is a psychiatrist who was associated with Richard Nixon prior to the 1970 presidential election. Early in Nixon's presidency, Hutschnecker suggested that all six- through eight-year-olds be screened for criminal tendencies. Those identified as potential criminals (by *whomever* was doing the screening) would be obligated to go to special classes designed to reform them. After a brief, but spirited controversy at HEW and elsewhere about self-fulfilling prophecies, the proposal was killed. "Guess it's good to keep remembering that just about any good idea can be used in a destructive way too," Maggie mused.

When she got home, Maggie dug through a file box until she unearthed a paper entitled "The Milwaukee Project: Early Intervention as a Technique to Prevent Mental Retardation." She looked it over carefully, propping the papers against the toaster while she cut up vegetables for dinner.

All forty children originally involved in the Milwaukee Project had been chosen because they were "high risk" in terms of the factors that, in combination, seem to land some children in EMR classes. The primary factor for selection in Milwaukee was that the child's mother had herself been considered retarded. The children all lived in areas of Milwaukee with high unemployment rates, poor housing, high density per living unit, and low per capita income.

The Milwaukee Project, directed by Dr. Rick Heber, had paid close attention to reasearch showing that children from high-risk backgrounds usually score in the "normal" range on tests when they are very young. These scores tend to go down as the children grow older. The main goal of the Milwaukee Project, then, was not to "raise IQs" but to prevent the children from being driven down by unfavorable conditions in their lives into the form of "retardation" the researchers called "cultural familial." Nearly 80 percent of all individuals defined or classified as mentally retarded, it was noted, fall into that group.

The children chosen for the project were determined through studies to be at a sixteen times greater risk for retardation than the average child, due to the fact that their mothers were of low verbal ability at that point and were therefore not likely to give them the necessary stimulation. So the Milwaukee Project had two parts — one for children, another for mothers.

The experimental-group mothers received job training and classes in child care, home budgeting, nutrition, community-oriented social studies, and interpersonal relations, in addition to basic academics. The experimental-group children participated in a year-round stimulating-day educational program from about six months of age through entry into public school. The children's educational program focused particularly on two areas: development of language and development of problem-solving ability. The control group children grew up as they normally would have, with periodic reviews by the Milwaukee Project staff.

From the beginning, the experimental-group children showed increasingly greater ability in both areas, as compared with the control group, which tended to lag further and further below "normal." The increasingly greater language command of the children in the experimental group was accompanied by increasing responsiveness in their mothers, many of whom had jobs by the time the children were four and were much more aware of the needs of their children. The experimental-group children, by that time, also spoke self-confidently and coped well with standard English.

The relationship between the mothers and children in the experimental group, after the children began to talk, involved much more verbal communication as compared with that of the control group. The families were breaking out of the cycle in which the mothers tended "to regulate behavior by using imperatives and restricted communcation — a behavior control system which can stultify intellectual growth" according to project literature. "The mothers showed significant improvement in their own personal self-image," wrote Dr. Howard Garber, one of the main researchers, "and a change to a positive attitude about child-rearing and the significance of their role in the family."

The IQ test comparison from two through five and a half years old, taken as a measure of achievement and ability to cope with such situations, showed the experimental group with an average mean score of 123.4. The average mean for the control group was 94.9. The difference between the two groups on this test, as on all other measures, grew greater as the children grew older, indicating that the losses of the control group were not due to some innate deficiency within the children but to the debilitating pressures of poverty and lack of opportunity for both mother and child.

Maggie put down her vegetables and thought for several minutes about what she had read. She became momentarily angry at the researchers for not giving the same opportunities to the control-group children. But then, on reflection, she realized that her anger was pointed in entirely the wrong direction. By giving a good early educational program to twenty children and training programs to their mothers, the researchers were mainly disproving the old notion that "these kids can't learn anyhow." They had taken those twenty children from a "control group" of countless thousands of children in similar circumstances all across the country who don't get the opportunities middle-class children usually do.

"Our study suggests that the conditions which are accepted as ordinary and necessary for a normal development in early life are not available to many children," wrote Dr. Garber. "This disadvantage puts them at greater risk than the average child. All children face developmental dangers, but our children faced them to a far greater extent.

"Our study shows that high risk families are responsive and benefit considerably from such a program and that their children have the capacity to achieve at normal levels upon entering school. The future success of the children with whom we have worked now remains very much in the hands of their families and the schools."

23. Accountability?

"We know of the ever increasing emphasis on programs for the severely handicapped. At the other end (minimally) we are all painfully aware of the pressure which is being brought to bear in most states, particularly those states which now receive a highly visible ratio of dollars in special education as compared to the general education budget. In effect, we are being forced to expand horizontally, which means that programs must move quantitatively, with little regard for quality.

"It isn't so much dollars or lack of them, but a combination of dollars, plus manpower shortages, and the whole educational spectrum's inability to adjust as rapidly as needed. I see us then, as expanding in both directions. Our field is being asked to assume responsibility for more and more children and youth, who, philosophically and professionally, have not been considered a part of the handicapped and gifted population. Almost daily, most of us probably say, 'What in the hell is special education?' "

— Herbert Nash, president, National Association of
State Directors of Special Education (NASDSE), 1974

MRS. CALDWELL had told Maggie about an incident that had bothered her. "I was at a directors' meeting with people from all over the state, and, in front of everybody, Sloan County got congratulated for having put the highest percentage of our children in EMR classes. Of course, that's not the way he said it. He said 'providing special services to the highest percentage of children.' Two different ways of saying it, you know. Well, I wasn't as pleased as I once would have been. I'd been thinking about the way the regular classroom teachers were just referring more and more kids to us. I want to be accountable as much as the next one, but I don't think you can measure accountability by the numbers of children you've got in your program. There's something backwards about that. It seems to me that when you've got more kids in a segregated special ed program, that means the general system is saying about an inreasing number of kids: 'I'm not willing or able to deal well with his child.' So, no matter how the accountability of the academic pecial ed program is going up, the accountability of the general ystem seems to be going down."

Maggie didn't quite grasp what Mrs. Caldwell was talking about. When she got home, she asked Anita, "What's 'accountability' mean o you?"

Anita had a different perspective on that word. Before coming to Copper County, she had taught in a school system that had tried to develop an accountability system. "The parents held meetings and demanded that the schools come up with some way of demonstrating that the children were getting the product the taxpayers were paying for," she explained. "And let me tell you, that ain't any easy ob."

"See, for one thing, parents have different ideas about what the schools ought to be doing. They'll all agree with the basic idea that a school should provide their child with an education and that its personnel should be held accountable for providing that education. But then they have to agree on what constitutes education, if a total accountability system's going to be set up. And that's where it gets tricky.

"Remember that controversy over textbooks in Kanawha County, West Virginia? All those people wanted the schools to be accountable, but they just didn't agree on what the schools should be accountable *for*. What one group called preparing children to deal effectively with real life, another considered immoral. But the whole issue may be a little different for special ed, I suppose. You'd have a different list of choices you could be accountable for. Reading achievement might be one thing. Self-concept could be another. How about social standing?"

Since at least the midsixties, educators have been suggesting that an accountability system is not only more easily set up for special education but that it's necessary, given the uncertainties involved. In an effort to begin building such a system, the federal law that will go into effect in 1978 requires an individualized, written plan for each child enrolled in a special education program. (Some states already require this procedure.) Under this system, theoretically, each child's needs will be assessed as accurately as possible and a program will be planned to meet those needs, interests, and learning styles *before* it is decided where to place the child. Ideally teachers, parents, and child will all participate in the process, and all might have certain agreed-upon obligations under the plan. It is expected that everyone involved will then keep checking to see if the child is actually progressing toward the state goals written into the plan. If it becomes apparent that satisfactory progress is not being made, the plan itself is examined to determine if it is inappropriate or inadequate.

Critics of the individual plan say, with reason, that the time and paperwork involved could actually cut program quality unless provisions are made to allow the teacher to carry both teaching and paperwork. Critics also feel that many teachers would have honest difficulty writing and carrying out a detailed plan. Supporters say that just the process of having to sit down and make a contract brings people together to communicate and to look at a child as an individual. They also feel that such a process should produce the kind of specific information on a child's difficulties that IQ tests usually do not provide.

Others agree with Mrs. Caldwell, who says that at the same time as people work to increase the accountability of a special education program, it's equally important to watch how the accountability of the general system is being affected.

Mrs. Caldwell kept saying that "finding new ways of working together is a vital, but very slow process. So many small steps. It can get frustrating, but it's a process," she told Maggie. "Start where you are. Do one thing at a time. Maybe the first thing to do is to decide where you want to go."

Maggie realized that the Copper County special ed program had never decided what they wanted to be accountable for. She called Sam Watkins and asked him if a local system could add its own regulations to the state's. "Sure. As long as you don't contradict the state regulations. But one thing — get your teachers involved."

So that's what was tried in Copper County. A small committee of teachers met several times to make a rough draft. They stated the goals, what they hoped to do, would do, and would not do. Then Maggie put the rough draft into regulation form. Next, all the children stayed home one day so the whole special ed staff could put the final product together. The teachers and aides divided into groups, each with copies of the tentative guidelines. Then each small group spent the morning tearing them apart sentence by sentence, adding, altering, omitting.

The amount of energy that went into that workshop was wonderful to see. The participants ended up thinking and talking seriously about every aspect of the Copper County program. There had been meetings before, but they'd been deadly affairs where people wouldn't say what they really thought. Maggie had directed those meetings, but this time, the teachers themselves had put together most of the input in advance, and it made a difference.

"Shoot, this sort of thing ought to be done at least once a year," Mr. Blankenship said. "It really makes you think."

The new guidelines, in their final form, included provisions for a three-stage evaluation process, including classroom observation. A working "teachers' special education committee" would be elected, along with a special education advisory board. The psychologist alone would no longer place a child in special ed. Buying materials would be channeled through the committee, and definite procedures for transferring children out of special ed were nailed down.

"Well, it's been fun, but the board and Warner will never go along with them," said one teacher as she was leaving.

"Naw, they'll go ahead and approve them," Mr. McCreedy said. "And then, as soon as they come into conflict with what the office wants to do, that'll be the end of them."

The board did approve the guidelines.

Abigail Robin asked Maggie if she felt good after the vote. "Well, I'm not sure," Maggie answered. "For right now, I'm glad, but in a bigger sense, something still doesn't feel right. The guidelines really don't do anything to get at the problems in the whole system that frustrate teachers and put a lot of kids in special ed in the first place." She was thinking about what Mrs. Caldwell had said.

"For Cripes' sake, Maggie. When are you going to start thinking in terms of what's possible *now?* It's a step-by-step process." She paused and smiled. "And by the way, you may have taken a step toward accountability, but you took a step backwards with Warner. You didn't invite him again." She shook her finger at Maggie. "You aren't being accountable to *him*."

"Well, I was afraid he'd intimidate —"

"Doesn't matter," Abigail insisted.

The next immediate step seemed to be doing something about the testing process. Maggie remembered that Mrs. Caldwell had said there was a possibility that Tim Higgins, the Sloan County psychologist, might be available on a part-time basis the following year. "It's not as good as having a full-time psychologist who lives right there, and it costs more than that IQ mill you're using, but you're dealing with children's lives," Mrs. Caldwell had advised. "His fee includes teacher consultation and placement assistance at the least."

Since Buzz Murphy wasn't a psychologist, a good case could be made for changing. Mrs. Caldwell had told Maggie that Higgins was a man "with boundless energy." After a few minutes' phone conversation with Maggie, Higgins gave her what he called his "no-politics speech" ("I don't have time to be wishy-washy, so I have a prepared speech").

"I will never even consider a job in which politics are involved," he began. "In other words, if I'm working with a special education program, I want to be directly responsible to a special education professional who will make good use of my reports. I don't and won't mail psychological reports to a secretary or hand them over to some administrator who has no direct involvement with the children concerned or doesn't know how to put the reports into actual practice.

"I don't do evaluations in order to produce a label or to supply numbers which make it easy to file children. My evaluations are constructed to be practical contributions to the children's ongoing programs. Because I feel this way, I write detailed reports in a language most people can understand. And I want to be there to explain it to the teacher when necessary."

Maggie began to think that Mrs. Caldwell hadn't been kidding when she said the Lord sent her this guy. "I keep getting all kinds and shapes of offers from school systems within a two hundred-mile radius of here," he told Maggie, "simply because I'm a psychologist and systems are desperate for qualified people to give tests. Most want me to come in for a few days, test some children, mail the reports, and collect my money. Nothing doing.

"I'll also quit at the first sign of administrative meddling in placement," he continued. "By meddling, I mean suggestions that I place a child for administrative purposes. I refuse to recommend special ed placement simply because an administrator orders me to get a child out of a teacher's hair. You'd be surprised how many people ask me to do that.

"If my evaluations are to benefit the child's program, I have to discuss them with the special ed supervisor, at the very least. I hope I will have the opportunity to talk with the child's teacher and parents to make specific suggestions for remediation.

"I won't discuss programs or child placement with financial administrators," he added flatly. "If at all possible, I like to have one pleasant discussion with that person about payment, get everything settled, and not bring politics in there either. I'll be glad to tell anybody about what I'm doing in general, but financial administrators, in my view, have no business using the purse strings to dictate educational policy.

"I guess I'd sum it up by saying that I'm there to help the children and teachers however I can, and not to play administrative power games. I am also not there as a convenient means of legally dividing children into categories. If that's the extent of services your county wants, then I'm not your man."

"I feel like I ought to stand up and clap," Maggie said.

Tim laughed. "You'd be surprised at how much grief that speech saves me. You've just gotten a rundown on the ways in which school administrators sometimes try to misuse us psychologists." He agreed to come over later in the month, superintendent willing, to evaluate some of the children who had been referred for the following year.

*

Abigail asked Maggie if she were happy about Tim's being hired. Maggie couldn't resist saying something about its only being a step in the right direction. Abigail put her hands over her ears, but didn't continue. She knew Maggie had been getting some pressure to expand the numbers of children in special education. April in Copper County was largely devoted to "screening" the children who had been referred to special education for the following year. Though screening was scheduled all over the county, some schools had referred twenty or thirty children, and others had referred only a few. Two schools didn't refer any children at all. One of the principals of those schools told Maggie diplomatically that she felt that "we can do more for our children here."

Some situations really highlighted the absurdity of labeling and transferring children rather than giving direct assistance. For instance, Maggie spent the second week in April at one of the high-referral schools, a three-room country schoolhouse surrounded by a row of fruit trees and filled with happy faces and good feelings. Redbud covered the hillsides, willows hung over the river, and many-colored flowers bloomed in chartreuse grasses. The school was at least ten miles from the nearest special ed class, so the teachers weren't familiar with the nature of the program. "We felt you should be aware of these children's problems," one teacher had told Maggie. "Maybe you can tell us what you could do for them."

On her second day there, Maggie arrived at recess and was immediately surrounded by primary-age children. "Are you going to take me today?" they called, tugging at her shirt. "Can I come with you?" They didn't know why she had come, but evidently had decided that it would be a big treat to "play games" with the stranger.

Maggie had a piece of information that made her wonder if the best of "evaluations" might not be beside the point that year. The children were being evaluated for placement at Goshen School, in classes that as yet had no definite location or teachers. A spillover of regular Goshen children had been assigned that year to a ramshackle building a few miles away, and their parents were demanding that the children be transferred back to Goshen. Mr. Birdwell was having trouble finding space, and there had been talk of housing those children in the special education rooms.

"But what about the special education kids?" Maggie had asked.

"We might have to bus them over to Gateway," worried Mr. Birdwell. "There might be no other alternative." Gateway was twenty miles away. "Of course," he added, "since one of those Goshen classrooms was renovated with Title I money, we probably can't use it for anything but special education." For the first time, Maggie was happy to have that Title I regulation. However, she was at a loss to justify reassigning children to a program with no specified teachers or guaranteed location.

One of Maggie's first customers was a girl Warner called "one of those Fairleys," a child who reminded her very much of Jenny. A shy, smiling pigtailer, Doreen Fairley was wearing a worn but clean dress. She and Maggie talked and went through the inventories in the cafeteria. The usual tests showed Doreen to be very low in vocabulary but quick to understand and make appropriate associations when the meanings of words were explained to her. Her academic skills were understandably weak in areas that depended on vocabulary and middle-class concept development.

Doreen shed her shyness within minutes and showed a great deal of curiosity about everything they talked about: spaceships and big cities, gardens, brothers, spiders, and sisters. She said with shy pride that she was "doing way better" in school. "But me and my sister are still in the slow reading group." Maggie asked if she liked her school. She nodded until her pigtails bounced. After Doreen went back to her classroom, Maggie sat in the cafeteria watching the children skip rope outside the window and thinking that her decision was made much easier by the fact that the school was so nice. What would I do if Doreen hated the school? she wondered. As it is, if I were to recommend special ed for her, she could only be guaranteed two things: a long bus ride and a mentally retarded label. The law says she has a right . . . to what?

The same was true for a little fellow named Donald, who kept threatening to fall asleep on the table. When he was awake, Donald's conversation was very entertaining. He talked about how he would get up in the early morning "when it's still misty out, and all the birds are hollering," to go capture his neighbor's pony for a bareback ride. He also discussed the horror movie on "The Late Show" the night before.

Donald's referral sheet said "Listless, wandering attention, can't seem to complete anything, low mental ability . . ." Donald went on to describe another late movie and told Maggie he stayed up almost every night to watch TV. His teacher hadn't been aware of the hours he'd been keeping, it turned out, but, in the light of the information, insisted herself that he shouldn't be transferred and made plans to get in touch with his parents and work from there.

Some children's problems were much more serious. Clyde, a large fifteen-year-old, had great difficulty with just about everything he attempted, from conversation to motor control. His low level of achievement in all areas made it very hard for him to participate in most sixth grade classroom activities. "Clyde's so unhappy with himself that he's begun to take it out on the other kids," his teacher told Maggie. "Poor guy," he added. "You know, he even leaves notes around the class saying, 'I'm ugly. Nobody likes me,' or 'Clyde can't do nothing.' I do everything I can to encourage him and make him feel accepted, but this has been going on a long time, and he's started to get into trouble outside school too." Maggie decided to refer Clyde to Tim Higgins, realizing that the new vocational school would be completed by the time Clyde was seventeen.

Before she left for the day, one of the teachers told her that she was very concerned about six Puerto Rican children who had arrived in Copper County via New York several weeks before. "They're all from the same family, and they don't speak English very well," she said. "I thought maybe they'd need to be in special ed for a while."

Maggie explained that it would be impossible, since the testing system depended on familiarity with English. To soften her reply, she added, "We don't have any Spanish-speaking teachers in special ed either. Let's give them an adjustment period and see how fast they pick up English. There's not a warmer atmosphere in the whole county for them." It was a pretty lame answer, and she knew it.

A few days later, she accompanied Tim Higgins to the school for the second stage of screening. Tim radiated confidence and competence. Maggie watched him consult with a teacher. After ten minutes, he had made the teacher feel much better about what she had already done for the child, as well as hopeful for the future. "It would be a crime to move the child to special ed when she's getting so much here," he complimented her. "It's true that every child who qualifies for special education won't need to go there, and thanks to you, this is one child who can stay where she is."

"Why didn't you eliminate that child when you screened her?" he asked Maggie after they left the school. "She was obviously ineligible."

"Her teacher wouldn't believe me when I told her. She wanted to hear it coming from you. She doesn't know me, after all. You're the psychologist and when you say the child can learn at a meaningful rate under her care, it means something." They smiled, but it was frightening. They both knew there should be some alternative to either transferring the child or just leaving her there.

Maggie and Tim came and went, testing and evaluating, with so many life stories depending on their findings, decisions, and particular biases and viewpoints. If we choose not to see what's going to happen to the kids, we're affected too, Maggie thought, looking out the window at the river as Tim drove back toward Davidson. She wondered when and if it would be possible to get a resource teacher stationed at that school.

Mr. Birdwell decided to hire Tim Higgins on a contract basis for the following year after reminding Maggie that it would be much preferable to have a full-time person. Maggie and Higgins went to the Yellow Castle to have that one discussion with the financial administrator.

Warner Jenkins was surprisingly ready to negotiate. His readiness even made Maggie suspicious. Tim complimented Warner on his willingness to take on such a thankless job, and Warner smiled and kidded about the difficulties of dealing with federal regulations that didn't fit local needs. Somehow, they slid very easily from there onto the subject of fees, and Warner determined that the entire bill for the upcoming year would amount to approximately $9000 for evaluation services. After they decided on a per-child figure, Warner licked his thumb and began riffling through a pile of papers.

"Now, I have to decide how I'm going to pay you," he said. "Let's see . . . I could take it out of last year's funds . . . or there's that in-service money left over from the year before, but that has to be spent before June . . . maybe I could transfer the unused salary allocations from last year over to evaluation . . . or I could always write it into next year's proposal . . ."

Finally it was settled. As they walked out of the Yellow Castle, Tim kept shaking his head as if he needed to clear it. "Holy baloney," he said. "It's just as if he has rows of cooky jars in there, with thousands of dollars tucked away in every one!"

Maggie stared down the street without answering. How much further had all those little improvements brought them toward providing something worth having for the children? She began to wonder seriously if all that activity — the guidelines, ordering materials, transferring teachers, employing Tim Higgins — wasn't just prettying up a program that would remain essentially counterproductive and unaccountable in important ways, as long as the children could be badly stigmatized by the separation from the regulars.

A few weeks later, Warner dropped a few comments to Maggie about making arrangements with the Mental Health people again for the fall.

"But I thought . . ."

"We may not be able to afford that psychologist you brought in here," Warner said briefly. "I've checked through the different places I could pay him from, and it looks like it may be too much. We'll have to wait and see." He looked up and said again, "We'll have to see. We need that money for other things."

Maggie fumed. Mr. Birdwell had said Higgins would definitely be employed and that he made the decisions, but uneasiness was building between Maggie and Warner again.

24. Due Process

"It is hardly too strong to say that the Constitution was made to guard the public against the dangers of good intentions."

— Daniel Webster

"If a person is judged incompetent by reason of mental disability, this has significant repercussions for him as an individual. Twenty-seven states have sterilization laws applicable to the mentally retarded, 37 states prohibit marriage of persons designated variously as 'idiots,' 'imbeciles,' and 'feebleminded,' and eight states permit the annulment of an adoption if the child is subsequently found to be 'feebleminded.' Although terms used in legislation are ambiguous and their references are not always clear, it appears that, in most states, a mentally retarded person cannot be issued a driver's license, nor can he vote, hold public office, or perform jury duty."

— Jane R. Mercer, *Labeling the Mentally Retarded*, 1973

UNTIL RECENTLY, filing a lawsuit against a school system has been the only recognized legal means, in most states, of raising the accountability question for special education. Lawsuits have been filed to force school systems to place genuinely handicapped children in special education programs, to take other children out of special education, and to move children from one type of special program to another. Between 1969 and 1975, more than seventy lawsuits relating to special education were filed in over thirty-five states.

Almost all of these lawsuits were filed either by parents of handicapped children or by advocacy groups representing the interests of the children. A high percentage have been successful, particularly those filed on behalf of severely handicapped children who had been excluded from programs. The lawsuits have led directly to the legal mandates requiring special education programs in all school systems, and to many benefits for handicapped children.

Unfortunately, in addition to the positive benefits, the lawsuits and mandates have also led to the notion in many systems that special education placement should be used to "solve" all the problems children experience in school. As Mrs. Caldwell pointed out, this notion can have the reverse effect of disguising the need for basic improvement in the whole system.

Mrs. Caldwell's basic concerns in a rural system are reflected on a broader scale in big-city school systems. In summer 1974, Merle Van Dyke, then assistant superintendent for special education for District of Columbia schools, said the effects of labeling more and more children are particularly noticeable in the big city schools. "Due to our court decree and other factors," he said, "the number of children enrolled in special education in the District has increased from 4,000 to 12,000 in only one year. Yet, when I meet with principals and teachers throughout the city, they tell me they don't see much difference, from one year to the next, and that begins to tell you something about the magnitude of the problem in inner city education. They really don't see that the rate of special education service has increased that dramatically, because, for them, as one person actually said to me, 'Look. Right behind every child you do give services to, I've got eight more of those little rascals.' And consequently, they just keep seeing more and more problems.

"The big city schools, and many others, are facing a literal crisis situation, which will be alleviated by nothing short of major changes in the entire system. The problem cannot be solved by special education alone. The relevant facts have to be taken into account here: First of all, 60 percent of the children in this school system come from families who are on public assistance of some form. Now, the relationship between poverty and what it does in terms of rendering a child capable of taking advantage of an educational situation, I think, is fairly well documented. So, with that as a given, add to that the fact that the drop-out rate in the urban areas is around 50 percent. Fifty percent of the kids who enter junior high school don't graduate from high school. Add to that, at the elementary level, the fact that at least 40 percent of the children are two or more grades behind in reading and math.

"This is the population of children who end up being highly problematic to the schools. We aren't talking anymore about handicapped children, as traditionally understood when you talk about profoundly retarded, severely emotionally disturbed, physically handicapped children. Those kinds of services are comparatively possible to provide, once the children are located. And they should be provided through special education.

"But the big problem in the cities are those kids who have remedial problems or curriculum problems, or have been subject to bad teaching, or whatever, so that they're reading on a first grade level when they're in the sixth grade. At that point, nobody really knows what to do with them, because you can't keep them in the elementary school forever, and so you get social promotions, or in some cases, the kid gets misplaced in a labeled program and he carries the label with him for the rest of his school career. Maybe he also becomes a discipline problem. Now, general education likes to do nothing more than dump these kids in special education. There are also many people who would like to have defined into special ed that group of kids who have been known as disadvantaged — or that group of kids who have remedial problems. Now I am not suggesting for a minute that these children should not receive individualized help. I'm saying that no one part of the school system can do an effective job of it alone, and that there should be resources available throughout the system — reading and math specialists, good guidance counselors, in-service training for all teachers. Unless we find ways of working together to make basic changes in the whole school system, problems of this magnitude are going to keep on happening. The general education system will stand still or become more rigid, and its accountability will suffer if more and more kids with minimal-range problems are shunted off to special education.

"It is indeed a very complex business, and it's not going to get any better. Because, at this point, these kinds of problems are no longer professional concerns. It's no longer simply a professional question of what kind of service to give, or whether you can, can't, should, or shouldn't. There are now all sorts of political and legal concerns too. And when all those things get thrown in with the child and his school, the complexity of the task becomes enormous. If most people could realize that, we might be able to minimize all this friction among various groups of adults, appreciate each other more, and find more effective ways of tackling these problems together."

In some cases, pressure is being appropriately applied to entire systems. In 1973, for instance, an eighteen-year-old high school graduate filed suit against the San Francisco school system for one million dollars because he was not taught to read above a fifth-grade level. The plaintiff, pseudonym Peter Doe, was in general more fortunate than the children of whom Van Dyke spoke. He went through thirteen years of public schools, making average grades, attending regularly, and never being involved in any disciplinary action. When his parents expressed concern about his obvious reading difficulties, they were told that he was comparable to his peers and had no problems to speak of. After graduation, however, two reading specialists assessed his reading ability at approximately fifth grade level. After a reading tutor was employed, he made rapid and significant progress.

Peter Doe v. *San Francisco Unified School District* contends that the plaintiff has been deprived of an adequate, basic education as a result of the acts and omissions of the defendants. The defendants include the San Francisco Unified School District, the board of education, the state board of education, the state superintendent of public instruction, and 100 persons alleged to be the agents or employees of the school's public agencies.

In "The Strangely Significant Case of Peter Doe," Gary Saretsky described the case as "the linking up of the militant consumer movement with the educational reform movement." Peter Doe, he noted, had led to the "founding of a new legal strategy for education reform, one that would use the judicial process not only to hold the public schools legally accountable for the results of the educational process, but would change the legal status of education from a privilege to a right."

The Peter Doe case was intended to raise important questions about the responsibility of entire school systems. In Copper County, Maggie mentioned the case to several people. "Well, they should have put him in special ed," Warner Jenkins said. "Then nobody could have sued."

As Maggie went from home to home that day, Warner's comment kept resounding in her head. The placement process for the following year was finished, and Maggie and the teachers were making home visits to the children who were to be transferred out of special education. In the process, she began to realize that Peter Doe–type lawsuits represent thousands of children who will never protest or even know what has happened to them. It became daily obvious that there were many reasons why parents might not be closely in touch with what was going on at school, much less thinking about filing a lawsuit.

Some kids had no one to take active responsibility for them. At Johnny Bragg's home, for instance, his grandmother, who was his legal guardian, nodded absently at the news of his transfer and said she never knew where the boy was anyhow.

Other children came from fairly unstable home situations. Thirteen-year-old Cary Ann Lawless went with the teachers to her apartment. She lived over an abandoned store, up a narrow, rickety staircase and down a long dark hall. "Sometimes there's people in the hall that scares me," she murmured. Inside her apartment was a man who scared her too. "That's Jack. He's not my father." Jack had moved in a month or so before and yelled at Cary Ann while the teachers were there. Her mother sat quietly throughout the entire visit. Jack watched Cary Ann closely and wanted to know why the teachers had come snooping.

At other homes, the immediate worries superseded considerations like quality of school programs. Maggie and Miss Adkins found Mrs. Watkins hanging clothes outside her house. "We've got some good news about your daughter Cheryl," Miss Adkins began.

"She's just like mine," interrupted Mrs. Watkins softly. "But she's really my brother's girl. He had to go out of state to work." Two children were playing in the dust in front of the house, while chickens pecked the ground near their feet. Maggie realized that Mrs.

Watkins wasn't much older than she was. At first glance, she had looked about fifteen years older.

"Good day for drying clothes, it's so hot," Miss Adkins said.

"Better'n yesterday," said Mrs. Watkins. "Hard to tell anymore when it'll rain."

After a few minutes' conversation, Mrs. Watkins visibly relaxed. When they got around to talking about Cheryl, she listened carefully, then said she was glad to know people were taking an interest in her. "I know the schools are hard nowadays," she added, pushing back her hair. "With so many other things pressing on me, I can't help her out as I'd like. You know, with all the people in this house, the only time I get a chance to rest and be quiet by myself is in the early morning hours. I'm up before anybody else is about, and that's my time." Her smile was lovely.

She asked if Cheryl was getting in any trouble and said Mr. Watkins would whale the daylights out of her if she was. "We want her to behave right, just like we do all the kids."

Jerry Bigelow and Maggie went to see Chet's mother in the morning before she went to work. Seated at her sewing machine in the family's wood-paneled den, she was delighted to hear that Chet would be in the half-day class. "I guess that's progress," she joked, gathering up odds and ends of cloth. "He's been reading up a storm lately. Working as a bank teller," she added, "lots of times I'm too tired when I come home to keep up with what he's been doing in school. But I do think it's wonderful that these children are getting extra help. It eases my mind, I'll tell you."

A few parents just didn't seem to care. No visit was tougher than the encounter with Brenda Haney's mother. Brenda's tremendous need to be touched and to touch had landed her in an isolated corner seat in Mrs. Quigley's room. ("Can't keep her hands off people . . . so we have to keep her off by herself.") After ten minutes with Brenda's parents, it was hard not to form definite opinions about the source of her need for affection.

"Child's no good, never has been," said Mrs. Haney flatly. "She's my husband's by his first marriage." Mr. Haney sat reading a newspaper during the whole conversation. "Ever since she was a little one, she's been that way," continued Mrs. Haney. "The Lord knows I've tried. None of my kids are like this one. It didn't surprise me a bit when they said she needed to go to Gateway. I suppose you know what you're doing, but if it were me, I'd leave her right where she is."

Other parents simply trusted the schools to do as well by their children as they did themselves. The visit with Mrs. Wilkins was a lovely experience. The Wilkins' house clung to a steep hillside outside Goshen. It was muddy season and Maggie jumped from stone to stone on the walkway bordered with daffodils. Mr. Wilkins, it turned out, had "gone to help, over to our neighbor's." Mrs. Wilkins was anxious to show Maggie the work she had been doing with her daughter Elizabeth, "to see if I'm going about it right." She obviously loved her daughter very much and was more than willing to do anything she could "to get her the things I didn't have." The most memorable impressions from the visit weren't transmitted through words. "Elizabeth's getting older," said Mrs. Wilkins, "and she's taking school seriously. I had a hard way at home, because my parents couldn't read. So I believe in doing all I can for her."

Some parents had had uneasy feelings about their child's placement but had not felt themselves to be in a position to question the school personnel. Other parents were, like Danny Brenner's, unaware that they had in effect given permission for placement. Luke and Preston Bennett's mother, for instance, was somewhat puzzled when Maggie asked if she had had any warning at all before her children were transferred. "Well, for some of them, there was that note . . ." she said vaguely, not quite sure what Maggie was talking about.

"Do you remember signing papers for the kids to get some testing done?"

"Well, there was something a long time back," she said, still puzzled. "And that paper didn't say they were going to send the children to Gateway." Though the permission-to-test slip did say the children might be "assigned to special classes," that term didn't carry the meaning "Gateway School" did.

Maggie told Mrs. Bennett that when she signed that paper, she had given permission to put the kids in Gateway if the test scores made it legal. "It does say so on the paper, but it's not quite clear . . ." Mrs. Bennett sat up straight in her chair, studying Maggie curiously. "Now, I didn't know that," she said finally. "My husband neither. It can't be so very clear if we, neither of us, knew it. We thought that paper meant the tests were to find out what kind of help they needed at Roosevelt School."

"If you ever get one of those papers on any of your other children," Maggie advised her, "don't sign it until you find out exactly what's going on. You could go over to the school and visit."

A few minutes later, Maggie and Miss Adkins got up to leave. "If you like it way out here," Mrs. Bennett said warmly as they got into the car, "come on back and see us again." Her littlest boy waved from behind her legs.

The two women rode in silence for several minutes before Miss Adkins sighed. "I don't think Mrs. Bennett would ever come look at the school," she said. "But suppose she did. She wouldn't really know what to look for. A lot of parents don't."

Maggie gave other parents the same advice about the permission forms as she had given the Bennetts. Most were reluctant to say much, but the day after she visited the Bennett home, Mr. Bennett came to the Yellow Castle to see the superintendent. Several hours later, Warner stopped by her desk. He hesitated for a moment before saying, "We really believe in home visiting around here, Miss Callahan. Too few of our teachers do it. But the purpose of any home visit is to *build up* support for school programs." The knuckles of his hand were white as he pressed down on the desk. "Do you *understand* that?" Maggie didn't say anything. "We had a *parent* in here all in a *dither* after a visit from you . . ." Obviously frustrated by Maggie's lack of response, Warner colored slowly and said, "Well, I just thought you should have known better. There are *other* ways of dealing with problems, so they don't come back the next day on *other* people's heads."

A little while later, Mrs. Frank Stone, wife of a real estate broker in town, stopped by to meet Maggie and inquire about future programs for her boy, who was blind. Mrs. Stone was one of the parents who did know what to look for in a special education program. She was in a position to do something about it too. As soon as the mandatory special education law had been passed the year before, she had begun to apply pressure very effectively to various politicians and board members. As a result, her boy, who had been born totally blind, was in an excellent state program for blind children.

Many parents, middle-class or not, haven't been as lucky as Mrs. Stone. Parents of handicapped children have traditionally banded together in some places into groups classified by disability: associations for the blind, associations for the cerebral palsied, and so forth. But even such groups have seldom carried enough political clout, by themselves, to secure educational programs for the children involved.

About the time parents began serious use of lawsuits to secure appropriate programs for their kids, different parent groups began to form coalitions. Their combined membership became a substantial political pressure group in many states and was a primary force behind the passage of many state mandatory special education laws. Parents' coalitions have flooded legislators' offices with phone calls and telegrams, organized highly effective marches, and filled the halls of state capitols.

The membership of coalitions tends to be made up of middle-class parents. Some parents in coalitions and other groups have also taken as part of their responsibility the protection of the rights of all children. In 1974, for example, Springfield, Massachusetts, parents formed PALDA (Parents Against Legal Drug Abuse) when it was discovered that "calming" drugs were being routinely prescribed for a very high percentage of minority and bilingual children through the special education program in the schools. PALDA pressured the school system and undertook various activities to inform the community about the practice. "I don't want the laws which helped my child to be used against others," explained one parent.

Parents in coalitions also report personal benefits from the consolidation of efforts. "We've been so separated before, in our different categories, both parents and children," commented Martha

Ziegler, a Massachusetts mother of an autistic child. "As we have come to know each other and know each other's children, I think that parents of children with different traditional disabilities have come to realize that our children have more in common than they have differences. We have begun to look at children as individual people, rather than label bearers."

Organized parents have become a much more powerful force in the past five years. Because of recent legal developments relating to special education, an individual parent can also have much more say-so about the type of program a child will receive — if the parent is willing and able to exercise that right.

As a direct result of the work of parent coalitions and other advocacy groups, federal law now requires a "due process" system for the protection of children, parents, and school personnel. The system was established to provide a means for parents and the schools to work out difficulties before resorting to lawsuits. The nationwide impact of such requirements on the schools was just beginning to be felt in 1975 and will have increasingly greater effects in years to come.

"Due process" is a term that has traditionally been associated with adult legal proceedings, with the right to a trial and legal representation. Applied to children, it now means that no change in a child's status relating to special education (or suspension from school) can be made unless certain procedures are first made available to the child's parents or guardian.

These procedures vary from state to state, but the basic rights guaranteed by federal law stem from a 1967 Supreme Court case (*In re Gault*) involving a boy who had been remanded to a state industrial school without a hearing. Writing that "the condition of being a boy does not justify a kangaroo court," the justices defined due process in its basic form as follows: notice of changes, right to counsel, right to confrontation and cross-examination, privilege against self-incrimination, right to an accurate transcript of the proceedings, and right to appeal. By federal law passed in 1976, each child to be transferred in or out of special education is entitled to those general rights, plus the following:

Before any alteration in the child's educational status relating to special education can be made, the child's parents or guardian (or surrogate parent unconnected with the school system) must receive prior written notice, explaining the proposed change in detail and must agree in writing to the change. If testing or evaluation is involved, written permission to place the child may not be obtained at the same time as permission to test. After evaluation is completed, parents must be informed of the results, after which another written permission to place the child must be obtained. The parent or guardian may request a hearing if at any point they wish to disagree with the school's recommendation. Parents also have a right to examine school records and (beginning in 1978) to participate in the creation of an individualized educational plan for their child, if the child is in special education. Schools, on their part, can ask for a hearing if the parent refuses special education placement and school personnel strongly believe that the child would suffer without the services provided in the program.*

All in all, with whatever drawbacks it may have, due process provides a readily available structure in which both parents and school personnel can raise questions in the normal course of events. And many school systems are welcoming the opportunity. "I think the whole thing is tremendous," commented Jim Huntley, chairman of the special education placement committee for Prince William County, Virginia. "It provides for a dialogue which we've never had before, and even if it does mean more work, I see a great deal of good coming out of it."

Mr. Huntley said that his county was making efforts to assure all parents that the schools would indeed welcome all inquiries and that there would not be any unpleasant consequences for the parents or the children. Such reassurance is needed. Dorothy Dean is a national information clearinghouse for parents of handicapped children. She has visited many parts of the United States as Project Director for Closer Look, commented on widespread reluctance, particularly among low-income parents, to insist that their child receive an appropriate education. "Once they stick their neck out and get out there where they're visible," she said, "well, job loss is one thing people fear may happen, but then there is also retaliation

*See pp. 329–34 for further details on current federal law.

against siblings, if you have other children in the schools. Welfare payments can be interfered with. There are all kinds of ways for a school system to, in effect, get even. Real or imagined, the threat of retaliation is often enough to keep a parent from demanding rights for his child."

As is true with the lawsuits, mandatory due process procedures will not automatically guarantee accountability. And like so many other terms in special education, due process can and will mean many things in actual practice. From the point of view of a dummy tech, it's important to remember that due process can be undermined, often unintentionally, as school officials are swamped with other duties. Warning against practices that nullify children's rights, Nicholas Hobbs observed in *The Futures of Children* that often, "the right of parents to consent to or dissent from the evaluation of their children and again to placement has been reduced to a farce. To 'save time,' those charged with obtaining parents' signatures coax parents into signing at the same time permission forms for evaluation and placement; thus the school has the freedom to place the child wherever it likes without having to solicit parental approval of the specific placement. When districts expect difficulty in obtaining parental consent, they may simply place the child *without* that consent. For example, while a survey of twenty-four school district EMR files indicated that 79% of all children enrolled in EMR programs had signed parent-approval forms in their files, in school districts with high concentrations of black children, the consent figures dropped to 55%. If all else fails, the schools have been known to coerce parents into agreeing to the school's desired placement by threatening to put the child on a program of 'home instruction' placement, which, oddly enough, requires no parental consent.

"We have chosen these dramatic examples to illustrate the ways in which institutions may not only distort the spirit, but also evade the letter of the law. One cannot assume that institutional officials instigate or cooperate with such subversion tactics for any other reason than to preserve internal structures of the institutions — to 'keep things running smoothly.' "

So, even with the new laws in place, it looks like the legal confrontations aren't over yet. "Ever since the lawsuits first started coming, people have been assuming that a law or a lawsuit can guarantee a child a good program," commented Jack Jones, chief of the Aid-to-States branch of BEH. "We're far enough down the road now to see that that just doesn't automatically happen. So I predict that the next round of lawsuits is going to hit the quality of programs, and it will be interesting to see if the suits are directed toward special education alone or toward entire systems."

"Even with the best of laws and regulations," agreed a representative of the Council for Exceptional Children, "each child can get a fair hearing only because people on the local level are committed to making sure that it happens." CEC is in the process of building up a state-by-state children's interest network they call the Political Action Network (PAN). Some states are putting together child advocacy organizations within the state government to mediate legal disputes between parents and schools with as much good will as possible. Massachusetts, for instance, was maintaining, as of 1975, an agency called the Office for Children, with over 200 employees dealing with child advocacy problems, both inside and outside schools. Other states employ one or two people for the whole state. Most states, however, as of this writing, do not employ official child advocates.

"Due process is going to mean many different things in years to come," Mrs. Caldwell told Maggie during one of their next visits. "But, outside all this new paperwork I see coming, I'm going to assume that the children need the same thing as before. What I mean is, no matter how many regulations you've got you've still got to have somebody right there who actually knows the kids and knows what's going on in the program. Somebody on the school side of things who's willing to approach each child asking, 'What if this were me? If this were *my* child, what would I do?'"

25. Hard Decisions

"Nobody in this business can ever realistically come to the conclusion that they've finished learning what there is to learn or that they've got the answer that's going to suit everyone. There's much more to know than we imagine, and everybody's got to find some way to get that fact into their bloodstream. Hell's bells, I wish I was twenty-five again, so I could go back and look at the situations I encountered then, with all of this information and understanding that I'm just beginning to put together in some kind of reasonable way."

— Andy Andersen, learning resource specialist,
Regional Resource Center, July 1975

ANITA FOUND OUT in early May that she had mononucleosis, so she stopped teaching and moved to the housing project where her husband was working. A teacher with a totally different educational philosophy was hired to finish out the year with the third grade. This woman was aghast to find that a "troublemaker" like Pickle was being "babied," and she refused to carry on any part of his special program. The result was predictable. Pickle became a teacher's nightmare. He threw things, started fights with the other kids, drummed on his desk while the teacher was talking, and wandered around the classroom — anything he knew to set her off.

"It just kills me to see it," Anita's aide told Maggie. "Pickle was doing so well, and if the new teacher would just keep up those little changes . . . but she says it's not her responsibility. She's paddled him three times this week already, and it just gets worse. It'd take her a lot less time to keep on doing what Anita was doing with him."

The new teacher couldn't even be convinced to let the aide take over Pickle's program. "I need her for *all* the children, not just a few," she said. "That's what's wrong with him in the first place. You've been coddling him."

Pickle lost a lot of his enthusiasm for the work he and Maggie were doing at home. "It's not the same," he said, and asked her again for reassurance that he wasn't going to be put in one of the retarded classes. His new teacher had said in his presence that he needed to go to special ed.

"No, Pickle, this year I decide who's going to special ed," Maggie told him. "And you're not."

A few days later, Pickle had a bang-'em-up fight with his dad. Maggie sat in her living room, flinching under the noise from across the street. The next morning, Mr. Dillard strolled into Pickle's classroom and told him he was going to play games with Buzz Murphy.

Buzz had been testing children earlier that spring, and the Stockdale people weren't aware yet of Tim Higgins' existence. So, in the same style that brought the refrigerator to Miss Adkins' classroom, somebody at Stockdale arranged, without informing Maggie, for Buzz Murphy to "evaluate" Pickle.

Pickle couldn't handle it. Buzz wrote in his notes that "the child seemed listless" and that "his attention wandered frequently." Pickle didn't answer the test questions right either. He told Buzz that nobody discovered America. He said that any kid, no matter what size, who tried to pick a fight with him was going to get creamed. Buzz asked him what he would do if his mother sent him to the store for bread and the grocer said there wasn't any. Pickle said he'd buy some snuff instead. And he told Buzz that peaches and plums are alike because you can mash both of them. Pianos and violins are alike, he said, because you can burn them. All apparently in a listless manner. Buzz read off series of numbers and Pickle repeated only the first two or three in each series. (He had been very adept at this in Maggie's kitchen.) He put together most of the sequence puzzles in the wrong order.

Pickle qualified for an EMR class. In his report, Buzz said this was a very repressed, hostile child, showing evidence of possible brain damage and/or emotional disturbance.

Maggie didn't find out what had happened until after Pickle shot her a third finger in the street after school, then ran the other way. Jenny finally told her. "He thinks they're going to put him at Gateway, and you're going to let them. I've got to go home now."

Nobody at Stockdale would claim responsibility for adding Pickle's name to Buzz's list. "But, my stars, he's been so disruptive lately," Mr. Dillard exclaimed. "I shouldn't wonder if it might not be a good idea to get some help."

Maggie visited Buzz for a heart-to-heart talk, hoping he'd be willing to drop the test. After she explained what had happened, he was. "Why, that's awful," he said with concern, showing Maggie his notes. "No wonder he didn't do well."

Pickle got off the hook. But he never trusted Maggie quite so much again, didn't come to visit very often, and was much more evasive. But he did get off the hook. By chance. If chance hadn't put him across the street from Maggie, he would undoubtedly have been placed in a class for EMRs the following year.

The incident had gone against the new guidelines the school board had passed. Maggie protested to Mr. Birdwell, and he said regretfully that it was hard to get everybody to agree on new procedures and that he was having serious problems of his own. The faction of the school board that opposed him was blocking one of his proposals after another. The controversy came to a head when the board refused to rehire a principal who had been working closely with Mr. Birdwell. These events had left the superintendent in a delicate position.

While Pickle was being due-processed, other children were being processed *out* of special ed into regular classrooms. It was no longer possible for teachers to look at special ed by itself. The regular system was a reality, and that was a bit much for some of the special ed teachers to cope with. Though they had been enthusiastic about their children's abilities and accomplishments, they got cold feet about transferring the kids out of special ed.

Eight children from Jerry Bigelow's class were making the change, some with half-day assistance, some with a lesser amount. "I don't know, Miss Callahan," his aide told Maggie. "I've seen some of these children come out of their shells this year, and I know they can do as well as other children their age. But I remember how they were when we first got them. I'm afraid that if we let them go, they'll just end up right back where they were. I'm afraid those teachers are going to ignore them all over again. Maybe we ought to keep them."

Some people have suggested that special education teachers frequently don't like to give up their children because they don't want to believe that the children can get along without them, and yet indifference to less fortunate children in the regular system is no fantasy. But should the children have to stay in classrooms for the retarded in order to "protect" them from the rest of the school system? Wouldn't it be better to try to change the basic approach? Once again, it seemed the children were being transferred with crossed fingers. "Maybe that will be true whenever special education and regular education exist as totally separate operations," speculated Jerry Bigelow.

Mr. Birdwell invited Maggie into his office during the first week in May to express his concern about the following year's enrollment at Gateway. "I need a definite figure," he said. "I understand that you're thinking about transferring a sizable group, and we must have enough children in special ed next year to justify the teachers' salaries. The salaries are being paid by the state, you know. If we send too many children back to the regular classrooms, we'll lose those funds."

Maggie's face registered shock, but she couldn't see Mr. Birdwell's expression since he was behind the *County Superintendents' Newsletter*. Raising her voice above the drone of the fan, she told him that placement was being made to the children's advantage, and threw in, "Most of those children shouldn't be at Gateway."

Mr. Birdwell looked up, slightly startled. "You know I shudder to think that some of those children don't deserve to be there. At the same time, we must be careful not to lose those salaries. That wouldn't be a good idea, if we wish to utilize that many teachers in the future." He added judiciously that he wasn't sure they could legally transfer *any* of the children without "making sure they can score appropriately on the intelligence test."

Maggie flinched. That was no random comment. Technically, the children were supposed to have another test. It wasn't spelled out in the state regulations, but, until they were tested again, they could be put back into special ed, any time, on the basis of the existing test, and it was obvious that Warner Jenkins wasn't likely to approve money to have those tests administered.

"At this point, it looks as though each of the teachers will have approximately twelve children," Maggie said. "And one classroom has been eliminated completely." Mr. Birdwell said in his judgment that was an acceptable number, not to be undercut.

"Well, if we do it that way," Maggie said, "then we should make a policy of not transferring any more children into Gateway or any other classroom unless they're severely handicapped and we know the program's there for them . . ."

Mr. Birdwell gave her an odd look and went back to his newsletter.

Preston, Jenny, Elizabeth, and several others were going from Gateway to Stockdale. Ten children, including Johnny (the "bright boy"), were going to the high school. Three were coming from Stockdale to Gateway. That put Gateway's enrollment at fifty-one children, and there was a list of at least six other children who were overripe to get out of there.

After the conversation with the superintendent, with no due process procedures to fall back on, Maggie had to decide on her own who would be considered retarded the following year and who wouldn't. She had talked with all the children's teachers about the various children involved, but still . . . "Thank God there's going to be a committee next year" kept going through her mind, as she realized that she would be likely to lean toward the children she happened to know best. Her deskwork went something like this:

The Unretarding Game

You must send three of these children to Stockdale School. Your choices will transform three children now considered EMR into Regular Children. Your choices will significantly affect the lives of all six. Nothing you do will be fair.

I. The children
   a. Elizabeth. Shy, white, 11 years old. Possesses much personal dignity, works diligently at any assignment. Overall fourth grade level, could bloom with an appropriate program.
   b. B.J. 12-year-old black boy. Clever, alert, distractable. Often

drunk, yet retains appealing childlike openness. Unchallenged at Gateway. May be acting out frustration. Would be in Jerry Bigelow's class the following year.

c. Shelly, 10 years old, white, Elizabeth's cousin. Has been subjected to much material below her capabilities and interests during the past two years at Gateway. Extremely low self-concept and motivation, quite cynical. Overall fourth grade academic level.

d. Mary. Quiet, white, 9-year-old from a particularly isolated home. Has drawn within herself this year. Capabilities and achievements exceed many of her third grade peers at Stockdale. Considers herself incompetent.

e. Sharon. Black 10-year-old. Mary's inseparable friend. Very friendly but afraid to go back to Stockdale. Entirely capable of handling it if she can overcome her lack of self-confidence.

f. John Bennett. Luke's brother. He never should have been at Gateway. Has fallen far behind, could make it up with Jerry Bigelow.

II. The schools

a. Stockdale

Positive: a phase-in program run by a well-qualified sensitive teacher; a chance to be regular again for students.

Negative: high enrollment, spotty quality teaching for children below grade level, probable discrimination against former special ed students.

b. Gateway

Positive: a much-improved program which would concentrate on individual needs to a much greater extent; the "security" of avoiding competition.

Negative: the stigma of being considered retarded and the possible losses in motivation and self-confidence which go along with that stigma. Less social and academic opportunity.

III. Other factors

Since this is the first year children have been officially transferred from special education, the regular classroom teachers will be suspicious of them and may look for any opportunity to send them back. The children's success will largely determine the ease with which children can be transferred out of special education in the future. All six children could make it, with varying degrees of support from the "phase-in" resource teacher.

This game should not be considered paperwork. After you have made your choices, think about the three who are left behind. What are your reasons for leaving them behind? Do these reasons justify continued placement in a class for the mentally retarded? Don't look for the answers in the back of the book. They aren't there.

Lack of due process left so much room for arbitrary decisions. A few days after struggling with transfers, Maggie and Miss Adkins were sitting on the edge of the gravel playground, watching a kickball game, when they noticed Cary Ann Watkins edging up to them. Maggie noticed Sarah Clendenin and several other girls from Mrs. Legg's class huddled together a few feet away, giggling and staring.

"You think they're going to ambush us?" Miss Adkins wondered aloud.

Suddenly, Cary blurted, "Miss Callahan, Sarah wants to know can she go to high school too." Her question knocked Maggie totally off balance. Beyond Cary, Sarah was blushing wildly and trying to occupy a smaller space. None of the girls took their eyes from Maggie's face. They were going to high school, and their friend Sarah wasn't. Maggie was speechless with the realization of how important her answer was to them.

A few seconds for me, four years for Sarah, she thought. So important for Sarah, but so far out of her control. Look at the helplessness in their eyes. The other children were yelling and cheering, but around Maggie it was awfully quiet.

She could hear these children's voices: Miss Callahan, let her live a life just like everybody else. She wants to know if she can go to dances. Can she socialize in the drugstore at lunch, can she sit in the classes with everybody else her age? Can she stop coming here?

They should never have to ask, Maggie thought. I should never have that kind of power over their lives. She looked at Miss Adkins and saw the same anger, frustration, and helplessness.

The girls stared. Maggie finally managed to nod and say, "I'll see what I can do." The spell was broken. The girls hugged each other, dancing and hugging. *"Does she mean yes? I think she does! You can go, Sarah! No, wait a minute! She said she'd see what she could do, didn't you, Miss Callahan?"*

They were so happy, and Maggie was playing God.

Sarah hadn't been scheduled for the high school because Mrs. Legg had told Maggie that she wasn't ready to handle it. That afternoon, Maggie brought up Sarah's case again, telling Mrs. Legg about the playground incident and asking her again if she felt Sarah could manage high school.

"Why, if Sarah wants to go that bad, just send her on," she said, scratching her ear.

"But I thought she was so far behind . . ."

"Oh, she'll get on, if she can get some help. Mostly, I thought maybe she was a bit shy to handle it."

Maggie dropped by the high school to talk with the principal, an outspoken, pragmatic man. "We'll take the girl," he agreed. "We're overcrowded, you know, and I just hope we'll be able to offer these Gateway kids the kind of help they're going to need to make the adjustment."

Maggie hadn't been by to see Warner for a while. The next day, when she went to his office to talk about setting up procedures for buying through the special education committee, he looked at her silently for a minute, as if she had brought up a subject he found it difficult to think about. Then he said, "We don't need to talk about that, because we can't do it that way." He tilted his head to one side and added, "I'm responsible for those funds, you know."

Maggie's blood pressure shot up again. "Warner, you can't do that," she spluttered. "The board passed the guidelines. The teachers are entitled . . ."

Warner's face also reddened. "I've read through those guidelines, and they conflict with Title I regulations." He started leafing through a catalogue, then looked up and added, "I'm not sure that the teachers are going to have *time* to do all the things those guidelines say. That's not their responsibility, and it seems to me that you're imposing on their time. We can't afford to take them away from their classroom program, you know."

Something had happened. "And I don't know what you think that committee is going to be spending," Warner continued, putting the catalogue down. "You've already added enough expense to the budget to more than take up any funds that might be available to special education." His remark lit a match, and they ended up going round and round again, just like old times — both coming up against the same shortages, but each making the other feel rotten.

Up at the Instructional Materials Center, Harry was his usual blunt self. "You may have noticed that the political situation is changing around here," he began, feet propped up on his desk. "Birdwell isn't in a position to act like a referee anymore." He shook his head. "Woman, Warner thinks you've been throwing your weight around again," he said. "Here he gave you all that money" — Harry's headshakes were becoming more exaggerated — "and then you go looking a gift horse in the mouth, bringing in some expensive psychologist —"

"But that money wasn't for *me!*"

Harry held up his hand for silence. He was ticking off, finger by finger. "— and getting little books of rules passed without even consulting him, stirring up parents . . ." He put his hands behind his head and stared at her.

Maggie let his words sink in. "Harry, do you think Warner's opposed to what's been happening, or do you think he's opposed to the ideas coming from me?"

Harry shrugged, gesturing with the ever-present Pepsi bottle. "It's hard to separate the two, isn't it? Ideas don't function alone. They're always connected to somebody. You've been pushing it way too fast. Now, it may be for the sake of the kids, but it's gotten to the point where the children get lost in the interpersonals, so it's counterproductive."

"Maybe Mr. Birdwell —"

"I told you, Birdwell can't afford to do anything about it any-more," Harry cut in with a matter-of-fact smile. "He might not be here that much longer himself."

"Holy cow, Harry."

"Holy cow, indeed. There's a lot about the politics of the system that you don't understand or you haven't been paying attention to," he continued, looking up at the ceiling. "You can't say that I didn't warn you. Boy, are you hardheaded. A slow learner, you might say, if my choice of words is correct." He stopped to consider that last statement. "Or then again, if you try hard to see that the 'random element' is just as important as theories about how things ought to be . . ." He held up a fat catalogue to ward off any flying objects. "We might be able to take you out of the 'educated fool' category."

The next day, Mr. Birdwell was more depressed than Maggie had ever seen him. "I've never seen such a school board in my life," he told Maggie slowly. He promised to encourage Warner to cooper-ate with her, but warned that, at the same time, he couldn't support policies that would disrupt the operation of the school system. "We have to deal with the realities of the situation," he added. "We all do."

"But if I read you right, that's pulling the ground out from under a lot of what's been built up —"

"We have to deal with the realities of the situation," Birdwell re-peated.

That afternoon, Maggie delivered some materials to Mr. Blan-kenship at Goshen School. It wasn't really necessary, but she wanted to catch a little of his positive outlook. The school buses were leaving as she arrived.

Mr. Blankenship and his class had been moved into a classroom at the beginning of April. For two months, the transfer from the cafeteria had always run up against the agricultural reference li-brary. Then, finally, for no discernible reason, Mr. Birdwell had called the Goshen principal and told him to make the transfer. (Somebody told Maggie later that one of the board members had been particularly interested in agricultural studies, and Mr.

Birdwell had had to work the problem out delicately so as not to antagonize him and jeopardize other projects.)

Blankenship was pleased to have the classroom. "You know, I didn't think I liked teaching before this year," he told Maggie, looking around the empty room. "I taught accounting at the high school. I didn't want to teach special education and certainly not the intermediate grades. But, after I'd been here a couple months, I found myself telling my wife and everybody else who would listen about these kids — what they want, what they care about, how they try."

He told Maggie about the marble tournament he had planned for the following week's math lesson and showed her the boys' work on banking procedure. Then he put on his baseball cap and leaned against his desk, looking around the room. "You know, if I get called back to work for the power company," he said, "financially, I'll have to take the job. But the way I feel now, I'd a whole lot rather teach.

"I have a favor to ask you," he ventured. "Three of my boys are over sixteen now, and I'm wondering what's going to happen to them. Joe, particularly, has made great advances this year. What happens to him? Can he go on and get a high school diploma?" Blankenship wanted Maggie to ask the superintendent what could be done for them.

Mr. Birdwell told Maggie that the county couldn't possibly give students who had been in special education most of their school years a certificate of any kind. "We'd look pretty silly if we gave these children a diploma without their finishing an established program, wouldn't we?" he asked. "Think about how the other students would feel. It wouldn't be fair to them, when they've had to take all the required courses. Our diploma has to mean *something*," he explained.

"Now, if any of these students has the perseverance to finish an established program, I'd be more than delighted to give him a diploma." He nodded, hooking his thumb under his suspender. "It might mean, of course, beginning in the ninth grade and working on through."

Joe hadn't had the option of persevering in an established program. The school system had placed him in an unestablished program, connected to nothing, leading nowhere. He was rapidly approaching the age where he would be expected to earn his own living. Under that setup, he was free to drop out any time, without so much as a piece of paper saying, "The boy was here, and he tried." He would just wander away, having received a special education.

"The vocational school will change all that," Mr. Birdwell said, as if he could read Maggie's thoughts. "I have to go by the law."

He's not in the political position to do anything that might rock the boat for the vocational school, she realized suddenly, looking at Mr. Birdwell's unhappy expression. He has too much to lose.

There were other questions Maggie needed answered. What about Gateway School? When could most of the children be mainstreamed? When could some of the teachers be converted to resource teachers in the elementary schools?

Mr. Birdwell shook his head slowly. "I would also like to see those sorts of changes made quite soon, but our hands are tied by Title I regulations. The only conceivable way we could use Gateway for anything else would be to put Title I offices there, and we've already planned to build our new school board offices elsewhere. Beyond that, we have to consider the overcrowded condition of our classrooms. It's a shame, but we're locked in, simply locked in. We have to go with what we have for now."

They looked at each other for a very long minute. "There's just one thing we've got to do then," Maggie repeated. "No more kids can be transferred into special ed from the regular classrooms unless we can be absolutely sure we have a good program to give them."

Mr. Birdwell took out his watch and studied it, rubbing the front with his thumb. "We are required by law to provide programs for children who qualify," he said finally. "I understand why you say that, but we really aren't in a position to make those kinds of decisions. Mr. Jenkins tells me there is a list of qualifying children." That gentle smile crossed his face, but his eyes looked sad. "Do you feel you could work with that?"

Everything was quiet, except for the clack of typewriters. *Clickety clack clack.* Mr. Birdwell spread his hands before him and studied them. Then he sighed loudly. "You and Mr. Jenkins have been at odds again . . ." He swiveled around in his chair and looked out the window. "It's not as easy as people believe to put these programs into effect, Miss Callahan. If the public could begin to understand some of the problems and shortages we encounter . . . and when you've got politics on top of that, I just don't know where the children fit in."

In the strong afternoon light, the superintendent's profile changed from reflective to businesslike. He swiveled to face her and told Maggie that he himself was considering another job offer. "I feel it my obligation to let you know what my own situation is. As for yours, we do have a lady with a great deal of experience working around school systems who has an application on file for the supervisor position. Now, if you feel you cannot live with the expansion of the program under the circumstances, it's going to be very uncomfortable for you in your position. You think about it, and see if you can be happy going with things the way they are."

Maggie went back to her desk and sat staring at the wall for a while, trying to sort everything out. Then she went home. Her ecological system was out of balance. All she wanted to do was sit and look at the mountains and the river for a long, long time.

A friend named Peter was waiting at home. He looked at her face and said softly, "Hey, don't say anything about school. We could talk about something funny instead . . . How about a chocolate-covered overshoe?"

Peter, Jenny, and Maggie took Brown Eye along the railroad tracks beside the river. They walked until they came to a narrow, dark hollow. When they followed the creek back in, they found a big waterfall, and there was a grapevine to swing on and large rocks to climb. Peter and Jenny climbed all the way up, while Maggie sat on a ledge about a thousand feet above the falls singing, "Some glad morning, when this life is over, I'll fly away." Brown Eye sat down at the base of the cliff, whining and barking every now and then.

They all walked back along the railroad tracks as the sun went down and waved to the engineer when the freight train roared by. The lightning bugs came out. And the hills curving up above the river looked too round to be anything more than a child's drawing of a mountain dream — floating above a river that goes past all those places you never have seen.

Later that night, Maggie woke up in the darkness, telling herself, "If you'd used a little more sense in working with the adults, things wouldn't be falling apart now. You've become a roadblock to your own efforts."

A week later, after two more emotional rounds with Warner, Maggie resigned, effective the end of the term, not entirely sure whether she'd be helping the kids more by leaving or by staying. Mr. Birdwell accepted her resignation gently. "You've been learning some rather hard lessons in school, Miss Callahan," he said, looking down at the papers before him. He promised to arrange for the following year's supervisor as quickly as possible.

Any school system has its long-term people who feel understandably attached to what's already been done and correspondingly defensive when a new person, an outsider, starts making critical noises. In that light, Maggie was lucky she didn't get kicked out of the Yellow Castle in the middle of the term. Shortly before she left, the assistant superintendent asked Warner if all the spice would go out of his life when he didn't have Maggie to duel with. Warner rolled his eyes, then ran his hand through his white hair. After considering a minute, he said, "Well, I'll tell you. It's too bad, but that girl could have done all right I *suppose*, if she could have gotten it through her head that things don't change overnight."

The assistant superintendent gave him an "are-you-really-saying-that?" look. Warner grinned and said, "No, I mean it. She worked hard enough, all right, but she just didn't seem too *bright* in the way she'd go about things. She'd get her feathers all ruffled up and start in here like she was going to turn everything inside out lickety-split without consulting any of us, and I'll tell you, my blood pressure'd go *up*, and I wouldn't feel like giving her one inch. Got a bad heart, you know. No telling *what* she'd do with that inch if you'd give it to her." He chuckled and shook his head. "Yup . . . she's got some interesting ideas though. Mr. Birdwell's got a real good woman lined up to take her place. Maybe this new woman'll be able to make use of some of those ideas."

That's exactly what happened. Mr. Birdwell had a good long talk with the new supervisor, who then established a good working relationship with Warner from the start. In the meantine, Abigail Robin got a reading tutorial program going in five of the regular schools. The new sixth grade teacher at Stockdale School got the fourth and fifth grade teachers interested in teaming up and scheduling kids into different classes at different times of the day to accommodate different needs. The special ed supervisor and the new resource teacher teamed up with the regular teachers, and the resource program was off to a flying start. Peggy Adkins decided to stay in special education, where she began to acquire a reputation as a fine teacher. Jerry Bigelow, as the new principal at Gateway, got together with his teachers to analyze each child's needs in each area, then work out a multilevel program for all the children. Warner wrote to Tim Higgins to tell him that his services were no longer required.

To the regret of all who knew him, Harry Blankenship had to take the job with the power company for financial reasons. Harry at the Instructional Materials Center resigned at the end of the year, and Mr. Birdwell left the following year. Both had some pointed things to say about politics in the schools. So some circumstances changed, others didn't.

Anita and her husband came to visit in Copper County the weekend before Maggie left, and they took a bunch of kids on a picnic in their truck. While the others played softball, Jenny and Maggie took a long walk along a creek bed. They came out by an old abandoned four-room schoolhouse. Its windows were shattered, and broken glass mixed with old textbooks was scattered on the floor. They picked their way from room to silent room. Jenny giggled at the cuss words newly painted on the old blackboards. She found a piece of chalk and began to draw. You could almost touch the quiet.

In a small back room, vines crept through the window above a low table and a couple of tiny chairs, one of them upside-down. A few children's alphabet blocks sat on the table, as if a child had left them there in his hurry to go out and play. Heavy dust covered everything. A sign on the wall read PRAYER CHANGES THINGS.

As they walked back to the picnic, Jenny was very quiet. She stuck flowers in her hair, and blew dandelion puffs into the air. Finally she asked Maggie if she thought Stockdale would be too hard for her the next year. She smiled when she said it, but Maggie caught a flicker of anxiety in her eyes.

"The only way it will be too hard for you, Jenny, is if you lose confidence in yourself. You're going to have another teacher there to help you." Jenny nodded, and Maggie thought about the children who weren't as far advanced as Jenny.

Anita and her husband stayed for dinner that night. After they ate, they went next door to visit a bit with Lucy on her front porch. Children were playing tag under the bridge. Jesse was pulling weeds down at the end of the street. Mrs. Krebbs stood by her screen door. The air was soft, and June bugs were yelling. Sitting on Lucy's porch steps, Maggie looked up above the bridge at Stockdale School and beyond, at the mountain. How did everything get this green so quickly? she wondered.

Lucy knew most of the neighborhood children, and their problems both in and out of school were real to her. That evening, rocking in the porch swing, she put some of her thoughts into words. "You know, you've just about sold me on this mainstreaming idea," she told Maggie and Anita abruptly. "It think it's probably worth a good honest try. You know why I think so? Because the kids who get sent to the classes they say are for dummies turn out to be the ones who've already got a tougher row to hoe because of the way life is outside school. I know the intentions are good, sending kids to the other place. But I know too, from talking to the kids around here, that it makes it harder for them to overcome the difference life's already set. I mean life's not fair, and some people are always born with less advantages. But, if the schools can't make it better, at least they don't have to make it worse. Maybe it's different in other places, but that's the way I feel for Copper County." She folded her arms and nodded her head with an "I have spoken" air.

"I do have a question for you," she continued. "Now suppose that I'm a third grade teacher, and I've already got thirty kids in my class. Even if my school has a good resource teacher, am I going to be able to handle those extra children? Especially children who've been having problems of one sort of another?"

"That question could have a whole bag full of answers," Anita said thoughtfully. "Seems like it would depend on the school, and the people involved. And in some cases, there might not be any good solution right away. People believing like you do would have to work together for a while to build a system they can believe in . . . so we won't have to think of any kids as 'extra children.' "

Maggie thought about the sign she and Jenny had seen in the abandoned schoolhouse and felt a funny kind of ache rise up inside. "Seems like we're really talking about some pretty basic problems of the whole school system as it reflects society," she said. "And mainstreaming's not going to be the final answer to those. But then, at the least, it may force schools to look at some questions it's been easier to ignore before. I'm thinking about questions like 'How come there are thirty kids in a class to begin with?' and 'If we have the money to hire a learning disabilities teacher, how come we don't have the money to hire another third grade teacher?' If we could hire another third grade teacher, then each teacher would have only fifteen kids, right? That way, it'd be possible to mainstream kids effectively, and a lot more could also be done for all the kids."

"You two are up on your soapboxes again, and it hasn't even been an hour since dinner," Anita's husband kidded them. Maggie turned red, and they all laughed.

Lucy said she had something else to say "before concluding *my* broadcast. It's obvious that there's no simple answer, but what you're saying is that the problem has something to do with the question of how come all of education can't be special. Is that it, Maggie?"

"That's close," Maggie said, smiling up at her. "At least for kids like the neighborhood kids."

"That's a very interesting thought," Lucy said. "But then, it's past my bedtime, and I try not to chew on any complicated ideas this time of night. I'll take it to bed with me and dream on it instead. How would that be?"

26. Toward Making It All Special

"When a regular classroom teacher asks legitimate 'How am I going to do it?' questions about mainstreaming, the last thing she needs to hear, and the first thing that's going to turn her off is some kind of response which implies that she is some sort of hard-line educational fascist who 'just doesn't like those kids.' "

— Frederick Andelman, Massachusetts
Association of Teachers, May 1975

"And yet, there's a basic insanity here. You take a seven- or eight-year-old child who has not signed a contract, who does not want to be in school, who isn't there voluntarily, who may have no prior preparation to be there. He's required by law to be there. He gets matched up against a person who has spent years preparing to be there, who has volunteered to be there, who is paid to be there and is even licensed by the state as a specialist to be there. And then, when the communication between the two of them breaks down, you automatically blame the kid and put a label on him?"

— Robert Prouty, Department of Special Education,
George Washington University, May 1975

As SPECIAL EDUCATION programs grow bigger, more complicated, and better funded, it's more important than ever to deal with the kinds of human relations problems that tripped up Maggie Callahan. At this stage of development, when widely differing opinions and points of view on mainstreaming are common, the impatience with other adults which handicapped Maggie in her job is something to be avoided.

Everybody is learning. Copper County is experimenting with mainstreaming today, and mainstreaming is bringing its own versions of the human relations problems in Copper County and far beyond. "My feeling is that the real make or break of mainstreaming will be in the attitudes of the teachers and the children," commented Ed Martin of the Bureau of Education for the Handicapped. "This means both of the teachers — the special ed teacher and the regular teacher. How are they going to talk together? How are they going to work together? How do they resolve conflicting feelings they're going to have about kids?"

I'd like to show how important these questions are. In spring 1975, Frederick Andelman of the Massachusetts Teachers Association (which represents regular classroom teachers) described the impact of mainstreaming on the members of his union in terms of the needs of his teachers. "Whatever finger-pointing is going on in this business," Andelman commented, "most of them end up pointing at regular education personnel, as if there is something wrong with those people or as if their attitudes are impeding progress. We just can't accept that, for a number of reasons.

"First of all, regular classroom teachers are being in many respects represented — and are being seen by the public — as being responsible for all kinds of circumstances that they have *no power or control over*. And all we're saying in regard to mainstreaming is, 'If you want to change the ground rules, if you want to impose a whole new set of expectations on the schools, then all we want is a chance to understand what it is that we ought to be doing. And we want to be provided with the resources necessary to fulfill those objectives. And teachers aren't being well provided with those sorts of things, not anywhere in this country.' "

Massachusetts is a good example here, since its special education law, Chapter 766, in effect since 1974, is very similar to, and even more extensive than, the national law effective in 1978. The Massachusetts regulations contain very strong provisions for mainstreaming (also called the least restrictive alternative), due process, and nondiscriminatory testing. Andelman emphasized his feeling that Massachusetts teachers had gotten to the point where they supported the intention of the state law and, on the whole, would like to see it work for the sake of the children. "In the beginning," he recalled, "lots of teachers in the union felt that it was a terrible law and that we ought to get rid of it. The initial response was one of fear and some real hostility. That response changed as teachers found out more about the purpose and specifics of the law and began asking legitimate questions. After they learned more about the law, they realized that it's a good law and that it can benefit all children if it is ever translated into reality. But teachers also know that it can't work well in a situation where the legislature votes a fraction of the necessary funding and resources. So, our organization has taken a very simple position: full funding and full implementation. Secondly, we have called for adequate teacher education and reeducation.

"I think, today, you will find that teachers are frustrated with the law and its regulations. Not because of the earlier kinds of concerns about 'those kids in my classroom,' but as teachers found out about this law, what it ought to do, and how it ought to work, they raised questions like 'My classroom is overcrowded to begin with. I am perfectly willing to do this, but what are you going to do to enable me to do it effectively?' "

The reactions Andelman describes among the members of his union do reflect reactions reported from many other parts of the country. Dr. Jean Hebeler, professor of special education at the University of Maryland, also had some important things to say in 1975 about the adult side of mainstreaming. "All along," she observed, "we talk about individual differences of kids, but we deny individual differences of teachers. Suppose, for instance, that a teacher likes to work with small groups. Instead of considering the way in which she works best or providing her with adequate help to make a comfortable transition what we do is just say to her, 'Now this is what we're going to do this year, and you're going to be doing that.' Equally bad, we do the same thing to administrators like principals. Now, that's enough to sabotage a mainstreaming program right there. It's totally inappropriate to expect a person to change immediately. We wouldn't expect children to do that.

"I think we are often naive about this human condition in school systems and state education agencies, in the federal agencies. We think we can say, 'Now this is what we want to do' and have it happen, without taking the necessary steps to assist the people who are supposed to make it happen. At this point, what we're saying is mainstreaming, which happens to be a good direction, one worth sticking with. I think 90 percent of the educators around the country would probably agree with the *concept* of least restrictive alternative. But that doesn't mean that they're automatically going to be able to do it. There will be a time lag between the commitment and the actual ability to do it.

"But see, what we do, is we decide that we want to do it, so we try to implement it administratively. Or we get a regulation passed that says it's got to happen. And then we hammer on the people who actually have to do it, day after day, saying, 'You're not doing it right! It's not working!' Well, in a case like that, of course it's not working. Lots of times, in my experience, these people didn't understand what it was that the administration wanted them to do.

"You can't have the planning done by one group of people totally in isolation from the people who are going to put it into effect and expect that it will come out as it was 'supposed' to. If we don't start paying attention to that fact, we may be heading for a big fiasco in many parts of the country with mainstreaming. Not because the concept is wrong, but because we're not involving the regular classroom teachers in the planning, giving them a piece of the action so to speak. We have a majority of the teachers in the schools at this time, working with a majority of the kids, who have been allowed no input into the specifics of their situations. As a result, on a national scale, I find general educators saying, 'Don't tell us about this mainstreaming unless you're going to help us make the adjustment.' And yet the basic willingness is there. So, the sooner we start seeing this as a process involving the entire system, the smoother it will go for everybody."

Andelman feels that the process could go even more smoothly if the special education association people would take time to get the support of the general education teachers' unions and associations. "One of the things which has interested me for a number of years," he observed, "as I've participated in activities of the Council for Exceptional Children on a state, regional, and national basis, is their incredible shortsightedness in failing to recognize our kinds of organizations. Now, this is more of a comment than a criticism, but most state departments and most teacher-preparation institutions, when it comes to special education, take their cue from CEC, which is the special education professional organization. And yet, CEC itself has not been able to recognize how schools are organized on a day-to-day basis, and how important it is to enlist the support of regular classroom teachers.

"While the state departments of education and the CEC people seem to do a lot of talking with each other about the installation of special education programs, they seem to regard general educators as impediments, as people who ought to learn how to do things right, rather than people who should be consulted and assisted. But, as teachers become organized, and as we have more and more to say about what happens in school districts, teacher organizations certainly shouldn't be ignored. Indeed, we can be a great help."

Andelman's warnings have much substance behind them. In her 1974 study of five Indiana-negotiated general education teachers' contracts, Julianne Clarke, assistant professor of special education at Western Michigan University, found that clauses were being written into the contracts that could have long-term negative implications for special education by seriously impeding mainstreaming efforts. Ms. Clarke and other reviewers of the contracts were particularly concerned about items that would have the child who caused discipline or control problems removed to special ed.

"This kind of thing wouldn't be happening if we'd just show the unions that we want to and will work with them, rather than try to impose things on them," commented Phil Burke of the Bureau of Education for the Handicapped. "And it's always the children who are the losers when we don't do that sort of thing."

Somehow, the finger-pointing on all sides keeps going back to teacher-training. "I think what's ultimately going to happen, after the full effect of the special education laws is felt," mused Andelman, "is that the process of diagnosis and evaluation of children's difficulties will be accelerated, while the process of actual program development will stay pretty much as it is. So we'll end up with sophisticated evaluation, diagnosis, and due process, with little change in what's actually happening in the classrooms. At this point, school systems are also having to backtrack and run in-service programs for their teachers, and regular classroom teachers in general are asking for assistance. Now, what all *that* means is that there will probably be pressure from teachers and school systems for a complete revolution in undergraduate teacher-preparation programs, so that all teachers coming out are equipped to handle individual problems of all kinds, in what we now consider the minimal range.

"At this point, for instance, any teacher ought to be able to do most of what many people called 'learning disabilities specialists' do. I didn't say anybody *could* do it now. I said they *ought* to be able to do it. But just any teacher can't work that way now, because most of the teacher preparation programs are loaded up with so much junk that there's no time to put in that kind of training.

"And yet, that's probably what's eventually going to have to happen. The focus of these laws is going to be changed to where it belongs. It does belong with the teachers. More basically, it belongs on the nature of the system that prepares all teachers to teach. Really, what we need now is a whole new kind of preparation for the people coming into teaching. In the meantime, one thing we need is a whole lot of consideration and diplomacy on all sides."

Efforts to backtrack and make up for deficits in teacher-training are under way in many places; many school systems, particularly the larger ones, are running year-round in-service programs. The state of Utah has developed a Title III training program (U–SAIL) for teachers already teaching, which orients them toward individualized instruction over a three-year period. Thousands of regular classroom teachers in several states have already gone through U–SAIL while still actually teaching. North Dakota's New School runs a program in which teachers in the field switch places with teaching students for a year. The Learning Resource System, the Council for Exceptional Children, and other sources have put together workshop "packages" to acquaint teachers with the various aspects of mainstreaming. The CEC's "Mainstreaming: Teacher Training Workshops on Individualized Instruction" and "How Can Tests Be Unfair?" are good examples. The Los Angeles County Schools' "Equal Opportunity in the Classroom" is a three-day packaged workshop with five follow-up classroom observations primarily designed to make a teacher more aware of the effects that stereotyped expectations have on the mainstreamed students. Taking another approach, a few systems like the Milwaukee Schools have experimented with a consciously designed minisystem in which a parent can choose for her child a school that suits the child's learning style — highly structured, open classroom, or other alternatives.

Taking a step toward the kind of training of which Andelman spoke, the Bureau of Education for the Handicapped, beginning in 1975, offered federal special education funds to colleges and universities that agreed to include special education courses in the preparation programs of regular classroom teachers. "Like everything else in special education, this one could go either way," commented Bob Prouty, a special education teacher-trainer at George Washington University. "It could either pave the way for new solutions or it could backfire beyond belief. So much depends on the actual content of the courses.

"I hope to God they don't teach categories. I can't think of anything worse that we could do to children than to spread categories and all the negative expectations that go along with them over the entire teaching profession. If that happens, it will be like a psych undergrad in his second year of psych. Four pieces of jargon, and he thinks he knows how to analyze behavior. That's what will happen with teachers if we go that route.

"I hope that instead of teaching categories, we begin to train *all* teachers to deal with a diversity of behavior and a diversity of learning styles. And 'diversity' doesn't automatically mean special education. If you take a look at the kinds of things which are now taught in good special ed training programs, outside the identifiable handicaps like deafness and blindness, they're no more special ed than the man in the moon. They're part of the general human knowledge about human beings, and would be useful to every teacher teaching.

"At this point, the 'least restrictive alternative' concept should have another concept added to it, and that's the 'least flexible or experienced teacher' concept. Because, unless we do that and provide that teacher with the kind of assistance she needs, what's going to happen is good planning on the top level, good regulations on paper, and actual programs that don't even resemble the intent of the people who made the policy.

"So we need to be fair to all teachers and provide them with the philosophy, expectations, and know-how to deal with mainstreaming. When that happens, we'll be in business."

Because of the special education laws, the present school situation is unique in our educational history. Many other trends and approaches have been tried in the past, but none has ever been required and funded by law. Whatever can be learned from earlier history also has to be seen in the light of the unique present circumstances. The laws are there and can be used either to the great advantage or disadvantage of individual children and adults in school systems. At this stage, the special education laws seem to offer schools a wonderful chance to do good things for a whole range of children, *if sufficient resources are made available to allow school system personnel to provide for the needs of all teachers and to make reasonable choices about the programs they will offer children.*

Whatever the "answers" might be for "minimally handicapped" children in each system, they do seem, in general, to be connected at this point to the fact that special education is funded at a much higher level than any academic area of general education. To say that problems would be eased if special education were funded at a lower level would be an especially perverse answer, just at the time when tens of thousands of severely handicapped children are getting their first chance at therapy and programs that obviously wouldn't be provided without the laws and funding. On the contrary, it could be argued that there has been no better time in the country's educational history to increase funding opportunities for all of education — specifically, funds *earmarked* for the needs of general educators involved in mainstreaming and for alternatives to labeled placement for "minimally handicapped" children. At the same time, funds could be well used to encourage the kind of revision of teacher-training of which Frederick Andelman spoke. Not to do so may well increase the possibility of more and more labeled children, with very little overall substantial change in actual programs (other than increased hostility among the adults and self-doubt among the children).

During the summer of 1975, Ed Martin recalled, "Years ago, I suggested to the learning disabilities people that they ought to expand the definition of *normal*, not expand the definition of handicapped, that this would be much better for the kids in the long run. What they ought to be insisting on is that the schools see as part of their normal responsibility the development of some supplemental reading and tutorial programs for kids who have some difficulties, but keep it in that ball park. Well, interestingly enough, their paranoia was running so high that they thought maybe I was against learning disabilities, and people were saying, 'Ed Martin doesn't want to let us in.' Well, what it amounted to is, I don't want to see those kids go *out!*"

There is one main problem in what Dr. Martin had to say. In a time when the government has already spent $3.2 billion on "research and development" of the B–1 bomber, there just is not much money being made available to general education for the alternatives Dr. Martin talked about. School enrollment is going down, and many school officials find themselves with extra classroom space on their hands. There is a surplus of teachers and widespread parent dissatisfaction with the schools in general. If adequate funds were available, systems would be able to hire additional third grade teachers, for instance, and lower classroom enrollment, thereby giving general education teachers more room for individual attention to their children. At this point, however, for systems that do want to do something extra for children who are having difficulty, the main financially feasible alternative is special education, with its open-ended categories. Unfortunately, this situation can force systems into "solutions" that plant additional seeds of self-doubt in children's minds.

So little money is allocated for teachers' salaries in many states that people like Harry Blankenship can't afford to teach. The problems and possible solutions seem to be infinite. Yet, maybe Bertrand Russell found one end of the whole tangled knot when he said, "If we took education seriously and thought it as important to keep alive the minds of children as to secure victory in war, we should conduct education quite differently. We would make sure of achieving the end, even if the expense were a hundredfold greater than it is."

Robert Prouty may have found another end of the tangle. "I think we're naive if we assume that what we're dealing with is a technical problem. We're dealing with very basic value problems. And those values don't arise from and aren't focused on education. They're across the board.

"Beyond that, there are so many motivations and vested interests tied in now. You're dealing with the pediatrician who is running learning disability programs on the side. Or the psychologist who suddenly can't test anymore in the public schools because the courts won't let him, so he's doing it in private. The whole educational materials market, and certainly the 250,000 additional teaching jobs projected for special education over the next decade. You figure that the guys who haven't been able to deal with delinquency as they'd like suddenly discover that they can blame learning disabilities for it. The parent who lacks skill in child-rearing can blame the fact that it's affecting her child on a learning disabilities problem. You could go on and on, and whatever grain of truth might be in any one of those situations, it gets so that we're using these kids as a scapegoat for the human race in the United States, and that's a tragedy.

"Seriously and multiply handicapped kids should continue to receive improved and modified programs. But, for the great population of mildly and moderately, who are basically victimized by the prejudices of our society against the poor, or the Chicano, the black, or even boys* . . . those kids are going to be victimized until people in general begin to see that society, and therefore the schools, is composed of a variety of human beings, and that different doesn't automatically mean being worse. It just means being different."

*Prouty refers to studies like the Mercer Riverside, California, study, which show that at least twice as many boys than girls are enrolled in EMR classes. This is usually attributed to the fact that boys tend to be more disruptive and are therefore more likely to be referred. Otherwise, one would have to conclude that boys are less bright than girls.

Afterword: Macon County —
Something Fine

A FEW YEARS AGO, a person I met by chance told me that material for the final chapter of *"Johnny's Such a Bright Boy, What a Shame He's Retarded"* might well be found in Macon County, Tennessee, I owe him many thanks for that suggestion, for this section is taken from two visits there in spring 1974 and late summer 1975.

During my second visit, a man who worked for the Tennessee state division of special education explained, "Macon County is a kind of yardstick for us all, as far as rural programs go. They haven't done anything so terribly unusual, as far as program structure goes, but they do go about things in an extraordinary way. For one thing, they don't waste any time. For the past five years, they've taken on new responsibilities well before most other counties have even thought about them. They were the first to have a mainstream program, they've got an excellent vocational education setup, and a program for severely handicapped kids well under way. Now they're moving into preschool handicapped programs, while the very idea is giving personnel in other counties nervous fits. Myself, I'm glad that none of their programs is set up in unusually complicated ways. They've done things in such a way that any other rural county could relate to and copy if they wanted."

When I asked him why that particular county was able to do so much so well, he hesitated and said, "Well, it isn't money, though they couldn't have done it without money. But they didn't start out with any more resources than anybody else. On the contrary, they've had less than most, as far as state and local funds go, though they sure know how to get them from elsewhere. But then, I could name you five or six counties off the top of my head who've had much more total money and have done much less. So Macon County's advantages have been mostly intangible, I'd say, the kind you couldn't buy, no matter how many grants you got." He ran through a list: resourcefulness, hard work, solid philosophical agreement about where the program should be going, and imagination. He ended with "Mainly though, I've never seen a group of school employees work with more good will and consideration toward each other. Now, the children do come first, and it's not that people don't disagree . . . I don't know exactly why it is that they get on so well, but I'd lay odds that Annette Cothran has a finger or two in that pie."

Annette Cothran, the woman of whom he spoke, is the main reason this section has been added to the book. As supervisor of the Macon County program, she daily exercises a natural talent for heading off politics, discouragements, squabbles, and the petty nonsense that so often drains the potential from a program like that of Copper County. She brings out the best in the people with whom she works, and the program has blossomed under her guidance. In that respect, she represents thousands of similar people in all parts of the country, the real heart and soul of special education's "quiet revolution."

Annette is a woman who does such things as show up outside the school board office at seven-thirty to watch the maintenance men unload file cabinets from the pickup truck. Why? "Well, they'd chased all over and had gone to a lot of trouble to get those file cabinets, and were excited about what a good deal they'd gotten us. I don't know how exciting a file cabinet is to look at, but I wanted them to know their efforts were appreciated." That wasn't an unusual incident. She approaches everyone that way, from the superintendent of schools to a first grader, and her attitude has its effect. The maintenance people are unusually willing to go the extra mile for the children in her program, and many others are too.

Annette Cothran is a Macon County girl — born there, raised there, married there, works there. She "dances on her own table," a phrase Anaïs Nin uses to describe a person who, like a flamenco dancer, dances always on the same tabletop, knowing every ridge and crack intensely and well and ultimately discovering the same truths that the world traveler finds far afield.

Macon County itself is much like Copper County — beautiful, hilly countryside and warm, straightforward people. The roads coming into Lafayette, the county seat, are lined with ploughed fields and flowering fruit trees in the springtime. An occasional child rides a pony by the roadside. Beer joints stand near white frame churches. Lafayette also has a courthouse — a red castle — in the town square. Old men sit out front, whittling and talking politics and high prices. The Dollar Store is just around the corner. The county population is fairly stable, conservative, and proud of its peaceful, tradition-rich way of life. A comparatively high percentage of the county population requires public assistance, and widespread negative feelings about "the welfare" exist there.

Mrs. Cothran has been working with children and their problems in Macon County for nearly three decades. During those years, she has gone through many changes in her ideas about education for children who don't fit the standard mold — changes that have come through hard work and painful reexamination. A short, gray-haired woman, she gestures expressively while talking. She listens as well as she talks. You get a sense that she cares. The story of her experience and philosophical changes is the story of the growth and metamorphosis of the Macon County program. Beyond that, in a real sense, her story also parallels the growth and changes that have taken place in the entire field of special education during the past twenty-five years.

"My involvement with special education started many years ago with homebound children," she explained to me one evening. "As I traveled around from home to home, some people welcomed me, some were ashamed of their handicapped children, some believed they were being punished by God, others ignored the children, and others were very concerned, teaching them as they could. One man threatened a teacher with a shotgun, another would have food ready for us when we came. There was more than one filth-caked child who was left to crawl around with the chickens because her parents didn't think she was going to be good for anything. So we had a lot of work to do.

"It was customary then to keep children who had problems at

home, so most of mine were severely handicapped children. Homebound was considered a very progressive program. But we also had children who just hadn't been succeeding in school, those who were not being allowed in school for disciplinary reasons, and some whose parents just wanted them at home, sometimes to work around the house or farm. I made the rounds for seven years before realizing that, for the most part, we were teaching children in the home who could get much more in the schools. After that, getting the children into school became my prime concern.

"Not long thereafter, the school system started the first class for EMRs and TMRs in the American Legion Hall. It was such a big step forward. You have to understand how proud we felt. I have a significantly retarded daughter myself, so I was all for it. About a third of the children in that class had never gone to school before. The other two-thirds were pulled out of the regular classroom, where they had been sitting coloring or doing nothing. At that time, nobody thought about individualizing instruction or resource assistance for the teachers. We just put the children together, all degrees of problems, and I was the teacher.

"At first we really felt that arrangement was tops. The children were learning to do a lot of craft activities, they were learning academically, and the parents seemed happy enough. We did have parents, however, mostly middle class, who refused to let their children participate.

"We were kind of like a big motley family, with the children ages six through eighteen, academic level about kindergarten through fifth grade. But after a year or so, I began to notice that the nonseverely retarded children were being badly stigmatized. They started telling me that the other children on the school bus said they were going to the dummy school. Other people told me that the kids ducked down in their seats as the school bus went through town, so people wouldn't see them going to the special education class in the American Legion Hall.

"But other concerns seemed more important at that period. I had begun to suspect that my curriculum wasn't what the children needed. I felt that we were too much oriented toward the traditional ideal of 'retarded' curriculum, a lot of crafts and a watered-down program. The crafts were fine, but the kids weren't getting the skills and language development they needed to get along in the working world. I suspected that, with all my good intentions, I might be denying them the chance to develop capabilities that would help them in everyday life. So I decided to go back to school myself, hoping that would provide the answer.

"When I first enrolled in Peabody College in Nashville for a master's program, my sole interest was improving the curriculum we had, with no thought about changing the structure of the program. I was teaching while going to school, so the Macon County program changed right along with me. We moved toward vocational education and developed strong ties with the vocational training school. But, even as I was rewriting the curriculum, my thinking was changing drastically.

"It started changing that very first summer in school. Dr. Lloyd Dunn had just written 'Special Education for the Mildly Retarded: Is Much of It Justifiable?' the article in which he questioned his own lifetime work with self-contained situations for EMR children. As you know, that article shook up a lot of people. I was one of the first to be shook. He was the director of the Institute for Mental Retardation and Rehabilitation at the time, and I had only been in school about three weeks when he delivered the paper for the first time ever, using our class as a guinea pig audience.

"Well, it completely rattled me out of my shoes. To tell the truth, he really antagonized me. I met him for coffee, and oh, I was really hot under the collar. 'Do you mean to tell me that my program is a complete failure?' I asked him. He said, 'No. Your program is not a complete failure. But there's a much better way of doing it.' And then he told me about mainstreaming for children in what was called the minimal range. Even though I couldn't agree with him at the time, he hit home. I continued to revise my curriculum, but all the while, I kept feeling those things Dr. Dunn had been saying.

"We went through three years of curriculum-changing at the American Legion after that. I was telling myself, 'Now we're going to make this program work. We've got the Vocational Training School, and we've got our workshop here . . .' I was dreaming that we could maybe change the whole image of retardation in the community, so that it wouldn't be a stigmatizing word. Then we could have our little self-contained program, and nobody would be ashamed to come. My daughter wouldn't be hurt, and neither would anybody else's child. But I was forgetting that people are afraid of what they have no experience with. And so, by separating all those children, we were making them into something mysteriously and negatively different.

"Soon several of the children in the EMR range were getting older and had left my class. These children had stayed in the special education class all the way through, so they were used to a rather isolated and artificial social situation. I couldn't help but see that they were having a tough time in the workaday world. Having been so sheltered, they weren't reacting well to situations they would have encountered as a matter of course in a regular school. For instance, the first day they got mad at their employer, or somebody said something unflattering to them, they'd simply go home. Mrs. Cothran wasn't there to take up for them or to help them stay. I was forced to see that they weren't really ready to be a part of the world around them.

"By that time, I'd hear myself telling children, 'It's necessary for you to be in this class if you're going to learn,' when deep down, I really didn't believe it anymore. And the stigma was more noticeable than ever. One incident made a particularly strong impression on me. One of my boys was a crack shot with a rifle and loved to go hunting. He went into the store one day to buy some ammunition, and the clerk told him that he knew he went down to the American Legion to school, and that store policy was not to sell ammunition to retarded people.

"By the time I'd finished rewriting my curriculum, my thinking had changed so much that I didn't want to use it within the American Legion structure. After all that work, I just threw the curriculum away and went back to school again. My husband thought I'd gone crazy.

"There were three things I wanted to do: to look at everything that had been done in regard to mainstreaming in the whole United States, to decide what type of supportive service would be best for our county, and to develop that program with the guidance of the professors at Peabody. During that stint at Peabody, we finally decided that resource rooms where the children could come for part of the day were best for Macon County. That was the start of the beginning of mainstreaming in the county.

"Now, the changeover didn't happen immediately. It took five years of talking to convince the superintendent and the board of education to restructure the program. And it almost got to the point where I said, 'Well, if I can't get this kind of change, I'm through with special education, and I'll go back to the regular classroom.' It had gotten to the point where, when I went to work, I went to work depressed, knowing that I was doing the wrong thing by my lights for most of those children. And, when you're working very hard, knowing all the time that you're defeating what you really want to do —

"It took some hard evidence to finally produce the change. We had a different superintendent back then and he had become very dedicated to the idea of special education. He knew that we wanted to expand the program, but didn't really understand the direction I wanted to go in. This created a rather unfortunate situation, because he began working toward getting us a new building, just for special education. He didn't tell me, because he wanted it to be a surprise.

"That dear man walked into my classroom one day, looking just like Santa Claus coming in for Christmas. He told me he had done a whole lot of talking and had convinced enough board of education members and county court members that money should be written into the budget for a whole new building for these children. 'You'll have it all to yourselves, Mrs. Cothran,' he said. 'Plenty of room, a shop, a home economics area, all the things you've been wanting.'

"I would have liked to disappear on the spot. I had to tell him I didn't want it. He was one of the most disappointed persons I've ever seen, and I felt as bad or worse than he did. But that building would have tied us down to a self-contained situation and we wouldn't have been able to restructure the children's programs.

How could we have explained to people why we weren't going to use a very expensive, relatively new building? And if we had started putting a lot of children in that building, we would have encountered much more resistance from the regular classroom teachers when we eventually tried to mainstream.

"Anyhow, after that, everyone was finally convinced to at least give mainstreaming a try. We went to work on the state department in Nashville and finally got a fourteen-thousand-dollar federal grant from Title III to purchase a portable classroom and all the necessary equipment, and set up a pilot project.

"We set up the portable classroom outside Central School, a middle school, grades five through eight. Of course, I would have preferred to have a classroom inside the school building, but I wasn't in any position to push further. It was large, well equipped, and air-conditioned, so we went forward with that.

"Now this change to mainstreaming is hard for a lot of people to understand, you know, and that's understandable. After all, five years ago, special educators were telling the regular classroom teacher that she didn't have the ability or facilities to deal with children with problems. 'We have,' we said. 'Give us the children. We can work the miracles.' And now we're coming back and saying, 'These children would be better off in regular classrooms.' No matter how sincere we are or how true that may be, you can't expect that people wouldn't be a bit confused and maybe resentful. In my particular case, even though I didn't have a big tradition of self-containing to reverse, I still felt that it was absolutely necessary to let everybody know what was going on and try to get their support before we even started.

"The hardest thing in some ways was visiting all the parents of the children involved. I'd been to them years before to say, 'Please let me have your child. We can do so much more for him out of the regular classroom,' and now I was coming back to say, 'Please won't you let us put your child back into the regular classroom with resource support? It will be much better for him.' It felt a little awkward, but after I explained, everybody agreed.

"We met with all the regular teachers in small groups and then again with those teachers who seemed sympathetic and who were considered good teachers. We placed the children with them initially. But perhaps the most important thing that was done was preparing the regular children themselves, to try to give them a positive feeling about the program from the start.

"Each teacher brought her class out to the portable classroom, so everyone could look around. We felt that if the children had the chance to ask all kinds of questions openly and get involved themselves, they would be more likely to accept the program and the children in it. So when they came in, they were handed a little checklist of areas where a student might need help and were told, 'This program is for boys and girls who think they might possibly need some help this year.' We explained that we would try to fit in as many students as we could during the year, but space was limited.

"They knew that the former American Legion children would all be participating, and we talked about the fact that they would be ahead of some of the children who would be coming new into their classes. They really seemed to accept and understand the idea that the most important thing is the extent to which a person can value himself and keep on learning. Those little sessions helped to set that sort of tone.

"That week, two hundred and thirty children asked to be included in the program. We were flabbergasted. It was such a change. In the American Legion class, nobody else had ever wanted to be included. But in this case, the new structure of the program excited the children enough that the stigma in great part fell away. After that experience, I began to feel that if children can understand what a program is about, and if they share the teachers' goals, they can make a decision for themselves rather than be shoved into the program. The new structure seemed to be much more acceptable to many parents too, people who had previously told me, 'I know my child has problems, and I'd love for you to help him, but I can't let him be stigmatized in that way.' So we were beginning to reach many more children who needed help in that minimal range.

"Not all of our children, of course, were transferred out of the self-contained structure. As is true now, we began to reserve the self-contained situation for children whose handicaps were truly so limiting that they required and benefited from full-time specialized assistance.

"I saw so many children bloom though, after they went back into the regular program. The name-calling almost disappeared. I'd feel a lot of joy whenever I'd see one of them just walking with a new friend. There was so much more there than any tests could show, and it was worth every bit of the effort.

"Most of the children came to the resource room approximately two hours a day, though some came for less time. Otherwise, their schedules were the same as everybody else's. That support was vital to them. We had talked a great deal about going back, but they had still been somewhat fearful that people would be mean to them, and I don't think they had any idea how much broader the range of opportunity would be for them.

"It's hard to say why we didn't have more trouble than we did. There was a lot of praying going on, I'll tell you, because we couldn't afford failure, since that was the first resource program. I'm sure those prayers helped, but if the groundwork hadn't been laid with regular teachers, the parents, the principals, and the children, I suspect that we would have had problems coming out our ears. More to the point, if we hadn't prepared people and tried to set a good tone in advance, we would have *deserved* problems. I don't think successful programs just 'happen.' It doesn't seem like anybody has the right to shove a new program in on anybody else, adult or child, without at least explaining it. The government makes a habit of doing that, and, in my opinion, that's a big reason why a lot of otherwise good ideas fail. You've got to consider everybody involved and include each of them wherever you can."

That year, as the first resource teacher, Mrs. Cothran worked double time, by all reports, to make the program work. But she tried not to let people know, and used to go home when the other teachers did, then come back later when nobody was around and work very late. "A resource teacher has to walk such a fine line at first, until she's accepted," she explained. "On one hand, the regular teachers suspect that you might be goofing off while they do all the work, since you have a smaller class load at any given time. I had a total case load of over thirty students, for instance, but no more than six students were in the room at once. That could look kind of cushy, at first glance. So it's important that the resource teacher make sure the regular teachers see that she's working at least as hard as they are. On the other hand, it's important that the resource teacher not give off a holier-than-thou feeling, implying that she's there to tell the regular teachers what they're doing wrong or to show them up. You don't want them to feel resentful of you, because you do hope some will rethink their ways of approaching certain children. It can get very tricky."

Four years later, the Macon County mainstream program included thirteen resource teachers and two liaison teachers with the vocational school program. In addition, the county vocational technical center gave on-the-spot job training to any older handicapped student or ex-student who needed it. There was also a self-contained program for severely/profoundly retarded children and a preschool program for children with any handicapping condition. Some of the teachers were running what were called "Advanced Study" sessions for kids who showed unusual interest and ability in any area. ("We don't believe in measuring 'gifted' by IQ scores, any more than retarded," Mrs. Cothran commented.) The entire mainstream program is called "Compensatory Education," since it is a consolidation of the special education and Title I programs. Mrs. Cothran directs the program, and the elementary supervising teacher, Mrs. Dycus, writes proposals and other important paperwork. "I give her the information and she puts it into good form," Mrs. Cothran said. "It's marvelous to have that relationship. Otherwise, I'd be chained to a desk, and I don't have enough hours a day to be out in the classrooms as it is."

The success of the mainstream program can be judged in part by one little girl who stood at the door of one of the resource rooms, staring resentfully at one of her friends inside and asking, "How come *she* gets to come here and I don't?" It could also be judged by the high percentage of children who had improved and moved from the resource program back into full-time participation in the regular program. One principal said he judged the success of the program in part by the decrease in behavior problems from older children who were finally learning to read. Another said he judged success by the much greater degree to which some of the regular classroom teachers were able to individualize their instruction now that they had resource help.

Actually, it had been Mrs. Cothran's hope from the beginning to get to the point where the program would work with the regular classroom teachers on a partnership basis as much as with the children themselves. By the 1975–76 school year, the quality of the overall program had improved so much that that sort of relationship was developing. "A few years ago, the resource teachers, a lot of them, weren't really sure of themselves, and so many regular classroom teachers would hesitate before cooperating with them," Mrs. Cothran explained. "Now, we've improved our own staff and skills so much that teachers in general seem to have confidence in us. They know they can expect real concrete help when they refer a child."

Annette had begun to take that concrete help right into the classrooms. "Last year," she explained, "we felt that we had every child in the resource-type setting who needed to be there. So, when I did my evaluation for the state team, I said we would give relations with the regular classroom teacher priority this year. I feel that we can take at least seventy-five children out of the resource room setting sometime during this year *if* we can provide the regular classroom teacher with meaningful materials and support.

"We got consciously started last year. For beginners, the teachers in my program began sending their aides down to relieve the regular classroom teachers so they could visit the resource room while their children were there and we could work out closer coordination of programs. But I felt that we ought to give actual concrete support if we really wanted the teachers to shed any reluctance to take the children back on a full-time basis. The science teacher at Central School gave us our first opportunity. She said, 'If you'll help me with the materials, I really do want to meet the needs of these children in my class. I've been trying, but I'm not doing it.'

"We got her a listening center and copied a lot of science materials geared to high-interest and low reading level. We provided cassette programs and all kinds of interesting worksheets at an easier reading level than her materials. She could select the ones that went along with the particular subject the class happened to be working on. It worked beautifully. She found that other kids in the room were also profiting very much from it, not just the ones who went to the resource room.

"The math teacher saw how well it was working," Mrs. Cothran continued, " and she asked if we could do the same thing with her classes. So we got started with math before the end of the year came around, and now she's all set to begin the school year with one hundred percent participation, and then we'll go from there."

"It's just like friends," the science teacher told me. "I give a little, and they give a little."

"We're going to keep on expanding this kind of relationship whenever there's interest," Mrs. Cothran said. "Don't be fooled into thinking that everyone's interested. We still encounter considerable resistance, but if we can eventually work in this way with four or five teachers in each school, it'll be great."

Toward that end, the resource staff puts out extra effort to make sure that their program schedule doesn't conflict with the regular classroom teachers'. "We do our planning together with the regular classroom teachers now, so we don't have any schedules that don't go exactly with theirs," one of the teachers told me. "If there are conflicts, we're all sitting there scheduling together, so we work it out to the child's best advantage. It's so simple if you do it that way at the beginning, before school starts. But if the regular teachers were to get their schedules set up, and then we'd go in and try to schedule overtop of them, it'd make impossible problems. I've heard real complaints from teachers in other systems where they pull the kids out of the regular classes to go to the resource rooms at odd times. Maybe that works in some places, but here it wouldn't. Everyone would get irritated, and then your whole program would be in trouble. You've got to think of these details. This way, scheduling together, we also get away from the attitude that 'this kid's going to the resource room, so he's not my responsibility any-more.' You might say we're gradually building a kind of community spirit among all the teachers."

"We'd never be able to do any of this without good teachers in the resource programs," Mrs. Cothran commented. "I've gone down to the wire at times to get good teachers for these programs. You hear about mainstream programs being used as a dumping ground for ineffective teachers, just like the self-contained classrooms were." She frowned. "Well, that destroys the whole program right there. And then people say, 'Mainstreaming isn't any good.' Here, I think people are convinced that good teachers in the resource programs benefit the entire school system."

To bring up and maintain the skills of her staff during the beginning years, Mrs. Cothran was constantly there, week after week, bringing materials, advising, even helping scrub classrooms. She arranged for several practically oriented college-credit courses to be taught in Macon County each year, and invited the school principals when appropriate. Regular meetings were arranged for the teachers on school time, so everyone in the program could get together to trade ideas and have a planned in-service session. Mrs. Cothran was very proud that her teachers didn't hesitate "to air their gripes to me. They don't seem to feel they have to wait till I get out the door to tell each other what they *really* think. And they tell me when they make errors too, maybe because they know I'm always making mistakes, getting all harum-scarum, and going in all directions. None of us tries to pretend we're never wrong, and that certainly makes things more comfortable."

"The morale is really high," commented one teacher. "We've got a kind of family feeling in this program. We all believe in what we're trying to do and we love to get together. And Mrs. Cothran is always exposing us to new things and even substitutes for us so we can take field trips or go over to the Instructional Materials Center."

(The regional Instructional Materials Center of which she spoke was set up by the state in 1975. Its new director at that time bought, catalogued, and computerized a wide variety of teaching materials so that a teacher could feed information about a particular problem into the computer and get back suggestions for materials that could then be borrowed from the IMC. Mrs. Cothran had also begun to set up a similar filing system, minus the computer, in Macon County. The regional IMC director also put on workshops and took a traveling van out into the counties. When the state suggested that the center might not be refunded for the following year, all the counties kicked in money to show how much they wanted it to continue.)

Besides the much-increased confidence level of many resource teachers and the new IMC, just one year had made many differences in the program. The most striking change was in the physical facilities. In 1974, several resource teachers had been literally teaching in closet-sized areas. A year later, all had been given good working space. There was also a new tricounty vocational school ("Regional cooperation is a godsend out here in the country"). Materials were centrally organized and catalogued, and children with "low-incidence" handicaps were receiving the same quality service that children with more common problems received. Thanks to specialized equipment and materials, for instance, a deaf child was adjusting beautifully to public school. ("The state division people came down to see if she ought to go to the state school for the deaf and said she was getting on too well to be disrupted now.") Placement decisions that year were being made by a "multidisciplinary team." ("We call it M-team or conferences, since people get put off if you go around using all those big old words all the time.") The team meetings included everyone involved with the child's program, including parents. ("We're really working hard to get more parents involved, and that often means us going to them.")

Significant changes were also taking place in the overall working of special education in Tennessee, as well as across the nation. During 1973–1974, the state had attempted to drop the categorical system of classifying children in favor of the "structural " system that had had success in Massachusetts (funding special ed on the basis of the kind of program: resource, self-contained, etc.) In Tennessee, the changeover happened with less than a year of preparation and very little means to regulate the new procedures. As a result, mass confusion broke out in many counties, and there was no real way to assess the validity of any child's placement. Though some counties did make good use of the change, there was enough overreaction and misuse to send the state division personnel hurrying back to categories. One county was even reported to have used their money to send employees to the Council for Exceptional Children convention in Los Angeles. It was agreed that future attempts would happen after much more careful groundwork was laid. "We were disappointed, of course," the Macon County superintendent commented, "but it's just one more proof that there's no simple answer to complicated social problems. The way we feel here though, we'll report those kids in categories on paper to the state and federal governments, if we have to, but those labels won't go any further than those papers."

In Tennessee, as in most states, the amount of paperwork was increasing dramatically along with more complicated regulation. "Special ed and Title I seem to be running a race to see who can pile on the most forms," Mrs. Cothran said. She had acquired a secretary in 1975. "There was a bit of opposition from the board when we first started talking about a full-time person to help with all this office work," Mrs. Cothran remembered. "So, when they asked me about it, I said, 'Sure, I could get the paperwork done if I had to devote my time to it, but that wouldn't leave much time for the children or teachers, and, when you get right down to it, you would have just bought yourself the highest-paid secretary this county's ever seen.'"

It would have done Maggie Callahan good to see the work Mrs. Cothran did outside the office. Like Mrs. Caldwell from Sloan County, Mrs. Cothran consciously makes efforts to figure in people's feelings and possible reactions along with their needs. One incident I shared while visiting gives a good picture of the way she takes people's feelings and their possible reactions into account, while trying to fill the needs of the program. She made a run over to one of the grade schools to deliver materials, talk with one of the teachers about the following year's program, and consult with the principal about a child who had been referred to the program. "But the most important reason I'm going over there," Mrs. Cothran told me, "is the man who's going to help us with our evaluations. He's a very bright, perceptive young psychologist," she explained, "and we're lucky to get his help. He's sensitive and usually supplies the teachers with good insights. But tomorrow will be the first time he's ever visited this school, and he happens to have long hair and a beard. This is a conservative area, and so you can see how we might have a problem.

"If he's going to be more than a test generator, the teachers will have to be willing to take what he has to say seriously. One of my missions this morning is to defuse potential negative reaction to his hair. It'll only take a few minutes. I'll just chat with a few teachers when I see them in the hall and mention, by the way, that we've been lucky to get a very competent person to come work with the children and say something about how funny it is that he happens to have long hair and a beard. They know me, so it should be O.K. But if I didn't do that, some people might see very little beyond his hair and write him off as a hippie with no sense before he ever opens his mouth. Reason I know this reaction so well, of course, is because I react to stereotypes myself. And I also like to be told what's happening as much as the next person.

"You know," she continued, "it doesn't take so much to head off negative reactions or get people ready for something before they have to deal with it. Sometimes it takes just a few seconds. But, if you don't pay attention to those little things, the big ones may fall through."

Many more such tales could be told of Annette Cothran — and people like her — to illustrate the gentle, constructive approach to human nature. Each story would show how much respect and consideration of co-workers can also advance the interests of the children. (Not that she is willing to put the interests of co-workers before the interests of the children. She can be very tough, as I saw when she risked a lawsuit rather than rehire a teacher she felt was inappropriate for the children.) Her usual way seems to be made up of dozens of daily considerate personal contacts, in addition to all the other aspects of running a program, and that's very lucky for everyone, children as well as adults.

Annette Cothran gives much of the credit for what success the program has had to the rest of the administrative staff. "If they weren't so supportive," she says, "we wouldn't be able to do much of anything. I know some very talented supervisors in other counties who are just constantly hog-tied in their efforts by politics, paperwork, and general lack of support. If they got the backing the staff here gives me, you'd really see some beautiful things happening." It's true. The superintendent, an unusually level-headed man, supports the program right down the line, and the elementary supervising teacher gives support in many ways beyond proposal-writing. Many of the clerical staff use their spare time to help make materials.

Yet I wondered if Mrs. Cothran realized how much her own good nature and hard work had to do with all that good will. People were willing to support her efforts in part because they knew their support would be well used. "There's not a lazy bone in that woman's body," said the judge of the county court. "If she asks you for money, you know it's going to be put to good use. We haven't turned her down yet." He was speaking in particular of revenue-sharing funds that were given to special education to remodel a large area in a grade school for the resource services.

"I don't see how we *could* turn her down, most times," said one of the board of education members. "Any time she asks, she's got everything so clearly planned out, and she's usually figured out how to get every nickel possible from other sources. Besides that, you know she'd keep on coming around, and I just hate to end up feeling guilty."

Toward the end of my second visit, in the fall of 1975, Mrs. Cothran and I sat in a glider on her front lawn, watching darkness settle over the fields in front of us. Her daughter, who had helped cook dinner, walked on the lawn behind us, playing with her cat. In this relaxed atmosphere, she philosophized a little about her job, drifting from subject to subject. "It's much harder to work directly with adults than with children, it's true," she said. "We're so much more complex and indirect. But that's what was needed most of all here, if we're going to see mainstreaming work well, so that's what I do. And after a while, you find that it's just as satisfying to help a big person open up as it is a little one. Anyhow, with all size people, this kind of work really becomes a part of you. At times I can just lie in bed at night, listening to my mind ticking along by itself, searching around, trying to solve little problems that have come up during the day."

I complimented her, and she pooh-poohed my remarks. "I've been accused of being unselfish before, but, when you get right down to it, all of us try to do what makes us happy, and one's no better than the next, most likely. Sometimes I think that maybe if my own daughter hadn't been born with such serious difficulties, I might not be feeling so much sympathy for hundreds of other boys and girls. But then, I know other people who don't have any handicapped individuals in their families who are just as involved. I guess it's not important *what* it is that makes you know that any of those children could have been you or your own child."

Annette's daughter had gone into the house, and her cat jumped onto the glider with us. The crickets were out in full force, and I could imagine Mrs. Cothran's mind ticking along with them.

"You know," she said abruptly, "I hope people are going to be able to work through all the complications that go along with these new laws without too much trouble. Hard to predict what's going to happen because of them. Us adults are learning along with the kids, aren't we?

"In the county, we're just beginning to get our programs for severely handicapped and preschool kids going well," she continued, "and I worry a lot about whether we're doing those to the best advantage. There's this little voice in my head that says, 'Look here, time's a-wasting, and look what we could be doing that we aren't!' But then, you can't be fast enough for everything, and you can't push harder than people are willing to bear either. That's why I've made such a point of establishing achievable priorities and sticking to them. A definite list of goals for every year."

The glider creaked as it swung back and forth in the darkness. "I'm a little nervous about being included in a book," she said after a short silence. "People might get the idea that I think I've got all the answers. But I don't know anybody who's got all the answers. You can say 'This works for me,' but you have to remember that the same thing might not work in somebody else's situation. And I haven't ever felt that we've arrived at the final answers even for us here in Macon County. Every day, the answers are changing, and so, every day, I'm looking for new ones. And I'm very lucky to have the kind of situation that lets me do that.

"At this point, the main worry I have is that funding for schools as a whole is going to stay very low. If that happens, it's going to be very hard for many systems to carry out a lot of these provisions in the law. We've got the commitment on paper, but I guess more and more of us are realizing that there have to be adequate resources available to entire school systems if special education is to function as it should. That may mean a shift in some of our legislative priorities."*

The stars were coming out, a few at a time. "Look how many there are tonight," Annette mused. "They really make me remember that each of us is here on earth such a short time. Gives me a good framework for judging what I'm doing." She sat quietly for a while, then added, "You know, over the last few years, I've started to understand that what we're trying to do here is part of a process which is far bigger than the public schools. It has to do with people who are different. You know, the day's going to come when most people will no longer want to automatically put people who have problems of one sort or another at a distance.

"Excuse me if I get corny or overgeneralize, but I'm feeling tired and like to paint rainbows to pick myself up. I do believe it all connects together. This is true in the public schools, the institutions, programs for older people — all the civil rights movements. But, for the children, it connects particularly well. Maybe sooner than

*For Mrs. Cothran, as for many people in Tennessee that year, those priorities were an especially sensitive issue. One of the big agribusiness conglomerates located in the state had told the state legislature that if the corporation weren't exempted from taxes, it would leave the state. The legislatures had passed a special bill exempting the corporation from taxes, and then had made up the difference through cuts in education and human services.

we think, we'll be able to take care of the needs of the so-called minimally handicapped child in the day-to-day course of general education, with the help of reading programs, resource teachers, or what-have-you. Then, there will also be special therapy and classes available in the public schools for the severely handicapped children who do need them. All of that is going to cause positive changes in teacher-training. And all of that also means that many parents will be spared the nightmare of institutionalizing a child. And then, don't you see, with so many less children in residential facilities, those places can also become much more humane and effective, if we keep up a good level of support, directed in the right way. And when you add on preschool programs and get at the children's problems early enough, maybe for many children, there will be no need for such intensive services."

Little flashes of light mingled in with the constant points of light before us. "Hard to tell the lightning bugs from the stars, isn't it?" Annette asked. "Well, that's the dream. But I've got my eyes wide open, as you know, and so I recognize all the problems between here and there." She stopped to stroke the cat. "That dream's shared by a whole lot of people all over," she said quietly. "And who knows, if enough people take a step toward it, even if it's only looking at the kids in a new light, well . . ." She smiled and shrugged. "Some day, that dream just might happen, mightn't it?"

Appendix, Notes
Bibliography, Index

Appendix

A Summary of Federal Law (Public Law 94-142)

THE MORE one understands the laws affecting special education, the more she is able to see sympathetically both the available possibilities and some of the problems now facing school personnel, children, and their parents. This is particularly true because the shortage of funds for schools in general makes it very difficult, in many cases, for school systems to do what they are required by law to do.

The Education for All Handicapped Children Act, effective in full in September 1978, is expected to have a significant impact not only on special education, but also on the schools in general. New solutions bring new problems, and this is certainly true as the special education laws grow more complex. Legal action or the threat of legal action is no longer unusual, and many fine teachers and administrators are forced into a defensive posture by multiple requirements combined with limited time, funds, or expertise. This often happens at the same time as the requirements upgrade programs and provide the means to protect children's rights.

State practices vary widely in particulars, since each state has its own laws, regulations, and policies. Federal laws passed since 1974, however, have required each state to include certain basic provisions within its law. As of summer 1976, each state division of special education had submitted a "five-year plan" to the U.S. Bureau of Education for the Handicapped. Each state plan is available to the public on request from the appropriate state division of special education. The Children's Defense Fund has printed a booklet called "How to Look at Your State's Plans for Educating Handicapped Children," to assist anybody who wishes to evaluate his state's commitments. The booklet includes information about state and local responsibilities and what an individual can do to assist the school system in meeting its responsibilities. The booklet is available from the Children's Defense Fund, 1520 New Hampshire Avenue NW, Washington, D.C. 20036.

One of the main general goals of the federal law and state plans will be to greatly reduce problems of the type encountered in Copper County and elsewhere in this book. In line with existing federal law, each plan must include, *at minimum*, the following provisions:

1. *"Full Services" goal.* The plan must show in specific detail how federal funds will be used to assure that each child is able to exercise the right to an appropriate public education. First priority for use of funds goes to children who are not receiving an education. Second priority goes to the children with the most severe handicaps who are not receiving an adequate program.

2. *Due Process Safeguards.* Each plan must provide assurances that children and their parents are entitled to *at least* the following procedures:

a. *Prior Notice.* Prior notice must be supplied in writing before a child is formally tested or assessed and before any change is made in the child's educational program or placement. The notice should explain fully the nature and implications of the proposed evaluation or program. The parent's written permission must be obtained *before* any testing or evaluation is done, and parents should *not* be asked for permission to place a child until after they have been fully informed of the results of the evaluation.

b. *Impartial Due Process Hearing.* The parent who does not agree with the recommendations of the school system in regard to her child is entitled to a hearing upon request, presided over by an "impartial hearing officer," usually appointed by the local school system.

c. *Access to Records.* Parents have a right to examine all school records directly related to their child. They also have the right to arrange for an independent evaluation of their child's difficulties if they feel the school system's evaluation is not satisfactory. This second evaluation may be used in the impartial due process hearing.

d. *Surrogate Parents.* When a child's parents or guardians are not known or are unavailable, or when the child is a ward of the state, the state must appoint somebody outside the school system as a stand-in parent to protect the child's rights, as a stand in-parent.

e. *Reevaluation.* Federal law now requires that beginning in September 1978 each child enrolled in special education have an individualized written educational plan. This plan, to be developed in conjunction with the child's parent(s) or guardian, must be reevaluated at least once a year. If parents or school personnel feel that the plan ought to be reevaluated at any point during the year, they can request and receive a formal review.

3. *Mainstreaming or Least Restrictive Alternative.* The plan must include the procedures the state has established to assure that "to the maximum extent appropriate," special education children are educated "with children who are not handicapped." The law notes that "special classes, separate schooling, or other removal from the regular educational environment" will be allowed only when "the nature or severity of the handicap is such that education in regular classes with the use of supplementary aids and services cannot be achieved satisfactorily."

4. *Nondiscriminatory Testing and Evaluation.* Each state plan must include the procedures the state has established to assure that the tests and other materials used to evaluate a child's special needs, to the maximum extent possible, are selected and administered without cultural or racial bias. Beginning in 1978, no child may be placed in special education on the basis of only one test or criterion. The federal law orders a comprehensive assessment, conducted in the child's native language or mode of communication.

5. *Childfind.* The plan must detail the procedures established to locate and evaluate all children with special needs in the state and to provide special education services to those children who need them.

*

Beyond the minimum requirements to be included in state plans, federal law also includes, as of 1976, the following provisions and features, among others:

a. Every state must provide a free public education for all handicapped children aged three to eighteen by September 1, 1978. A free public education must be available to all children aged three to twenty-one by September 1, 1980. (If the federal law conflicts with state law in the 3 to 5 and 18 to 21 age ranges, the federal law does not apply.)

b. The state education agency is responsible for guaranteeing the development and maintenance of an individualized written program for handicapped children being served in agencies other than the local education agencies.

c. Under existing federal law, the amount of federal funds distributed will increase each year from 1978 through 1982. The amount of funds will also be based on the "national average expenditure per public school child" times the number of children enrolled in special education. The percentages of each child's education costs which the federal government is authorized to pay range from 5 percent in fiscal 1978 to 40 percent in fiscal 1982. However, the Congressional Appropriations committees are well known for slicing children's services authorizations, and so, each year, there will be the definite possibilities that the legislation will be funded at a lower level.

d. Recognizing the potential for "overcounting" children as handicapped in order to get more federal dollars, the federal law limits the number of children for whom any one state or individual school system can receive federal funds to 12 percent of the total school-age population between ages five and seventeen, inclusive. This does not limit the number of children who may be counted for state or local funding.

Being particularly sensitive to the loosely defined nature of the category of learning disabilities, the authors of the federal legislation directed the Office of Education either to develop a more precise definition or to impose a 2 percent limit on the number of children to be funded in that category.

e. In contrast to past practices, a substantial portion of the federal money goes directly to the local school systems, without being administered by the state. In fiscal 1978, 50 percent of the funds will go directly to local school systems. In fiscal 1979, and thereafter, 75 percent will go directly to local school systems. The state education agency has the responsibility to refuse to "pass through" the local money when the local system is in violation of federal law, fails to meet its application requirements, is considered to be providing inappropriately for children's needs, or does not generate at least $7500 in federal funds (in which case the system would be obligated to consolidate services with other districts). Before passing through the federal money, the state must also ascertain that the local school system is spending at least as much local money on each handicapped child as is being spent on each nonhandicapped child.

f. Each local school system must submit a written document containing all "assurances" of compliance with all the federal requirements. The state division is responsible for monitoring local school systems to insure that they are complying with these assurances. Correspondingly, the U.S. Commissioner of Education is required to cut off funds to a given state if that state is found to be in "substantial noncompliance" with any of the major requirements of the federal law.

g. Additional "incentive" funds will be supplied for the development of programs for preschool handicapped children, based upon the number of children, aged three to five, being served.

h. Money has also been authorized for grants from the U.S. Commissioner of Education to pay for all or part of the cost of altering existing buildings and equipment to eliminate architectural barriers in educational facilities. Such alteration makes it possible for certain handicapped children to be educated in the "least restrictive" environment.

i. Private elementary and secondary schools may receive federal special education funds if the children involved are referred by the state or local education agency *as a means of carrying out public policy,* if the special education services are free to the parents, and if the school meets all the standards set forth in federal law.

j. Each state must have an "advisory panel" composed of individuals involved in or concerned with the education of handicapped children, including handicapped individuals, teachers, parents, or guardians of handicapped children, state and local education officials, and administrators of programs.

Notes

ALL QUOTATIONS from individual persons were taken, with much appreciated permission, from taped interviews or written comments, unless otherwise specified.

Preface (Pages ix–xviii)

xi   The Office of Civil Rights data was analyzed and reported by the Children's Defense Fund in *Children Out of School in America* (Cambridge, Mass.: 1974). As summarized on pp. 4–5 of that report, "The extent of misclassification that we found alleged among all children was serious. Among minority children it was alarming. When we analyzed special education data submitted to the Office for Civil Rights (OCR) in the fall of 1973 by 505 school districts in Alabama, Georgia, South Carolina, Mississippi, and Arkansas which had children enrolled in classes for the educable mentally retarded (EMR), we found that:

- In 190 of the districts (37.4 percent), the probability that a black student would be in an EMR class was five times as great as for a white student. There were 51 districts in which the probability of being in an EMR class was ten times greater for a black student than for a white student.
- Over 80 percent of the students in EMR classes in these districts were black, even though less than 40 percent of the total enrollment in these districts were black.
- 46 percent of these 505 districts reported that 5 percent or more of their black students were in EMR classes, but only 4 districts (less than 1 percent) reported 5 percent or more of their white students in EMR classes.
- At least 10 percent of the black students were in EMR classes in 64 of the districts.
- Not only are the probability rates different for black and white students, but the number of black children affected by these rates is significant. Using the percentage of white students who are in EMR classes as a standard, the number of black students in EMR classes in excess of the corresponding ratio is 32,381. In only 13 districts

were there fewer black students than would be implied by the white ratio.

xii "For now the only." Local public support for schools has decreased dramatically in the past ten years. For instance, approximately 50 percent of all municipal school bond issues were voted down in the early seventies, in contrast to approximately 25 percent in the mid-sixties. (See Irene A. King, *Bond Sales for Public School Purposes,* U.S. Dept. of Health, Education and Welfare, 1974, Pub. # (OE)–73–11406).

Special and Regular
Chapter 1 (Pages 1–16)

1   "What is true." Dr. Jane R. Mercer, *Labeling the Mentally Retarded: Clinical and Social System Perspectives on Mental Retardation* (Berkeley: University of California Press, 1973), pp. 53–66.
1   "The answers to." *Labeling the Mentally Retarded,* p. 257.
13 "Many terms." Ronald W. Conley, *The Economics of Mental Retardation* (Baltimore: The Johns Hopkins University Press, 1973), p. 7.
13 "Such an array." See Herbert J. Grossman, M.D., ed., *Manual on Terminology and Classification in Mental Retardation,* Special Publication Number 2, American Association on Mental Deficiency, 1973 Revision.
14 "The President's Committee." *The Six-Hour Retarded Child,* published in 1970 by the President's Committee on Mental Retardation, is available at 65¢ a copy from the Superintendent of Documents, Government Printing Office, Washington, D.C. 20402 (Publication #36.8: M52/R342.)

According to Regulations
Chapter 2 (Pages 17–28)

17 "The track system." *Hobson* v. *Hansen* (269 F. Supp. 401) U.S. District Court, Washington, D.C., 1967, p. 473.
18 "Regular teachers." Lloyd Dunn, "Special Education for the Mildly Retarded: Is Much of It Justifiable?" *Exceptional Children,* September 1968.
19 The chart of the "cascade system" was taken from *One out of Ten: School Planning for the Handicapped,* Educational Facilities Laboratory, New York, October 1974, p. 7. The "cascade system" concept of special education was originally proposed by Dr. Evelyn Deno of the University of Minnesota in 1970.

Facts and Opinions

Chapter 3 (Pages 29–37)

29 "Children who are." Nicholas Hobbs, *The Futures of Children: Categories, Labels, and Their Consequences* (Report of the Project on Classification of Exceptional Children) (San Francisco: Jossey-Bass Publishers, 1975), p. 3.

Copper County

Chapter 4 (Pages 38–49)

38 "Deviance is not." Kai Erickson, "On the Sociology of Deviance," from *The Wayward Puritans: A Study in the Sociology of Deviance,* reprinted by permission of John Wiley and Sons, Inc., 1966, pp. 13–18.

49 "According to." *The Futures of Children,* pp. 31–32, with reference to: (a) "A majority of Americans." J. R. Feagin, "God Helps Those Who Help Themselves," *Psychology Today,* 1972, 6 (6), p. 101. (b) "An 18-month study." S. R. Wright, "Social Psychological Effects of Labor Supply in the New Jersey–Pennsylvania Experiment," Paper presented at the annual meeting of American Sociological Association, New Orleans, Louisiana, August 1972. (c) "We are still apt." *The Wayward Puritans,* p. 198.

Referrals: From the Regular System to the Special System

Chapter 5 (Pages 50–64)

50 "A child who." From a letter to Senator Jacob Javits, U.S. Senate, Washington, D.C., from Rims Barber, David Rice, and Charles E. Jenkins, Directors, Mississippi Head Start, January 17, 1974.

51 "In a nine-year." *Labeling the Mentally Retarded,* pp. 53–66.

51 "Mercer also found." *Labeling the Mentally Retarded,* p. 105.

52 "The Children's Defense." *Children out of School in America,* pp. 106–107.

63 "In July 1975." Washington *Star,* "Aiding Minority Problem Pupils, and What Should Be the Limit?" July 29, 1975.

Dummy Tech

Chapter 6 (Pages 65–76)

66 "As long as." Simon Olshansky, Jacob Schonfield, and Leon Sternfeld, "Mentally Retarded or Culturally Different?" in Reginald Jones, ed., *Problems and Issues in the Education of Exceptional Children* (Boston: Houghton Mifflin, 1971), pp. 111–12.

74 "Catch 22." The original article, "On Being Sane in Insane Places," was published by D. L. Rosenhan in *Science* magazine, Volume 179, January 19, 1973, pp. 250–58. Copyright 1973 by the American Association for the Advancement of Science. The *National Observer* story appeared January 27, 1973, p. 5.

"Johnny's Such a Bright Boy . . ."

Chapter 7 (Pages 77–86)

77 "The traditional categories." *The Futures of Children,* p. 103.

78 "A California researcher." David L. Kirp, "The Great Sorting Machine," *Phi Delta Kappan,* Vol. LV (8), April 1974, p. 524.

78 "In those systems." Carl Milofsky, "Why Special Education Isn't Special," *Harvard Educational Review,* Vol. 44 (4), November 1974, p. 473.

78 "The Lawyers' Committee." The Lawyers' Committee will assist anybody who has some question about use of federal funds for disadvantaged children in their school district. Write: Federal Education Project, The Lawyers' Committee for Civil Rights Under Law, 733 15th St. NW, Washington, D.C. 20006. The project also publishes a free monthly newsletter.

85 "As reported in." *Children out of School in America,* p. 109.

Beautiful Teachers in Not-so-Beautiful Situations

Chapter 8 (Pages 87–101)

100 "About the same time." Norris Harring and David A. Krug, "Placement in Regular Programs: Procedures and Results," *Exceptional Children,* March 1975, pp. 413–17.

The Influence of Dollars

Chapter 10 (Pages 108–115)

111 "A few examples of funding." Information about the various funding procedures used by different states were obtained through the Bureau of Education for the Handicapped, Summer 1975.

112 "Maynard Reynolds." *The Futures of Children,* p. 101, taken from undated report, pp. 10–11.

112 "A national project." *The Futures of Children,* p. 265.

114 "It's such." Interview, Anne Hocutt, research assistant, Senate Subcommittee on the Handicapped, June 19, 1975.

School Psychologist

Chapter 11 (Pages 116–125)

Psychological reports quoted without identifying information in this chapter and elsewhere were actually used to place children in EMR classes in the early seventies.

118 "Persons with these skills." *Labeling the Mentally Retarded,* p. 15.
118 "Testifying before." Dr. Lewis Klebanoff, assistant commissioner, Massachusetts Department of Mental Health, testifying before the Senate Subcommittee on the Handicapped, May 7, 1973, Boston, Hearing record on S. 6, p. 434.
120 "In 1975, HEW." The reference is to the GRIT (Guidelines Regulations Input Team) guidelines, sent to each state in 1975 for use in the construction of state five-year plans for special education. The guidelines were put together by a group of people representing many professions associated with exceptional children.
120 "One grade school." Taken from observations of the project coordinator, Rita Grismer, Hyannisport, Massachusetts, October 1973, as well as Richard A. Johnson and Rita M. Grismer, "The Harrison-University Cooperative Resource Center," a chapter in *Mainstream Special Education,* ed. Philip Mann and published by the Council for Exceptional Children in 1974.
125 "The picture for." For more information about the Buckley Amendment to the Family Educational Rights and Privacy Act (20 USC, 1232 (g)), write The Children's Defense Fund, 1520 New Hampshire Avenue NW, Washington, D.C. 20036, for their free booklet, "Your School Records: Questions and Answers About a New Set of Rights for Parents and Students."

IQ Tests and Testing

Chapter 12 (Pages 126–139)

126 "[The] four step process." H. Goldstein et al., "Schools" in *Issues in the Classification of Children: A Sourcebook on Categories, Labels, and Their Consequences,* ed. Nicholas Hobbs, pp. 33–34.
127 Details of the following lawsuits were taken from Alan Abeson and Nancy Bolick, eds., *A Continuing Summary of Pending and Completed Litigation Regarding the Education of Handicapped Children,* #8, The Council for Exceptional Children.

Larry P. v. *Riles,* Civil Action No. C-71-2270 343 F. Supp 1306 (N.D. Cal., 1972). "This class action suit was filed in late November

1971 on behalf of the six named black elementary school–aged children attending classes in the San Francisco Unified School District. It was alleged that they had been inappropriately classified as educable mentally retarded and placed and retained in classes for such children. The complaint argued that the children were not mentally retarded, but rather "the victims of a testing procedure which fails to recognize their unfamiliarity with the white middle class cultural background and which ignores the learning experiences which they may have had in their homes." The defendants included state and local school officials and board members.

"It was alleged that misplacement in classes for the mentally retarded carries a stigma and 'a life sentence of illiteracy.' Statistical information indicated that in the San Francisco Unified School District, as well as the state, a disproportionate number of black children are enrolled in programs for the retarded. It was further pointed out that even though code and regulatory procedures regarding identification, classification, and placement of the mentally retarded were changed to be more effective, inadequacies in the processes still exist."

In a California case, *Diana* v. *State Board of Education,* similar charges were made on behalf of the nine Mexican American children and "other young and pre-school bi-lingual children who will be given IQ tests which 'will inevitably lead to their placement in a class for mentally retarded.'" The children were retested in English and/or Spanish, and seven of the nine scored well above the cutoff point of 70. The eighth child scored 70, and the ninth 67. The average gain on retesting was 15 points.

*   *Stewart* v. *Philips,* Civil Action No. 70-1199-F (D. Mass., filed Sept. 14, 1970).

"In this 1970 class action, seven poor children placed in Boston public school classes for the mentally retarded, protesting the manner in which they were tested and placed in those programs were subdivided into two groups: (1) 'Poor or black Boston children who are not mentally retarded and . . . have been, are or may be denied the right to a regular public school education in a regular class by being misclassified mentally retarded' and (2) poor or black Boston children who had been misclassified mentally retarded, and incorrectly placed in special classes for the mentally retarded while in fact they were in need of special programs, but for the remediation of handicaps other than mental retardation. It was further alleged that the plaintiff children were so placed because they were perceived as behavior problems."

Specific allegations in this case were as follows:

1. The process of classification "is based exclusively upon tests which discriminate against (plaintiffs) in that the tests are standardized on a population which is white and dissimilar to the (plaintiffs).
2. The administration and interpretation of the tests by Boston school officials fail "to distinguish among a wide range of learning disabilities, only one of which may be mental retardation."
3. Classification and placement is made on the basis of a single test score standard and other necessary information is neither gathered nor considered.
4. Boston's "school psychologists" are unqualified to interpret the limited classification devices used in the Boston schools.

Further, the complaint alleged that children in "special classes," which are segregated from the regular class population, receive a substantially different education than children retained in regular programs. Such placements, it was alleged, result in "substantial educational, psychological, and social harm," which is cumulative. Thus, the longer children are incorrectly retained in special classes, the greater the damage. It was also indicated that even when such children are returned to the regular class, they remain irreparably harmed because counterpart children will have continued to make academic progress while the former remained in the special class, educationally static."

128 "Somebody with." Remarks contained in Bernard Asbell, "Is Your Child Brighter Than Teachers Think?" *Redbook,* March 1973, pp. 92–93.

131 "In a study under." Jerome Kagan, "The IQ Puzzle: What Are We Measuring?" *Inequality in Education,* Number 14, July 1973, Center for Law and Education, Harvard University, p. 7.

131 "Jerome Kagan." *Ibid.*

137 "We take a Stanford-Binet test." Oliver Hurley, testimony before the Senate Subcommittee on the Handicapped, May 14, 1973, Columbia, South Carolina.

Log in Somebody's Eye

Chapter 15 (Pages 157–165)

157 "Psychologists, psychiatrists." Seymour Sarason, *The Culture of the*

School and the Problem of Change (Boston: Allyn and Bacon, 1971), pp. 156–57.

Teaching Teachers in School

Chapter 17 (Pages 176–187)

176 "In 1968." Robert Rosenthal and Lenore Jacobson, *Pygmalion in the Classroom: Teacher Expectation and Pupils' Intellectual Development* (New York: Holt, Rinehart & Winston, 1968).

Mainstreaming

Chapter 18 (Pages 188–205)

188 "Basically." Winter report, 1974, Closer Look, National Information Center for the Handicapped. Closer Look provides free information services for parents of handicapped children and to parent groups or to groups-in-the-making. To be included on the mailing list for the periodic Closer Look newsletter, write Closer Look, Box 1492, Washington, D.C. 20013.

191 "When mainstreaming programs." Interview, Whyla Beman, January 16, 1976.

200 "In 1975, *Mainstreaming: Idea and Reality*," an occasional paper from Commissioner Ewald B. Nyquist, The State Education Department, Albany, New York, 1975. "Looking first at the studies of the effectiveness of special class placement," the authors continue, "it is clear that there is some reason to question the use of those classes for mildly handicapped children. Although few educators deny the value of classes for severely impaired children, studies of their effect on less severely disabled children are at best inconclusive. Rarely is it possible to show clear-cut academic or social gains for mildly handicapped children in segregated classes, and, in some instances, it is claimed that children on waiting lists improved more rapidly than did those in special classes. However, in other cases, growth and improvement, especially in self-concept, is attributed to special class placement. Although there is a general lack of clarity in this controversy, in recent years, there has been a definite trend toward questioning how much the mildly handicapped child gains from these classes. While some mildly handicapped children have made significant gains in special classes, it is possible that the same benefits might be achieved in integrated settings . . . Although mainstreaming will not cure all the ills of special education or magically provide a remedy which will help all handicapped children, it is reality oriented, and can help a child learn to cope with the outside world.

"Numerous studies illustrate the idea that a handicapped child will begin to perform more adaptively in a mainstreaming setting. Dramatic increases in spontaneous speech, increased vocabulary and greater proficiency in lip reading are reported by parents and educators working with deaf and hearing impaired children in regular classrooms, for visually handicapped children in public schools, increases in ability to use other senses and progress in mobility are reported. With other handicaps such as neurological impairment, orthopedic handicaps, and chronic health conditions, children in mainstreamed settings show increased ability to use their innate strengths and to live with their limitations."

201 "Four adult." "Person to Person," *The Exceptional Parent,* May/June 1973, pp. 9–10. Dennis Bowling, Evelyn Aronow, Fred Fay, and John Kemp were interviewed by Stanley Klein.

202 "The Bureau of Education." Interview, Martin Kaufman, April 30, 1976. For further information contact Martin Kauffmann, Bureau of Education for the Handicapped, 400 Maryland Avenue SW, Room 3155, Donahoe Building Washington, D.C. 20202.

The following examples of successful mainstreaming arrangements for children in the "minimal" and "moderate" range show that good mainstreaming programs come in many forms:

1. When a new school opened in the early seventies in Pontiac, Michigan, students were assigned to their classroom areas by random selection. Nobody but the special education teachers knew which children had been diagnosed as moderately retarded, emotionally disturbed, or learning disabled. The school was set up in "areas," each of which had 140 students and 6 teachers, including a special education teacher, on a "team." Other special ed teachers operated a special resource station in the school called the "Learning Center," which contained all the special equipment and resource material. Teachers in the classroom areas could send students to the Learning Center for specific training and therapy.

At the end of the first year, the district's department of special education asked the regular classroom teachers to pick out the handicapped students and assess their progress. The surveyors found that the achievement levels of special ed children who had previously been in segregated classes had gone up 25 percent. They also found that the regular classroom teachers picked out 33 percent more children with problems than had previously been identified for special education. Beyond that, almost 30 percent of the children who had been in special education before weren't on the teacher's list of handicapped children. They had disappeared into the mainstream.

2. Like many other rural regions, five counties in northern Virginia have pooled resources to hire specialists in the various kinds of handicapping problems found in their area. These specialists serve as a central base and resource, while other consulting teachers organize and participate in resource programs for "minimally handicapped" children in each individual county's schools. The emphasis is on working with the regular classroom teacher, as well as with the child to adjust the child's total program. After the adjustment is relatively stable, the consulting teacher concludes her part in the child's program (follow-up occurs later) and takes up another child's case.

3. In Fountain Valley, California, nonspecial education pupils are mainstreamed into schools designed for special education. Each school is equipped for a particular type of disability. The Plaven School, for instance, contains open space, barrier-free facilities for physically handicapped and cerebral palsied children. In 1974, 330 nonhandicapped children attended Plaven with 96 orthopedically handicapped children, preschool through eighth grade. An independent orthopedic clinic operated by the local Crippled Children's Society was also housed in the building. According to a 1974 report, through Plaven's consolidation of services, "The society gets free space, the school gains from the clinic's special equipment and expertise, and the community benefits from the extra services provided in the new center. According to school officials, a natural mix of students integrated into a common program reinforced with special equipment which serves them all benefits every student. Each child is simply felt to possess a peculiar set of potentialities and shortcomings, and the extra equipment and personnel provided in the school apply to all the children."

4. Many regular classroom teachers are starting their own mainstreaming "program" for children in the minimal/moderate range. "We don't have an overall school plan yet for mainstreaming," commented a fifth grade teacher in Silver Spring, Maryland, "so you might say I mainstream from the other end. I ask to have kids who otherwise might be sent to special classes. The other teachers see that it works out well for me, and they get more interested. Three of us have volunteered so far in my school."

5. The success of Santa Monica's "Madison Plan" for mainstreaming has attracted much attention and speculation. Named after the

California elementary school where it was developed, the Madison Plan involves three "centers" near the regular class area. Children who are assigned to special ed go first to the main learning center, where the special education staff decides which center would best suit the child's needs.

One of these centers is designed to help children develop the capacity to work together productively with other children. A second center actually teaches children "classroom survival" techniques like sitting still, taking turns, following directions, and raising hands. (The program developers had found that a child who lacks these behaviors is less likely to be accepted back into a regular classroom than a child who is academically deficient only.)

The third station, to which a child moves before going back into the mainstream, is set up to closely resemble the situation into which the child would be returning. This gives the special education teachers a final chance to spot and help a child with any of the problems or behaviors which originally brought him to the learning center.

As each school year begins, all the children in the Madison School start in the regular program. School staff report that, many times, a child will have outgrown the previous year's problems over the summer, and therefore will not be rereferred to special education.

6. Most laws encourage school systems to develop what is called a "continuum of services," a variety of program types to suit the varying degree of problems involved. The Lexington, Kentucky, public schools have developed a continuum of services in the area of behavior disorders. For children with minor classroom behavior problems or emotional difficulties, "liaison teachers" (similar to "resource teachers") work with teachers and children. Each liaison teacher is responsible for helping the regular classroom teacher adjust a child's program and for working directly with the child whenever problems which seem to involve emotional difficulties arise. The next step beyond the liaison teacher is a self-contained classroom; however, a child may not be considered for such placement until the liaison teacher approach has been tried for at least a month. "And sometimes we've been able to resolve difficulties by simply transferring a child across the hall to a different classroom and teacher, or moving him to another school better suited to his learning style," commented Natalie Patterson, Lexington's director of special education. The next step would be

the Parent-Child training program (offered to all children in self-contained classrooms) in which the parent(s) of a child with severe behavior disorders make a commitment to come to school *with* the child, to work with the teacher and child, on the assumption that attempting to change the child alone may be ineffectual at best. A child usually goes directly from the Parent-Child program back to the regular classroom program, where he or she is placed with a sympathetic teacher. A few children suffering from extreme behavior disorders go to programs in residential centers out of the public schools.

Severely Handicapped Children and Comprehensive Planning

Chapter 19 (Pages 206–220)

206 "The special educator." Philip H. Mann, ed., *Mainstream Special Education,* The Council for Exceptional Children, 1974, p. 2.

207 "People in agencies." Interview, Wayne Largent, state client officer, Aid-to-States Branch, Bureau of Education for the Handicapped, July 11, 1975.

207 "You can't always." Interview, Jane DeWeerd, coordinator, Early Childhood Education Programs, Bureau of Education for the Handicapped, May 1975.

215 "The cost of." Interview, Ronald Conley, April 14, 1976.

216 "Childfind." The information gathered at the March 1975 Childfind conference was published by the Coordinating Office of Regional Resource Centers and is available for $1.00 through the National Association of State Directors of Special Education, 1201 16th Street NW, Washington, D.C. 20036. (ERIC #E.D. 117 910).

217 "A BEH official." Interview, Wayne Largent, July 11, 1975.

217 "I contend that." Interview, Frederick Weintraub, assistant executive director, The Council for Exceptional Children, March 1974.

219 "A representative." Leopold D. Lippman, *Attitudes Toward the Handicapped: A Comparison Between Europe and the United States* (Springfield, Illinois: Charles C. Thomas, 1972), p. 12.

219 "Depending on." Visits to the Brookmont School, Brookmont, Maryland, July 1975, and interview with Mrs. Peg Gorham, Montgomery County Association for Retarded Citizens, July 1975.

Buying

Chapter 20 (Pages 221–231)

221 "Materials and media." *Mainstream Special Education,* p. 116.

228 "Robert Audette." Robert Audette, "Trick or Treat? A Call for Advertising Standards and Product Evaluation," *The Exceptional Parent,* July/August 1974, pp. 19–20.

230 "Barbara Aeillo." Interview, April 23, 1976. *Teaching Exceptional Children,* edited by Ms. Aeillo through the Council for Exceptional Children, carries a feature four times yearly entitled "Off the Shelf," in which commercial products are evaluated in terms of their actual program usefulness.

230 "There are now comprehensive." For information about IGE, write Director of Implementation, Wisconsin Research and Development Center for Cognitive Learning, 1025 West Jackson Street, Madison, Wisconsin 53706.

231 "The Regional Resource Center." As of this writing, there are five national centers working specifically with educational materials. Three of them are responsible for wading through the flood of new, old, and revamped materials. They're charged with keeping track of, testing, and evaluating all commercial materials "alleged to have educational value" for children with particular types of problems. There's a center for visual impairments, one for hearing impairments, and one for other handicaps. A fourth center, the National Center on Educational Media and Materials for the Handicapped, is set up to develop training activities for teachers, related to the use of media, materials, and educational technology and to be a "clearinghouse for the nation's problems, ideas and solutions" in this area. No small job. The fifth center is mainly a warehouse in which samples of all the educational materials in the country will be stored, waiting for people to examine them.

All the information for these centers is fed to Area Learning Resource Centers (ALRCs), which are supposed to work closely with the state divisions of special ed. If the whole system is working as planned within a few years, it could wipe out much of the personnel time now spent digging through catalogues, fielding through sales pitches and office politics, and ordering materials with the constant suspicion that there's something on the market you don't know about that would be much better for the children than what you're buying.

Beyond the materials questions are all the how-to questions raised by changing practice. The other responsibilities of the information system are aimed at answering these questions. There is a central coordinating office, whose duties, as of 1975, included the following:

• Assembling and storing the most useful information available on effective ways of dealing with specific handicapping conditions, for instance, techniques for working with a hard-of-hearing child in the regular classroom; methods of evaluation; different approaches to mainstreaming

- Keeping track of programs in different systems that have already found effective nuts and bolts ways of approaching problems other systems are just starting to wrestle with. What's happening in Kansas that could be used in Nevada?
- Using this information to put together workshop-type training packages that an individual school system could order and use with teachers, parents, or administrators
- Keeping in close contact with state and regional needs and advising HEW in some realistic way on how to use their funds to encourage certain practices
- Holding regional or national workshops for administrators and other relevant people, where different ideas and successful programs can be examined and traced

The Coordinating Office for Regional Resource Centers (CORRC), based in Lexington, Kentucky, feeds its information out to the Regional Resource Centers throughout the country. These centers are designed to actually get the accumulated expertise and help to the local level. They were authorized in 1975 to:

- Make sure school systems that need the accumulated information get it
- Come in and actually work with state division people who want help organizing statewide programs
- Help coordinate all the services from the different agencies in their area
- Upon request, provide evaluation and program planning for any child for whom the local and state agencies aren't able to put together an appropriate program with available resources
- Consult with parents and teachers on request

Officials emphasize the fact that, like all systems, some parts are meeting great success, and others haven't yet gotten off the ground. But the potential is there. "This is all part of a comprehensive effort to provide state school agencies with the kind of technological support they're never had before," commented specialist Andy Andersen who works with the entire system. "Other parts of our society —

notably business and the military — have long been using these techniques very effectively to develop products, to improve efficiency and effectiveness. Complex weapons systems and so forth. Why not education? We've got to learn to combine both the human factor and technology. Eventually, a teacher who works in a little school district would be able, by means of traditional communication devices like the telephone, to get access to computer-stored information dealing with specific problems literally overnight."

Information about the Regional Resource Center serving your state can be obtained by writing your state department of education, division of special education.

All descriptions of the Learning Resource System come from materials and information supplied by the National Association of State Directors of Special Education (NASDSE), July 1975. Though details of the system will change, the description gives a picture of the scope and direction of BEH's efforts.

State Level Headaches

Chapter 21 (Pages 232–239)

233 "Alan Abeson." Interview, Alan Abeson, July 11, 1974.
234 *"Legal Change."* Alan Abeson, ed., *Legal Change for the Handicapped Through Litigation,* State-Federal Information Clearinghouse for Exceptional Children, The Council for Exceptional Children, 1973, p. ii.
238 "Having heard two." "Grass Roots Politics," produced by the NPACT division of WETA-TV, Washington, D.C., as part of the "America '73" series aired nationally by the Public Broadcasting Service (PBS) on April 25, 1973.

Parents and Early Intervention

Chapter 22 (Pages 240—253)

251 "The Milwaukee Project." Howard Garber and Rick Heber, University of Wisconsin, "The Milwaukee Project: Early Intervention as a Technique to Prevent Mental Retardation," Technical Paper, National Leadership Institute, Teacher Education/Early Childhood, the University of Connecticut, March 1973, Storrs, Connecticut.

Also see R. Heber et al., *Rehabilitation of Families at Risk for Mental Retardation,* part of the University of Wisconsin Monograph Series of the Department of Studies in Behavioral Disabilities and Rehabilitation Research and Training Center in Mental Retardation, 1972 (revised).

Dr. Howard Garber, one of the chief researchers on the Milwaukee Project, emphasizes the fact that each early intervention project must be designed to suit the particular circumstances. "Our project can't be used as a cookbook which could be followed step by step, anywhere in the country. Indian children are different from black children, rural kids are different from city kids, and circumstances vary from place to place, so there have to be adjustments to suit local circumstances."

Though very little money is available for early intervention at this point, the tremendous potential shows up in many projects to date that have been concerned with the damaging effects of early nutritional deprivation and lack of mental and sensory stimulation on a child's development. A few such studies are briefly described below:

1. Joaquin Cravioto and Elsa DeLicardie, in their study of children born in 1966 in a small rural village in southwestern Mexico, found that the twenty-two children who were most severely malnourished during the first two years of their lives fell far behind the other children in language and concept development. It was discovered that these children also had received a much lower level of stimulation in terms of direct human conversation and variety of activities and games in which the child was involved.

2. Stephen Richardson and others, in their study of Jamaican children, reconfirmed the finding that a low level of stimulation in the home can have bad effects not only on a child's intellectual development but also on the child's social development. The combination of a low level of stimulation and malnutrition in the early years of life, they found, can have a devastating effect on a child's overall development.

Studying boys aged six to ten, who had been hospitalized for malnutrition before age two, researchers Richardson, H. G. Birch, and C. Ragbeer of Albert Einstein College of Medicine in New York also found that the formerly malnourished boys were seen by their mothers as much less socially adept. In comparison with a group of better-fed classmates of the same age and sex, the boys were much more prone to behavior like wetting, bad temper, and heavy fidgeting, were much less aggressive and frequently teased by classmates, and were less liked by brothers and sisters. The evidence of these studies suggests that the damage inflicted by malnutrition is not necessarily limited to social development.

3. Adolpho Cavez began his Mexican study of the effects of malnutrition on children while the mothers were still pregnant. He gave participating mothers food supplements during pregnancy and continued them until the children were over two years old. The children involved were about 8 percent heavier than the village average, walked at an earlier age, showed superior language development during their first year, and (on a measure of movement) were three times as active as the average child in their village by age one.

4. In Seattle, Washington, children born with Down's syndrome (mongolism) have entered public school on a developmental par with their peers. These children, in other circumstances, would have been written off as incapable of developing in such a fashion. As of 1976, the Seattle children had participated for five years in an intensive, long-term, early-intervention program at the University of Washington, directed by Norris Harring and Alice Hayden. The program has involved high-stimulation infant-learning programs, parent training, and support programs, and continuous sequential instruction. The implications of what has already been accomplished in this program and others like it are enormous, as it is no longer possible to maintain that Down's children are necessarily "low functioning" children.

Accountability

Chapter 23 (Pages 254–264)

254   "We know of." *A Call for Unity in Special Education,* National Association of State Directors of Special Education, Washington, D.C., 1975.

Due Process

Chapter 24 (Pages 265–277)

265   "Lawsuits have been." The exact number of lawsuits relating to special education since 1969 is not available as of this writing. The most nearly complete listing (with accompanying descriptions) is published through the Council for Exceptional Children: *A Continuing Summary of Pending and Completed Litigation Regarding the Education of Handicapped Children.*

268   "The Strangely Significant." Gary Saretsky, "The Strangely Significant Case of Peter Doe," *Phi Delta Kappan,* May 1973, p. 589.

273   "In 1974." For more information about misuse of drugs with children labeled hyperactive, see Lester Grinspoon and Susan B. Singer,

"Amphetamines in the Treatment of Hyperkinetic Children," *Harvard Educational Review,* Vol. 43, No. 4, November 1973, pp. 515–55.

276 "The right of parents." *The Futures of Children,* p. 177. Dr. Hobbs was summarizing the evidence compiled by Kirp, Buss, and Kurliloff in their chapter in *Issues in the Classification of Children.*

Toward Making It All Special

Chapter 26 (Pages 296–305)

All quotations from Frederick Andelman (Assistant Director of Professional Development, Massachusetts Teachers Association) are taken from a taped interview, May 11, 1975. Mr. Andelman's remarks are backed by substantial constructive action on the part of the Massachusetts Teachers Association. The MTA has done a great deal on its own initiative to help its members deal productively with mainstreaming requirements.

All quotations from Dr. Jean Hebeler are taken from a taped interview, June 20, 1975.

All quotations from Robert Prouty are from an interview on May 13, 1975.

300 "Andelman's warning." Julianne Clarke, "Special Education and Professional Negotiations in Indiana: A Case Study of Five School Districts," submitted to the School of Education, Indiana University, August 1976.

304 "If we took." Bertrand Russell, in *Great Issues in Education,* Volume one (Chicago: Great Books Foundation, 1956).

Afterword: Macon County — Something Fine (Pages 306–326)

All conversations in the Afterword have been taken from tape or paper recordings of the school personnel, parents, and children of Macon County, Tennessee, made in April 1974 and August–September 1975.

Bibliography

THIS SHORT BIBLIOGRAPHY is included for anybody who would like to know more about the various topics listed below. The books and references were chosen because they're readable and useful in a practical way. Most of them also contain additional references for the person who wants to read even further. (The list isn't meant to include all the best sources. It's just to help you get started.)

Mainstreaming Programs: Organization and Operation

Aeillo, Barbara, ed. *Making It Work: Practical Ideas for Integrating Exceptional Children.* 1976. Available from the Council for Exceptional Children, 1920 Association Drive, Reston, Virginia. $5.50.

Jones, Reginald L., and Wilderson, Frank B. *Mainstreaming and the Minority Child.* 1977. The Council for Exceptional Children. $5.00.

Jordan, June B., ed. *Teacher, Please Don't Close the Door. The Exceptional Child in the Mainstream.* 1975. The Council for Exceptional Children. $9.75.

Paul, James L., Turnbull, Ann, and Cruickshank, William M. *Mainstreaming: A Practical Guide.* 1976. Syracuse University Press. $9.95.

Mainstreaming: Practical Ideas for Every Day

Barnes, Ellen. *Teach and Reach: An Alternative Guide to Resources for the Classroom.* 1974. Human Policy Press, P.O. Box 127, University Station, Syracuse, N.Y. $3.50.

The Creative Sixth-Grade Teacher: A Practical Guide to Classroom Activities. (A similar book is also available for every grade level from kindergarten through sixth grade.) 1974. Milliken Publishing Company, St. Louis, Missouri 63132. $3.00 apiece.

The Teacher Idea Exchange: A Potpourri of Helpful Hints. From the "Teacher Idea Exchange" section of *Teaching Exceptional Children* magazine. 1977. The Council for Exceptional Children. $5.00.

Mainstreaming: Other Books of Interest

Places and Spaces: Facility Planning for Handicapped Children. 1976. The Council for Exceptional Children. $3.25.

Reynolds, Maynard, ed. *Mainstreaming: Origins and Implications*. 1976. The Council for Exceptional Children. $3.00.

Deviance and Treatment: Cautions

Bowles, Samuel, and Gintis, Herbert. *Schooling in Capitalist America*. 1976. Basic Books. New York. $13.95.

Center for Law and Education. *Classification Materials,* rev. ed., 1973. Harvard University Press, $7.00. *Supplement*, $3.00.

Kittrie, Nicholas N. *The Right to be Different: Deviance and Enforced Therapy*. Johns Hopkins Press, 1971. Penguin paperback, $4.50.

Ryan, William. *Blaming the Victim*. Vintage Books, 1972, revised 1976. $2.45.

Szasz, Thomas S. *The Manufacture of Madness*. Harper and Row, 1970. Dell paperback, $3.45.

IQ Testing and Other Evaluation: Examination of Controversy

Black, N. J., and Dworkin, Gerald, eds. *The IQ Controversy*. Pantheon Books, 1976. $6.75.

Samuda, Ronald J. *Psychological Testing of American Minorities: Issues and Consequences*. 1975. Harper and Row, New York. $7.95.

Schrag, Peter, and Divoky, Diane. *The Myth of the Hyperactive Child and Other Means of Child Control*. 1975. Pantheon Books, New York. $2.25. Particularly significant in its examination of "learning disabilities" assessment techniques and the use of amphetamines and other drugs on children in the schools.

Programs for Severely Handicapped Children: Resources

Haring, Norris G., and Brown, Louis S., eds. *Teaching the Severely Handicapped*. 1976. Grune and Stratton. New York.

Sontag, Ed, Smith, Judy, and Certo, Nick, eds. *Educational Programing for the Severely and Profoundly Handicapped*. 1977. Division on MR of the Council for Exceptional Children. Reston, Va.

Thomas, Angele, ed. *Hey! Don't Forget about Me. Education's Investment in the Severely, Profoundly, and Multiply Handicapped*. 1976. The Council for Exceptional Children. Reston, Va.

Programs for Preschool Handicapped Children: Resources

At this point, the best source of information and practical resources on programs for preschool children is the Technical Assistance Development

System (TADS). The current address for TADS is University of North Carolina, 500 NCNB Plaza, Chapel Hill, N.C. 27514.

Special Education and the Law

> *A Primer on Due Process: Education Decisions for Handicapped Children.* 1976. The Council for Exceptional Children.
> *The Exceptional Child and the Law, An Annotated Bibliography.* 1977. United Cerebral Palsy Associations of America, Attention: Marie Moore, 64 E. 34th St., New York 10016. Free, with a self-addressed, stamped envelope.

Parents of Handicapped Children: Support

Two of the best places to start are:

> Closer Look (see p. 341 for description). Write them a letter.
> *The Exceptional Parent* magazine. P.O. Box 4944, Manchester, N.H. 03108. One year's subscription: $10.00.

The major references used directly in the writing of this book are listed in the Notes section. However, it's worth reminding the reader of *The Futures of Children: Categories, Labels and Their Consequences*, along with its two "background" volumes, *Issues in the Classification of Children.* (*The Futures of Children* is a summary of the other two volumes.) The three volumes were put together by a large task force of doctors, lawyers, and educators, along with many of the major figures in the field of special education. Together, they are the most comprehensive and significant work available on the classification system and its effect on children.

Index